NEGRO LIBERATION

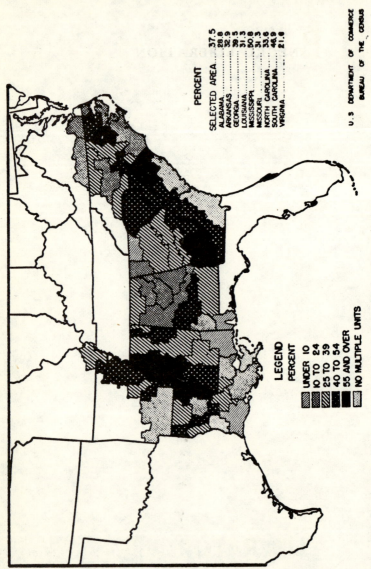

PERCENT

SELECTED AREA	37.5
ALABAMA	28.8
ARKANSAS	32.9
GEORGIA	39.5
LOUISIANA	31.3
MISSISSIPPI	50.8
MISSOURI	31.3
NORTH CAROLINA	33.6
SOUTH CAROLINA	46.9
VIRGINIA	21.6

U. S DEPARTMENT OF COMMERCE
BUREAU OF THE CENSUS

LEGEND

PERCENT

- UNDER 10
- 10 TO 24
- 25 TO 39
- 40 TO 54
- 55 AND OVER
- NO MULTIPLE UNITS

The plantation area in 1945 showing the percentage of total farm land in
multiple units. The area shaded for over 40 per cent forms the core of the
Black Belt and includes the principal plantation region.

NEGRO
LIBERATION

by Harry Haywood

Chicago, Ill.

Printed in U.S.A.

CONTENTS

To the Memory of My Mother Harriet
Born in Slavery,
She Taught Me To Fight
for Freedom

Preface to the
Second Edition

I wrote Negro Liberation in 1948, while working as a merchant seaman. I wanted to show the revolutionary character of the Black struggle for equality, to trace this struggle to its roots in the oppression of a Black nation in the Deep South, and to show that nothing short of Black political power in this area could guarantee equality for Blacks, North or South.

While making these ideas available to the general public, the book was also part of a struggle to bring the old Communist Party USA back to this position—a position it had abandoned during World War II under Browder's leadership. This position was partially restored and sparked the CP to lead some impor= tant struggles like the Martinsville 7 case, the Henry Wallace campaign in the South and the "We Charge Genocide" petition to the UN. But after a decade of struggle the revolutionaries in the party were defeated and the party became revisionist—indistinguishable from the Kennedy liberals on the Afro-American qeustion and most other issues.

At the same time that the party dropped their revolutionary position and suppressed my book, the masses of Black people launched a campaign of struggle culiminating in the Black Power Revolt of the 1960's. This revolt confirmed the main points of this book, particularly the national revolutionary character of the Black struggle which was shown in the movement's growing link to the national liberation movements in the Third World. The Black Belt continued to be the heart of the movement, the place where many turning points of the '60's occured.

The "long hot summers" of the '60's showed that the crisis of the plantation system had displaced millions of Southern Blacks, fueling a ghetto crisis which threatened the urban nerve centers of the establishment. Ford Foundation president McGeorge Bundy pointed out at the time that if the uprisings continued, "the white man's companies will have to take the losses."

The plantation system was the historic root of Black oppression in the U.S. The crisis of this system generated massive migrations to Northern and Southern ghettoes, strengthening the Black working class, the natural leader of the Black liberation movement. But these migrations didn't dissolve the roots of the movement in the survivals of the slave system. These survivals can only disappear in two ways: either there will be a century or two of capitalist prosperity opening up the possibility of peacefully assimilating Blacks; or the Black liberation movement, together with the working class movement, will overthrow the system of white supremacy in revolutionry struggle. The reader can decide which of the two perspectives is more realistic.

Out of the Black movement and other movements of the '60's (themselves often inspired by the Black movement) emerged a new generation of Black and white revolutionaries who understood the national character of the Black struggle and the bankruptcy of the old CP which denied Black people their birthright as a nation. They initiated the new communist movement of the '70's which has once again popularized the revolutionary Leninist position of Black liberation among thousands of Black, working class and other progressive people. I'm proud that republication of this book is part of this process.

PREFACE

THE AMERICAN NEGRO faces the most crucial decision in his entire history. All of the gains so painfully won by him through years of struggle and sacrifice stand in jeopardy as the specter of World War III looms sinisterly above the skyscrapers of Wall Street.

During the late war the Negro took his stand in overwhelming numbers against fascism. He turned a deaf ear to the siren voices that would have swerved him from his true interests and rejected the counsel that the war was a "white man's war" and that he stand on the side lines while the fate of humanity was being decided. He understood that his deepest aspirations for freedom would be achieved only by wholehearted participation in the struggle against fascist reaction. But even while he fought the enemy abroad he had to contend with his traditional enemy at home who sought to retain the Nazi-like system of Jim Crow.

This bitter experience in the war saved him from illusions. He knew that with the defeat of the Axis slave powers his battle was far from over. The victory in the war marked an historic advance of the democratic peoples of the world. The system of imperialist oppression was broken through on a wide front, in India, China, Indonesia, and the liberated countries of Eastern Europe. Here at home the Negro's own forces and those of his democratic allies were strengthened. But the end of the war also brought a resurgence of reaction and fascism frantically striving to stem this new worldwide advance of the common people. This new threat stems no longer from Berlin, Rome, and Tokyo, but from his own country, from the handful of Wall Street monopolists who stand in mortal fear before the advancing tide of democracy in the world.

These "wilful men," served by a venal Congress and national administration, have now taken over the imperial baton of world aggrandizement knocked down from the hands of the recent foe. Once more they are ready to plunge the world into a bloody holocaust for the enslavement of nations and peoples, and in the interest of profits and privilege to carry the banner of Mr. Henry Luce's "American Century" to the four corners of the earth. They seek to mask these sinister aims by the hypocritical use of the slogans of "democracy" and "freedom"; to extend to benighted humanity the "blessings" of "our American democratic way of life," to stem the rising tide of "bolshevist totalitarianism" upsurging from the East; these, according to the oracles of big business, are the noble aims which inspire the present crusade of the imperialist cohorts for world supremacy.

But the bitter facts are that today the United States has become the rallying and organizing center of reaction, plotting subversion of democracy on a global scale; and through the bi-partisan Marshall-Truman plans it is seeking to throttle the rising peoples' movement for peace, security, and national independence.

This new "democratic" moral stance, assumed by America's profit-hungry rulers in pursuit of their expansionist program, is viewed with profound suspicion by the Negro. He is disgusted with the spectacle of Truman's lip service to Negro rights which is designed to mask a dastardly sell-out to Wall Street and its feudal-minded bourbon hangers-on. He is not ignorant of the fact that among the warmest supporters of the "new crusade" for world "emancipation" are the most vicious poll taxers and Negrophobes of the country. To him, therefore, the words of democracy and "free" elections in the mouths of men who deny the most elementary rights to millions of America's Negro citizens are a mockery and a swindle.

These self-dubbed knights of Anglo-Saxon "race superiority" do not even trouble to conceal their cynical flaunting of the Hitlerian race lie. And yet, they are cunning. Unfortunately there are those among the Negro people whose acts and words help to conceal the true character of the course and policies which America's present rulers would impose upon the country and world. They would minimize the mortal threat of this course to the Negro and thus deliver him disarmed and helpless to the tender mercies of the enemy. They would dull the sharp edge of the mass struggle for Negro rights by distorting its aims, by setting before it narrow and illusory goals and thus isolate the Negro from his true allies in the struggle against the common enemy—American imperialism. Clearly, the interest and future of the Negro people lie with the camp of democracy the world over, with the colonial and semi-colonial millions of Africa, Asia, Latin America, now on the march for freedom.

The Negro must choose. He cannot in any way permit himself to become an instrument in the service of the new fascism. He must become an active force on the side of people's democracy. The Negro in the United States has been historically a potent force for progress. The full weight of his democratic influence and strength now must be thrown into the scales against imperialism. To permit the imperialist forces to triumph is to allow the return of slavery. Since the war, the evidence of reaction's plans to put the Negro "back in his place" has accumulated overwhelmingly.

The entire Negro world looks to the American Negro, situated in the center of world reaction, to strip the cloak of false democracy from the imperialist vultures and to expose their real predatory aims. Africa is being prepared openly as an advanced base for the new war of enslavement to American capital. Fascism undisguised and supported by the Marshall-Truman doctrines rides the saddle in the Union of South Africa. To help thwart this barbarous dream of world conquest is one of the most vital conditions of Negro freedom.

The common people of the world have long been able to see through the hypocritical pretense at democracy by America's rulers in their odious oppression of the Negroes. The Negro can and must make an historic contribution to the titanic world struggle for peace and democracy.

Under the circumstances, the need for clarity on the Negro question is more urgent than ever. The Negro must know not only his general interest, but who is the enemy and what are the specific prerequisites for the achievement of freedom. This alone can clarify the path.

For progressive Americans generally, and especially for the white workers, understanding of the Negro question is crucial, since it is above all a question of unity. It is pre-eminently a question of how to rally the masses of laboring people for joint struggle for common goals against a common enemy. American white labor can no longer ignore the fact that the unsolved Negro problem is a main hindrance to the development of working-class unity, a continuous brake upon the struggle for democracy and socialism, a mainspring of Wall Street domination over the working class and the masses of the American people.

The Negro question, the fight of 15,000,000 black Americans for land, equality, and freedom, can and must become a potent force in the struggle for the maintenance and extension of American democracy against fascist reaction. The Negroes, once their full strength is brought to bear, can become a decisive element, tipping the scales on the side of progress.

The vast potential of Negroes for democratic struggle, however, has only been tapped. Their full resources can be brought into active support of the cause of labor and American democracy only to the extent that the white workers and progressives understand and uncompromisingly support their full and just demands.

This book is a modest effort to restate some of the fundamentals of the Negro question, and to refocus attention especially upon the basic requisite of the Negro struggle for equality—the fight for democratic land-redivision and the liberation of the Negro nation in the Southland—which has not been sufficiently emphasized in the recent past. The author is fully aware of the limitations of the present study, and offers it purely as a contribution to the discussion and clarification of this crucial question.

In the preparation of this book, I have received invaluable assistance from many quarters, for which I am duly grateful. I have made full use of very excellent standard works, which I have cited. This book could not have been written without extensive and fruitful discussion with my friends and colleagues. In its general line and approach this book is a collective product. For any deficiencies in the development of the general thought I alone am responsible. Some of the many friends who have read the manuscript and whose suggestions and criticisms have been invaluable are: Henry Winston, William Z. Foster, William L. Patterson, Benjamin J. Davis, Jr., Elizabeth Lawson, A. W. Berry, Alexander Bittelman, Edward Strong, David Gordon, James Allen, John Pittman, Herbert Aptheker, Theodore Bassett, Herbert Wheeldin, Maude White, and Otto Hall.

I wish especially to express my appreciation to:

Doxey Wilkerson, for careful and critical reading of the manuscript and his many invaluable suggestions based on his vast knowledge and experience in the field of education.

A. Landy, the editor of this book, whose wide store of theoretical and practical knowledge I found indispensable in the handling of the many difficult questions discussed in this volume.

Elizabeth Green, for much of the research in this work, particularly on monopoly control in the South which is included in the appendix.

Erik Bert, statistician and writer and close student of the agrarian question.

For technical assistance in preparation of the manuscript for the press I am grateful to Rhoda Lewis and Ann Rivington.

I wish also to thank Doris Feldman for more than ordinary interest in typing the manuscript.

Finally, my thanks go to my wife, Belle, whose constant encouragement and practical help made this book possible.

CHAPTER I

The Problem

THE NEGRO QUESTION in the United States is agrarian in origin. It involves the problem of a depressed peasantry living under a system of sharecropping, riding-boss supervision, debt slavery, chronic land hunger, and dependency—in short, the plantation system, a relic of chattel slavery.

It presents the curious anomaly of a virtual serfdom in the very heart of the most highly industrialized country in the world. Slave-whipping barbarism at the center of "enlightened" twentieth-century capitalist culture—that is the core of America's "race" problem.

The Black Belt

Today, long after the abolition of slavery, about five million southern Negroes of the fifteen million total Negro population of the country[1] still live in the Black Belt, historically a continuous area of Negro majority. It holds a Negro population equal to that of the whole Negro population of the North and West, and almost a third of the entire country's Negro inhabitants. This Negro population is larger than the total population of such countries as Switzerland or Norway. Embracing the central cotton-growing region of the South, the Black Belt is the area in which plantation economy is most firmly rooted; the peon farms of today correspond to the slave plantations of yesterday.

The Black Belt shapes a crescent through twelve southern states. Heading down from its eastern point in Virginia's tidewater section, it cuts a strip through North Carolina, embraces nearly all of South Carolina, cuts into Florida, passes through lower and central Georgia and Alabama, engulfs Mississippi and the Louisiana Delta, wedges into eastern Texas and Southwest Tennessee, and has its western anchor in southern Arkansas.

The Black Belt is the center of America's Negro problem, the core of its greatest concentration. Here is the seat of the infection from which the virus of Negro persecution spreads throughout the country, contaminating all phases of Negro life. Here, in the status of the Black Belt Negro, is the clue to the economic, social, and cultural inequality of America's black millions. To quote Arthur F. Raper, well-known southern scholar:

"The Black Belt sketches the section of the nation where the smallest proportion of adults exercise the franchise and it defines the most solid part of the Solid South." Here is the stronghold of white supremacy, where the Negro is excluded from political life and his children are denied adequate educational opportunities; all institutions are designed to keep the Negro "in his place," and violence and the threat of violence always hang over his head.[2]

The Black Belt is likewise the matrix of the nation's number one economic problem—the cradle of southern economic and cultural lag. And, as a growing body of southern white liberal opinion is coming to understand, its depressing influence bears down fully upon the white population of the South. Says Raper:

"Human relations in Atlanta, Birmingham, Montgomery, Memphis, New Orleans, and Dallas are determined largely by the attitudes of the people of the Black Belt plantations from which many of their inhabitants, white and Negro, came. The standard of living in these cities does not escape the influence of this area of deterioration. No real relief can come to the region so long as the planter, who wants dependent workers, can confound the situation by setting the white worker over against the black worker, and so long as the industrialist, who wants cheap labor, can achieve his end by pitting

urban labor against rural labor. There are literally millions
of farm laborers in the Black Belt who are eagerly
awaiting an opportunity to work for wages even smaller
than are now being paid textile and steel workers in
southern cities.[3]

It is not surprising, therefore, that wages in the traditionally
"lily white" textile industry "grow progressively lower the further one penetrates into the Deep South".[4]

The County System

The Black Belt is arbitrarily broken up by a mass of state
or county boundaries and administrative, judicial, and electoral subdivisions. These divisions in no way correspond with
the economic and political needs of the oppressed majority
population and are artificially maintained and gerrymandered
by the real rulers of the South. Their avowed purpose is to
perpetuate the political impotence of the region's predominant
Negro population.

The role of the county government as an instrument of governmental power for Bourbon planter interests and the decisive
influence of the county in the state politics of the region were
dramatically brought out in the results of Georgia's guberna-
torial primaries of July, 1946. Through a county unit system
of voting,* in which elections are rigged in favor of downstate
planters, the rabid Ku Kluxer, Eugene Talmadge, was nomi-
nated, despite a statewide popular vote majority for his op-
ponent, James V. Carmichael.

The Skeleton in the Closet

Shackled by a common slavery and bound by a common history, ethnic origin and aspirations, the Negro people have
problems which are matters of growing import, not alone to
the South but to the whole country.

The explosive political material in this condition has never

*The county unit system assigns two to six votes to a county, depending
upon population (206 unit votes are needed for a majority). The fact that
counties can have a maximum of only six penalizes the heavily populated
urban counties.

been ignored by the leaders of southern Bourbonry, and it is the skeleton in the closet of the rabid "white supremacists" of the Talmadge-Bilbo breed. Here is a condition which their obscene racism is designed to hide. Political power in the hands of the black majority, the same specter that haunted their slave-trading forbears, dogs them today; for even a breath of genuine freedom for the millions of black bondsmen would change the social face of the South.

One can only marvel at the cynicism of our erstwhile Secretary of State, James F. Byrnes who, in the name of "free elections," attacks the peoples' democracies of eastern Europe. If applied to his own Black Belt state of South Carolina, "free elections" would mean the end of the stolen power of the Bourbon clique which Mr. Byrnes really represents. Let it be remembered that the first milestone in the meteoric political career of our eminent ex-Secretary of State was in 1922, when he was elected to Congress with only 4,163 votes cast in a congressional district with a population of 300,000![5]

The great mass of American people remain in deep ignorance of the existence of the huge vassal Negro community in the Black Belt, and of its blighting influence on our country's democracy. The truth concerning the Black Belt, so essential to any serious analysis of the Negro problem, remains buried in the works of authors not widely read by the general public. Vital statistical facts are unstated, distorted, or obscured in a mass of inconsequential minutiae by federal and state agencies (the United States Census Bureau not excepted), from which they can be extracted only by the most painstaking research. As Karl Brandt, a critic of agricultural statistics, pointed out in *Social Research* a decade ago:

> "In counting farm operators the census makes no distinction between the sharecropper on the one hand, and, on the other hand, the farmer who operates his property either personally or with the aid of a manager and the tenant who operates a rented farm. By this procedure the census has erased from the whole picture one of the most distinctive features in the constitution of agriculture in this and in many other countries. *Strange as it*

*may seem, in current American agricultural statistics
the plantation does not exist.*"[6] (Italics mine—*H. H.*)

This is only one of the respects in which census statistics fail
to reveal the important characteristics of the Black Belt population.

The Negro Community

In order fully to understand the Negro question as a whole,
one must first see clearly that, despite state and county borders,
the Black Belt is an entity in itself, comprising a population
chiefly Negro and constituting a stable community of Negro
Americans.

According to the 1940 United States Census, the Black Belt
contains 180 counties of proved Negro majority, ranging from 50
to 85 per cent. The total population of the counties of absolute
Negro majority in 1940 was 4,237,739. Of this total 2,642,808
(or 63 per cent) were Negroes.[7]

The extent of this Negro concentration is, however, by no
means limited to those counties having a clear Negro majority.
Such counties constitute only the core of the community.

Obviously, population concentrations do not stop short at
state or county lines. The compact Negro community overflows
such lines into neighboring counties. This is borne out by the
1940 Census which lists some 290 counties having populations
which are from 30 to 50 per cent Negro.

The area of concentration of the Negro population spans
about 470 counties with an over-all average Negro population
of 48.7 per cent of the total. We make no attempt rigidly to
fix the boundaries of the Black Belt. However, anyone not
completely blinded by the present arbitrarily erected state and
county lines can see that within the territory embraced by these
counties there is a well-defined, compact and stable Negro
community.

In 1940 the population of the entire Black Belt area (including both Negro majority counties and the peripheral areas)
totaled 10,256,289, of which 4,993,612 (or 48.7 per cent) were
Negroes.[8]

The following table, compiled from U. S. Bureau of Census

population statistics for Black Belt counties from 1860 to 1940, by James Allen, in an article in *Political Affairs*,[9] clearly indicates the existence of an historically continuous Negro community.

Census year	Total population	Negro population	Per cent Negro of total
1940	10,256,289	4,993,612	48.7
1930	9,525,865	4,790,049	50.3
1920	8,968,132	4,806,565	53.6
1910	8,387,958	4,842,766	57.7
1900	7,498,900	4,488,991	59.9
1890	6,465,307	3,866,792	59.8
1880	5,750,410	3,466,924	60.3
1870	4,431,597	2,560,263	57.8
1860	4,362,009	2,461,099	56.4

The "Mass Exodus" Theory

It has been asserted that this Negro majority in the Black Belt is rapidly disintegrating as a result of "huge migrations"—a veritable "mass exodus" of Negroes, especially during the late war.* This contention is refuted by the table of figures shown above, and also by the latest estimates on these Negro migrations.

It is true that there has been a decrease in the *ratio* of Negro to total population in the Black Belt area over the years, a trend which has been in evidence since the Civil War. It is also true that there has been a steady, and even sharp, decrease in the number of counties of Negro majority, particularly between 1900 and 1940, when it declined from 300 in the former year to 180 in the latter, or 37 per cent. Despite these facts, how-

*Dr. Edwin R. Embree, president of the Julius Rosenwald Fund, contends that "in fifteen years we may see the ratio of Negroes North and South reversed, with nine million in the North." (See *The Negro Digest*, Feb. 1946, p. 6.)

ever, the total Negro population did not decline; in fact, it even increased, although the increase was slight as compared to that of the white population. And as for the area of Negro majority, although its shrinkage has continued, its rate of decline fell off sharply in the decade of 1930-40 which also showed an increase in the total Negro population for the first time since 1900.

While these facts indicate the necessity of going beyond bare statistics for an understanding of what is happening to the Negro community in the Black Belt, they do not indicate a disintegration of the Negro concentration in this area. The figures in our table show a decline in the total Negro population during the decades 1910-1930 only, the period during which there was also the sharpest decline in the number of counties of Negro majority. This was the era of "the great migration" connected with the industrial boom of World War I and the prosperity period of the 'twenties. This decline clearly registered the "flight" of those elements of the population who were able to break away from a backward, depressed agricultural area and, in response to the needs of capitalistic industrial expansion, were drawn to urban centers of industry. When the boom of war and post-war prosperity gave way to the great crisis and depression of 1930-40, there occurred an absolute growth of the total Negro population in the Black Belt and a marked slowing up of the rate of decline of the counties of Negro majority.

It is obvious, therefore, that the movements of decline and growth of the Negro population and its concentration in the Black Belt have been conditioned by the economic fluctuations accompanying the development of monopoly capitalism in the United States. Any substantial disintegration of this concentrated Negro community would depend entirely upon a continuous and uninterrupted process of industrial expansion and prosperity in the country as a whole. But there is absolutely nothing in the perspective of capitalist development to warrant such an assumption. If, therefore, we confine ourselves to the facts rather than to wishful thinking, the feature that stands out is *not* the breaking up of the Negro concentration in the Black Belt, but its stubborn persistence.

Migration during the Second World War

Have the migratory movements of World War II affected the stability of this region? According to a special wartime survey (1940-1944), released by the Bureau of the Census in 1945,[10] the non-white resident population in "ten congested war production areas included less than 300,000 Negroes moving into these areas." Three of these cities were in the South.

Even if generous allowance is made for migration to other commercial and industrial centers not included in this survey, there is no evidence of a major decrease in the total Negro population of the Black Belt below that of 1940, that is, of a breakup of the concentration there. Moreover, the factors responsible for such a possible decline have clearly come to an end with the close of the war, and have been replaced by the immobilizing influences of coming crisis and depression. Monopoly capital, which is responsible for the conditions encouraging mass migration, at the same time imposes an automatic check on these migrations through the "bust" which follows the "boom."

The latest census figures available show that even during the war-dominated years of 1940-47, with their impetus to large-scale migration, the total Negro population of the South remained essentially stationary (a total of 9,530,000 in 1947 as compared with 10,007,323 in 1940).

The main wartime shift was away from agriculture into other occupations. The extent of this shift was largely a matter of conjecture until a January 1948 release of the Census Bureau (*Series P-20,* No. 9) brought to light the fact that 60 per cent of the nation's non-white population (96 per cent of which are Negroes) had become urban by April 1947, as compared to about 48.0 per cent in 1940. In spite of the fact that the non-white population was expanding at a rate of 50 per cent more rapidly than the white (11.6 per cent increase in seven years as compared to 7.5 per cent increase of the white inhabitants), the rural-farm Negro population declined by an estimated total of 1,270,000, or by more than 26.0 per cent, while the urban population increased by 2,550,000, or by about 40 per cent. There was some movement from the farm to rural villages.*

The survey of 1940-44 further shows that not all the Negro migration was from the Black Belt, or even from the rural areas of the South alone. In fact, it revealed a change in the direction of Negro migration which had prevailed from 1870-1941. The migrations of World War II broke away from the purely South-to-North pattern which characterized the early migrations. Thus, although the latest movements had their origin in the South, three of the ten terminal areas mentioned in the survey were in the Black Belt itself: Charlestown, S. C.; Hampton Roads, Va.; and Mobile, Ala., or in the periphery of the Black Belt.

On the whole, there was no northward migration of Negroes

---

*PER CENT CHANGE 1940-1947

URBAN AND RURAL RESIDENCE OF THE NON-WHITE POPULATION

Area	Total	Urban	Rural	Rural non-farm	Rural farm
United States	11.6	39.7	−14.2	12.3	−26.3
North East	66.1	79.5	−51.0		
North Central States	49.9	57.7	5.2		
South	−4.8	16.6	−16.7		
West	67.1	76.9	56.6		

Most of the non-white population who are Chinese, Japanese, etc., live in the West. The percentage increase of the Negro population was of course much larger.

URBAN AND RURAL NON-WHITE POPULATION FOR THE UNITED STATES BY REGIONS, CIVILIAN POPULATION, APRIL 1947, AND TOTAL POPULATION, APRIL 1940

Region	1947			1940		
	Total	Urban	Rural	Total	Urban	Rural
Northeastern States	2,342,000	2,271,000	71,000	1,410,009	1,265,142	144,867
North Central "	2,253,000	2,016,000	237,000	1,503,362	1,278,105	225,257
South	9,530,000	4,233,000	5,297,000	10,007,323	3,631,238	6,376,085
West	892,000	489,000	403,000	533,711	276,394	257,317
Total	15,017,000	9,009,000	6,008,000	13,454,405	6,450,879	7,003,526
Total *Rural Farm*		3,481,000				4,752,726

Source, Department of Commerce, Bureau of the Census, *Release*, Jan. 19. 1948, No. 9, p. 20.

during the recent war comparable in size and significance to that of World War I. The entrance of Negroes into war industries was considerably delayed, because of a tremendous reserve of unemployed white workers in the cities, both North and South, and because of the age-old policy of employers which decrees that the Negro must be the "last-hired."

In 1942 Charles S. Johnson reported that:

> "When placements through the U. S. Employment Service reached the highest peak, Negroes and other non-whites composed only 3 per cent of the placements in 20 large war industries, and they were less than 3 per cent of the referrals for pre-employment training courses. They are at present about 1 per cent of the total in those pre-employment and refresher courses. In one city . . . with two large shipbuilding concerns, there were nation-wide requests for shipyard workers, in spite of the fact that the U. S. Employment Service reported 6,000 Negro workers available in the active file of the Employment Service in that city."[11]

Plainly, those in search of an easy solution of the Negro question in the South—through peaceful out-migration of the Negro people—have "overlooked" the profound economic and historical causes which have shaped the Black Belt as the main region of Negro concentration in this country—*forces which still operate to maintain it as such.*

The explanation—and solution—is not to be found in dry statistical data alone. The explanation lies, on the one hand, in the over-all operation of monopoly capital which closes the door to out-migration as quickly as it opens it, and, on the other hand, in the plantation economy which dominates the Black Belt region and its relation to the economy of the country as a whole.

CHAPTER II

The Plantation—
Instrument of Oppression

THE SOUTH is a "pretty country," as the saying goes. It is a land with an abundance of natural resources, a land of rich soil on which anything can be grown. Its fields of waving cotton, its balmy climate, its vaunted hospitality, its "happy and carefree banjo-plunking Negroes," have long been the theme of poetry, folklore, and song.

But the sweet fragrance of its magnolia blossoms and honeysuckle vines cannot hide the stench of the real South: the South of decay, of crushing poverty and blighting ignorance, of plantation torture camps. Of all the nation's people, the Southerner is the poorest fed, the poorest housed, the poorest clothed, and has the lowest income. These low wages, substandard homes, inadequate diets—in short, all the vast misery of the majority of the South's inhabitants rests upon and takes sustenance from the existent agrarian relationships in the plantation regions.

The Great Southern Gamble

The South's plantation system is a form of large-scale commercial farming.

Cotton, the chief money crop, is produced for the world market. Although by the mid-thirties cotton was replaced by corn as the leading money income crop of the whole country, its importance to our nation's agricultural economy is illustrated by the fact that in 1944, the cotton and cotton-seed crop gave America's farmers one-and-a-half billion dollars equaling the one-and-a-half billion from wheat.[1]

More than half of the South's crop land is used for cotton growing; more than two million of its farm families (nearly a third of all farm families in the United States) live on cotton farms.[2]

Historically, the main bulk of Negro soil tillers have always labored in the realm of King Cotton, upon whom they have been entirely dependent. The country's central cotton-growing region lies within the Black Belt area of Negro majority population.

Although Negro owners, tenants, and croppers cultivate no more than a tenth of the southern farm land, in 1929 they produced on this land almost a third of the nation's total cotton output. Negro farm laborers also produce an additional quantity of cotton on farms operated by whites.[3]

The plantation system is notorious for the most reckless and shameless exploitation of its labor forces, because it requires an abundant supply of cheap, substandard, subservient and dependent labor. Here, as we shall see later, it is not a question of normal capitalist profits, but of super-profits.

The tremendous profit garnered from Negro plantation workers is similar to the imperialist tribute exacted from backward colonial labor—all of which goes to support a vast swarm of parasites on the back of the lowly soil cultivator. These range from the overseer, local planter, country banker, and time-merchant up to the Wall Street financier and coupon-clipper. To this shining array must be added, of course, the professional cotton broker or speculator. The size of their "take" is reflected in the fact that the actual cotton producer receives but fifteen cents of the consumer's dollar spent on cotton products.[4]

Serf-like exploitation of the Negro is insured by a combination of legal and extra-legal pressures whose antecedents reach back into the dark past of chattel slavery. Bound and gagged by all sorts of semi-slave proscriptions, the sharecropper is the central figure in the modern plantation labor scene, and he is delivered to the present-day slave driver as "fit only for cotton and servitude."

"Mule and One Row"

Cotton is cultivated in most of the South by a most primitive and labor-consuming technique which has not changed essentially since the days of slavery. There is a low degree of mechanization in the country's cotton-growing region; the "mule and one row" system is still typical of the methods under which our nation's cotton is produced.

The persistence of archaic and out-dated techniques has operated to force labor and living standards in the cotton belt to a level lower than anywhere else in the country, with the result that the region has become the base for a huge depressed agricultural "reserve," pulling down labor and cultural standards of the entire South, and constituting a threat to the gains of organized labor—even in the North.

This one-crop plantation system requires more labor than any other. For example, if the same acreage directed to cotton production were in corn, it would require less than one-half of the time required by cotton. If seeded to oats or hay, it would require one-sixth to one-fifth as much labor as is needed for cotton.[5]

Cotton is a world-market crop. The competition of other cotton-producing lands, and of new cotton substitutes (for instance, nylon) has meant an intensified exploitation of the working cotton farmer and farm laborer. These victims have been forced to compete with imperialism's colonial serfs in other cotton-growing regions of the world. It is not surprising, therefore, that the starvation standards of the Egyptian fellah, the East Asia coolie and the Brazilian peon, have served to reinforce the traditionally low standard of the southern sharecropper based on the semi-slave character of plantation economy.

The Single Crop

This one-sided dependency upon cotton is at the bottom of some of the region's major ills, for the production of cotton nowadays is a risky undertaking.

Says the report of the National Emergency Council on *Economic Conditions in the South:*

"No other similar area in the world gambles its welfare

and the destinies of so many people on a single crop market year after year.

"The gamble is not a good one. Few other crops are subject to such violent and unpredictable price variations as cotton. In 1927 cotton farmers got 20 cents a pound for their crop; in 1929 they got 16 cents; in 1931 they got 6 cents; in 1933 they got 10 cents. Only once during the last decade did the price of cotton change less than 10 per cent between pickings. Three times in 5 years it jumped more than 40 per cent—once up and twice down."[6]

In the summer of 1946, cotton went up to 39 cents a pound. That this was an inflated price became woefully apparent in the cotton panic of the fall of the same year—the worst panic in twenty-five years. Cotton slumped to 29 cents, and in a few weeks hundreds of millions of dollars in cotton values disappeared, bringing disaster to thousands of cotton producers. The average price per pound on April 15, 1947, was 32.26 cents. The same day, a year later, it was 34.10 cents.

Without doubt, the plantation landlord is able to carry on this gamble year after year because of the presence of a labor force composed of virtual serfs on whom he can inflict the brunt of his risks.

The Not-So-Good Earth

Inherent in the plantation's single crop system are its wasteful production methods which have been called the most reckless exploitation of natural and human resources known to history.

It is an established fact that cotton, tobacco, and corn use up the natural richness of the soil with great speed. Fields planted to these crops, year after year, wear out and waste away much more quickly than fields on which vegetables or other leguminous crops are planted in rotation with the chief money crops.

Soil decadence is already far advanced in most of the cotton areas. Much of the once-rich land of the region is left bare and unprotected from erosion, its fertility syphoned away by soil-destroying methods of cotton culture.

According to a sample study made in 1933, about one-third of the southern land was eroded, and more than one-half of all eroded land in the country was in the South.[7] In this connection, the Emergency Council's report pointed out that every year the South was losing through erosion fertile soil valued at over three hundred million dollars.

Quantities of fertilizer are used in a hopeless effort to preserve the soil. The South has only one-fifth of the income of the nation, but it spends three-fifths of the total fertilizer bill.[8] For the owner of the land this amounts to what Herman Clarence Nixon has called "selling his soil in annual installments."[9]

Added to the above evils is that of agrarian overcrowding. The pressure of population upon the meager resources of limited land area—particularly in the Black Belt—assumes a degree unrivaled in other agricultural sections. "Since 1860 there has been little change in the amount of land in the southeastern farms, new land is being cleared about as rapidly as old land was exhausted."[10] But as we have already seen, the population of the Black Belt more than doubled in the same period.

Gunnar Lange in his study, "Trends in Southern Agriculture," sums this up as follows:

"We may therefore conclude as changes in land in farms have been rather insignificant, that the agricultural population and among this population the Negroes in the old South at present have less land resources to support themselves on than they had a generation ago. The trend is continuing in the same direction, indicating that if strong action is not taken to prevent further erosion the farm population will have in the future even less land resources at its disposal than at present."[11]

These special features of the South's agrarian structure left it peculiarly vulnerable to ravages of the world-wide agricultural crisis which has been chronic since the end of World War I. This crisis is one from which the South has suffered more and recovered less than any other sector of our nation's agrarian economy.

An estimated 85 to 95 per cent of the best farm land of the region is tied up in the tight-fisted control of a few thousand big planters, less than 10 per cent of all white owners.[12] There are thousands of small family-sized farmers struggling on the poorest land on the fringe of the big plantations, living in chronic insecurity at a bare subsistence level. Completing the picture is the great mass of landless tenants denied ownership of the land by various kinds of social and legal strictures, many of which go back to the days of chattel slavery.

The Plantation System

The plantation system, the dominant form of large-scale farm ownership in the Cotton South, enables the plantation landlord to operate all his land as a single unit through a peculiar type of tenant tenure system known as sharecropping and share tenancy.*

More than half of the South's farmers are tenants of a special kind. Sixty per cent of the region's working farmers must part with one-fourth, one-third, one-half, or more of the products of their labor for the right to work the land.[13] Thus a division of labor has been created in which those who own most of the land perform no agricultural labor and those who do most of the work own no land.[14]

*Bureau of Census agricultural statistics, as pointed out in Chapter 1, do not recognize the existence of the plantation. Thereby they obscure the real class relations prevailing in southern agriculture. Karl Brandt, in his critical study of current statistical practices in the field of agriculture, observes: "Paradoxically enough, it [the plantation] lives statistically under the disguise of its direct competitor and adversary, the small family farm. Because the census calls the sharecropper a farm operator, and calls a 'farm' the average tract of 22 acres of crop land or 42 acres of all land on which he works, nobody knows how many plantations existed in the United States in 1920, 1925, 1930, or 1935." (Karl Brandt, "Fallacious Census Terminology and Its Consequences in Agriculture," *Social Research*, p. 22, February, 1938.)

The 1945 Multiple-Unit census of the Department of Agriculture provides the raw material for an analysis of the plantation economy but it continues the obscuring approach of the preceding censuses. Competent students of the South, however, have found it necessary to reckon with the existence of the plantation. Holley, Winston, and Woofter, in their study, *The Plantation South, 1934-1937*, define a plantation as containing five or more resident families, including that of the operator. It is true that the defect in this definition is that it excludes those enterprises which embrace a landowner and from one to three resident cropper, share-tenant, or wage earner families, but what it excludes is the smallest cropper operations.

The special U. S. census of plantations, taken in 1910, showed the high degree of concentration in land holdings in the region.* In the area surveyed, only one-twelfth of the owners controlled as much as one-quarter of the plantation economy.[15]

The tenacity of the plantation sharecropping system is shown in the extent of tenancy in the South as compared with the rest of the country. Furthermore, this tenancy is increasing, a fact which until 1930 was one of the most striking trends visible in southern farm life. This increased tenancy is registered particularly in the sharecropping category, the principal land-lord-tenant relationship found on the plantations.

Census data for the decade 1930-1940 show a reversal of this trend to increased tenancy, resulting from the eviction of thousands of tenants and croppers during the crisis years. But a breakdown of the census data for the Black Belt Negro population, according to James Allen, shows that despite the

*The 1945 Multiple-Unit Operations Census of the United States Department of Agriculture arrived too late for purposes of utilization in the present study, although there seems to be no indication of any reversal in the tendency of concentration of land ownership. A sample of the data in this census indicates that in Mississippi, for example, 69 per cent of the cotton acreage belong to multiple-unit farms. In the five main cotton states east of the Mississippi, 40 per cent of the cotton acreage belong to plantations. This does not include the large-scale "single" units which employ wage labor instead of croppers.

The 1910 special census of plantations showed that 39,073 plantation operators owned one-third of the improved land in 325 southern communities. (33,908 of these were in 270 counties in the seven leading cotton states.) Their plantations averaged 724.2 acres, 405.3 of which were acres of improved land. On these plantations were a total of 398,905 tenants. Almost one-third of the plantations had ten or more tenants and contained 18 per cent of the improved land in the counties surveyed. Further inspection of these total figures shows that of the total number of plantations: 68.09 per cent had from 5 to 9 tenants; 23.49 per cent had from 10 to 19 tenants; 7.5 per cent had from 20 to 49 tenants.

Four hundred and twelve plantations (1.1%) had 50 or more tenants, and an average of 2,084 acres of improved land. The average value of each of these larger plantations was $103,002. (See T. J. Woofter, Jr., *Landlord and Tenant on the Cotton Plantation*, Research Monograph 5, WPA Division of Social Research, Washington, D. C., p. xviii; Anna Rochester, *Why Farmers Are Poor*, International Publishers, New York, 1940, p. 64; James S. Allen, *The Negro Question in the U. S.*, p. 40, International Publishers, N. Y., 1936.)

decrease in the number of sharecroppers during that decade (1930-1940), there was a percentage increase in sharecropping. For example, sharecroppers constituted 43.6 per cent of all Black Belt Negro farm operators in 1925. In 1930 they were 45.6 per cent and in 1940 they were 48.3 per cent of the Negro farm operators in the Black Belt.[16]

The Plantation in the Black Belt

The plantation system centers in the Black Belt, coextensive with the old cotton belt in the South, except for the Yazoo-Mississippi Delta, the plantation area *par excellence* which developed mainly after 1880. Here the plantation organization has been most persistently retained as the regnant form of farm organization, dominating the economic, political and cultural life of the area.*

Here one finds the highest degree of concentration of land ownership with a consequent highest proportion of tenants, and with the entire plantation system resting predominantly upon Negro labor. Nine of every ten resident families on the plantations, and at least as large a proportion of the non-resident laborers, are Negro.[17] It is here in the Black Belt that one finds the root of the South's land problem.

Fortunately, a number of excellent field studies are at hand that gave a detailed description of the land question in this region.

Raper summarized this land distribution in two typical Black Belt counties of Georgia as follows:

> "Only one out of every ten Negro farmers owns any land, and scarcely half of these have enough to make a living on . . . The ownership of the best land is in the hands of a comparatively small group of white families; landlessness and chronic dependence is the lot of over half

---

*"Plantation customs and ideology set the pattern for relationships in smaller farm units. Large planters persistently emerge as political and economic leaders of the cotton areas. Even if there are only four or five large plantations in a county, the ownership of these considerable properties and the prestige of success on a large scale make it easy for the planters to assume prominence in community control." (T. J. Woofter, Jr., *op. cit.*)

the white families and nearly nine-tenths of the colored. . . ."[18]

An investigation of a Black Belt county by Allison Davis, Burleigh B. Gardner, and Mary R. Gardner, authors of *Deep South,* revealed the high degree of land monopoly, typical of the entire region. Of the nearly 2,000 farm operators in the county, nine tenths of whom were Negroes, less than 400 persons owned any land in 1935. Of these 400 landowners, 36 persons owned or controlled practically half of the land and almost a third of the cultivable land! Moreover, seven of these 36 persons owned or controlled 22.2 per cent of all the land, although they constituted only one-third of 1 per cent of all farm operators. Taking the property-owning unit as the family and not the individual, the authors found that probably as much as three-fourths of all the land was owned by these 36 families.[19]*

"Let's Keep It in the Family"

The role of the plantation as the basis for a hereditary feudal oligarchy is brought out by Davis and the Gardners. Ownership of a plantation is a symbol of aristocracy. Therefore, these authors observe:

> "This concentration of the ownership of . . . almost all of the most desirable land within a relatively few families . . . has been strengthened by extended kinship relations among the old planter-families and by frequent intermarriage between collateral lines in the same family . . . These extended kinship groupings have operated so as to prevent disintegration of large estates through the selling-

---

*In the Yazoo-Mississippi Delta, which comprises an area of some five million acres, including all of ten counties and parts of nine others in the northwestern part of Mississippi—which Frank J. Welch described as the "real concentrated super-plantation area of the country," he found that "83 per cent of all farm land is in the hands of planters, 81 per cent of the cotton acreage is under the plantation system, 91 per cent of the 'farms' [census "farms"—H.H.] are tenant units, and more than 90 per cent of the plantation labor force is Negro." (Frank J. Welch, *The Plantation Land Tenure System in Mississippi,* Bulletin 385, State College, Miss., June 1943. p. 52.)

off of land to economically mobile farmers and to new-
comers . . . The ownership of an old plantation, a large
tract of land, or an old plantation mansion has been
considered the most essential trait of a white person of
the upper class."[20]

The big planter of today, like his ante-bellum predecessor, is
a parasite. Although he owns not only the land, but practically
all the other means of production, including work stock, farm
implements, seed and fertilizer, and controls the source of credit,
the big planter is almost completely functionless and makes no
pretense of any useful activity in actual production, such as care
and development of the soil. Quite the contrary, all facts prove
that plantation landlordism intensifies the misuse of the land and
its deterioration.

The direct management and supervision of the plantation are
usually carried on by a manager or overseer. In most cases, a
purely parasitic claim is made on the working farmer by the
actual landlord—the villain in the plot in many cases is far
removed from the scene of his crime.

Woofter found "6 per cent of the plantations to be absentee-
owned, and 9 per cent of the landlords were classified as 'semi-ab-
sentee, since they made infrequent visits to the plantations."
Under absentee-ownership, his study further points out, "land
abuse is particularly prevalent and operation is especially un-
stable in times of crisis."

"Another characteristic of absenteeism," observes Woofter, "is
the extent to which landowners engage, at least partially, in
other occupations," the most important being that of a merchant.
The study revealed that "31 percent of all operators devoted
more than one-fourth of their time to occupations other than
farming."[21]

The proportion of absenteeism varied in different plantation
areas covered by the survey, the highest proportion being in certain parts of the Black Belt and the lower Mississippi Delta.[22]

Raper found that in Green County, Georgia, out of 837 white
owners having more than 50 acres, only 278 were listed as farmers by the 1930 agricultural census. In Macon County, in the
same state, of the 702 white owners only 320 were listed

as actual farmers. Several resident white owners had rented out all their acreage and were therefore not entered as farmers. A much larger number of these owners, particularly in Greene, lived in Atlanta, Macon, or even farther away.[23]

The Agricultural Ladder

In the cotton belt the tenure ladder presents a complex picture of the most varied and multifarious man-land relationships.

> "It is possible," says Rupert B. Vance in *All These People,* "to name thirteen separate 'rungs' . . . all the way from the unpaid family labor of a son working on his father's cropper farm to the status of casual wage hand, regular wage hand, cropper, share tenant, standing renter, cash renter, manager, part owner, mortgaged owner, full owner of a small farm, landlord, and large planter."[24]

Although the plantation regions contain a number of small owners of family-sized farms, these are not decisive in the cotton belt economy. In prosperous times, they eke out a precarious livelihood. In the main, they belong to the marginal farming class, relegated to the poorest soil on the fringe of the rich plantation land—and this is usually heavily mortgaged. The crisis and depression years saw many of these groups wiped out and pushed down the ladder into the various tenant groups, or off the land entirely.

The 1940 Census shows 173,000 Negro farm owners, compared to 220,000 in 1910—a decline of more than 20 per cent. Preliminary estimates for the 1945 Census of Agriculture indicate an increase to 186,000, still far below the number in 1910.

At the bottom of the agricultural scale is the wage laborer. In 1940, there were 507,303 Negro agricultural laborers in the thirteen southern states compared to 565,655 white, a number altogether out of proportion to the Negro population.* These figures do not include the large number of wageless child laborers below the age of fourteen.

These farm laborers, however, are scattered throughout the

---

*This figure includes 70,777 white and 29,177 Negro laborers unemployed during the Census week. (U. S. Bureau of Census, *Sixteenth Census of the United States, 1940, Population,* Second series, Vol. III, pp. 94, 96.)

South and work under varying conditions. In this study, we are chiefly concerned with the farm laborers, resident and non-resident, in the cotton belt, a large part of whom work on the big plantations and in most cases side by side with the sharecropper. Here they comprise the second and most numerous group.

Generally, the plantation laborer is not a wage worker in the modern sense of a man receiving cash wages. If he is a resident laborer, he gets his "wages" in terms of a cabin for his family and credit for food at the plantation store, and seldom sees cash.

Unlike the cropper, the farm laborer is assigned no particular patch of land, and he usually gets the worst cabin. His hours are just as long as those of the cropper; his wife and children are forced to labor in the field; and he is subject to the same riding-boss supervision and the same caste restrictions.

The non-resident or occasional laborer serves as a seasonal labor reserve for the plantation. Such a supply of local town labor relieves the planter of having to maintain laborers when they are not needed. In addition, it has been used to eliminate the labor of a sharecropper.*

The highest tenant category is the cash renter, who owns his own tools and work animals, rents the farm and dwelling outright, supplies his own food, seed and fertilizer, and supervises his own farm. In some cases he hires labor or lets out a part of his tract for sharecropping. This type of farmer most closely approaches the tenant in more developed capitalist areas. A few of this group are well-to-do. But most of them are poor, and in "hard times" face the danger of losing many of their possessions and being pushed down to sharecroppers. But as they are cash tenants, their social status and relations are entirely different from those in the share-tenant or share-

---

*Welch and Miley found that by the intensive use of seasonal labor for chopping and picking, a few Mississippi Delta planters in 1940 were able to operate with one cropper family for each 100 acres instead of the usual ratio of one family for 27 acres of crop land. Thus, by using transient labor to meet the peak labor power requirements, they were able to reduce the number of resident families required to operate a given acreage by 73 per cent. (Frank J. Welch and D. Gray Miley, *Mechanization of the Cotton Harvest*, Bulletin 420, June, 1945, State College, Mississippi, p. 22.)

renter categories. It is revealing that only one-eighth (12.7 per cent) of all Negro tenants were in this group.

Closely related to the cash renter is the small class of standing renters who also furnish their own equipment and production costs but pay rent with an agreed-upon amount of bales or pounds of the product.

The other cropsharing categories, namely the share tenant and the sharecropper, are distinguished from one another by the share of the crop going to the landlord. The share tenant owns his work animal and a few primitive tools, provides his own seed and feed and more than half of his fertilizer, and since theoretically he is reimbursed out of the product for the use of his workstock and tools, pays only one-fourth or one-third of his crop for rent. The sharecropper is entirely propertyless, fully dependent upon the landlord for his means of production, housing and credit, and therefore pays half or more of the main cash crop to the latter. Both the share tenant and the sharecropper are subject to landlord and riding-boss supervision.

A large section of sharecroppers are compelled to supplement their income by also hiring themselves out for wages on the landlord's crop. This practice is so extensive that statisticians have coined the term "cropper-laborer" and "combination worker" to describe those sharecroppers who secure more than half of their annual income in this manner. This is strikingly akin to the division of the feudal serf's labor between his lord's crops and his own.

It is not uncommon for landlords to restrict the acreage allotted to the sharecropper and share tenant in order to assure that their labor will also be available for employment on the landlord's "home farm."

In 1940, there were 1,449,000 tenants in the census South (16 southern states and the District of Columbia) and of this number 506,638—a little over a third—were Negroes.[25] Forty-one per cent of the South's white farmers as against 75 per cent of its Negro farmers were tenants. On the basis of color and tenure they were divided as follows:

	White	Negro	Percent Negro of total
Cash	189,667	64,684	25.4
Share-cash	32,131	6,547	16.9
Share tenants	389,561	89,483	18.7
Croppers	242,173	299,118	55.3
Others	89,123	46,806	34.4

This table shows that the great bulk of the South's tenants fall into the cropsharing categories. Negroes, comprising a little over one-fourth of the South's population, *constitute nearly a half of all its tenants, and more than one-half of the sharecroppers*. The higher the ascent on the agricultural ladder the fewer the Negroes; they comprise only a fourth of the cash tenants.*

The central and most typical figure in the landlord-tenant setup is the sharecropper. Landlord-cropper relations overshadow all others in the agricultural landscape of the old South. Share-cropping is the main form of southern tenancy, a form peculiar to the plantation.

The point of departure for any fundamental approach to the Negro agrarian question, therefore, must be an examination of the nature of plantation sharecropping.

Close supervision over the sharecropper, his abject servility and blind obedience to the slightest whim of the landlord, are requisites of "successful" cropper farming. The decision as to what shall be planted and when remains with the landlord. "Furnishing" the cropper means that the landlord determines what food he shall eat and the amount.

*Preliminary estimates on the 1945 census of Agriculture show no essential change. Negro farmers in the South made slight gains in their tenure status during the years of war prosperity. In 1945, 72.4 per cent of the Negro farmers were tenants as compared to 74.5 per cent in 1940, and 39.8 per cent were sharecroppers as compared to 44.0 per cent in 1940. However, white farmers benefited far more during the war boom. As a result the *relative* position of the Negro farmer in the South deteriorated. Negroes represented 40.9 per cent of all tenants in 1945 as compared to only 35.0 per cent in 1940, and 61.0 per cent of all croppers in 1945 as compared to 55.3 per cent in 1940. There were only 7,000 fewer Negro farm operators in 1945 than in 1940, but nearly 100,000 poor white farmers escaped into industry. (U.S. Bureau of the Census, *Release*, July 30, 1946.)

He decides also the tools with which the cropper works, the amount of fertilizer he uses, the mule he is allowed for plowing. The landlord also sets the length of the cropper's workday which, in the cropper's own language, is "from ken see to can't see." In many cases, the overseer is a "pistol-totin' " deputy, devoted to carrying out the landlord's edicts.

The burden of sharecropping, to a large degree, is carried out by the wageless labor of women and children. The family system is prevalent in both the cotton and the tobacco-producing areas of the South. The landlord prefers large families to meet labor demands of peak seasons. On the 38,000-acre Delta and Pine Land Company plantation in Mississippi it is taken for granted that all children six years old and over must help at least in the picking.[26]

Actually, sharecroppers are tenants only in form. In reality, they are laborers paid with a share of the crop, lacking the legal rights of the modern tenant and the wage laborer's right to collect a cash wage and spend it in the open market. The sharecropping "contract," in most cases a verbal one, is only a fiction designed to conceal what is in effect a kind of slavery.

Sharecropping Economics

Present-day Negro sharecropping is a hybrid form, combining the most primitive features of capitalism with survivals of chattel slavery in the exploitation of the soil cultivator, under conditions of the over-all domination of monopoly capital. Its capitalist features are expressed in the "contract" between tenant and the landowner in which they confront one another ostensibly as legal equals; in the monetary transactions between them in the sale of the product; in the advance of capital by the landowner to the cropper for purposes of production;* and, finally, in the relation of the landowner to the cropper as merchant-usurer. What determines the real character of the

---

*Langsford and Thibodeaux have found that "a large item in the crop-expense loans both to cropper and share tenants was for hired labor to supplement the family-labor in picking cotton." (E. L. Langsford and B. H. Thibodeaux, *Plantation Organization and Operation in the Yazoo-Mississippi Delta Area*, U. S. Department of Agriculture, Technical Bulletin, No. 682, May, 1939, Washington, D. C., p. 48.)

relation between the sharecropper and the planter, however, is the fact that these relations rest upon an elaborate system of Negro subjugation already inherent in the historical origin of the sharecropping form.

Historically, the pattern for the plantation sharecropping system was set as a result of the failure of American democracy radically to solve the land question in the South at the time of Reconstruction following the Civil War. A democratic solution of this question would have meant the confiscation and breaking-up of the big plantations—the redistribution of the land among the ex-slaves and the landless poor whites.

The carrying through of such a measure would have meant the establishment of a system of small "freeholders," i.e., independent farmers as the dominant pattern in southern agriculture.

It is plain that only such a radical agricultural reform would have broken the economic and political power of the former slaveholders. Only such a measure could have brought freedom to the ex-slave, clearing the road for a *new* truly democratic South. It was around this issue of land for the Negro freedman and his poor white allies that the revolutionary wave of Reconstruction beat in vain and was finally broken.

The land question was eventually "solved from above" in favor of the former slaveholders. The Negro freedman, left without the land, *i.e.*, cheated out of his chief means of livelihood, was forced back upon the plantations into a position of semi-slave servitude but slightly removed from that of his former chattel bondage. The promise of "40 acres and a mule," the watchword of his battle for the land during Reconstruction, remained unfulfilled.

> "The abolition of slavery," observes Rupert B. Vance, "was merely an episode in the history of the plantation system. . . . The plantation was staggered by the shock of the abolition of slavery, and after a brief interval reorganized its labor supply into a tenancy and share cropping system."[27]

The end of Reconstruction found the former slaveholders still largely in control of the land. The masses of landless ex-slaves and impoverished whites were left in a position where they were forced to pay for the privilege of working the land with a share of the crop. The outcome was the development of the sharecropping and the crop-lien system—a new and more refined type of slavery.

If in its origin, therefore, Negro sharecropping was the predominant form resorted to by the former slaveholders to maintain the old slave relations under the new conditions of legal emancipation, economically it made possible the continuation of a type of exploitation which in its intensity and form were akin to slavery. It has enabled the plantation owners to appropriate not only half or more of the product of the cropper's labor, but enough of the remainder to keep the cropper and his family below the level of sheer physical subsistence.

This super-exploitation, so characteristic of slave-serf relations, involves a combination of direct exploitation through production and an outright robbery by usurious credit, buttressed by an odious system of national oppression, a state of perpetual indebtedness and dependence. The difference between this system and chattel slavery is simply that the ante-bellum landlord owned not only the land and the instruments of production, but the person of the slave as well. But this "advantage" of the slaveowner over his modern successor is considerably offset by the system of legal and extra-legal sanctions, including peonage, by which the landlord can either hold the cropper on the land, throw him off at will, or reduce him to the status of plantation work-hand.

The Credit Trap

Franklin Delano Roosevelt, referring to southern agricultural labor, said that "the agricultural ladder of these American citizens has become a treadmill."

This treadmill is powered by the credit system which is little more than legalized robbery. The landlord is in absolute control of credit and in many cases he combines the role of usurer, credit merchant, and landlord. "Usury laws are inoperative," says Woofter. "The legal rate of interest is a fiction."[28] The sharecropper is completely dependent on the planter or time-merchant from planting time to the marketing of crops.

The landlord markets the crop, and from the cropper's "share" he deducts enough to cover all advances and "furnishings" plus heavy interest charges on everything advanced. The sharecropper receives what is left in cash. However, at the end of the season, instead of having cash in his pocket, the cropper usually finds himself just "breaking even" or in debt. This "debt" is then charged against the tenant's next crop!

The landlord's investment in "furnishings" is more than insured by the exorbitantly high interest rate he charges and by the virtually complete helplessness of the tenant.* Frequently, as much as 50 per cent is added to the prices charged for supplies.[29]

A central cog in this vicious system is the plantation commissary. More than a fourth of the plantations studied by Woofter had commissaries. Completely dependent upon credit extended him at the planter's commissary, or at the store of a time-merchant designated by the planter, for the necessaries of life, the cropper has no choice but to pay the prices charged. In fact, he does not even see his "share" until the amount of the advances to him has been deducted. He has no choice but to accept the landlord's accounting without question. The landlord's word is the law; for the cropper even to question

---

*In 1934 the average annual interest rate paid by all croppers and tenants on subsistence advances was 37.1 per cent. A plantation study for 1937 gave the planters' interest rates on advances as amounting to two or three times those paid by the operators (landlords) for short term credit. Even this high estimate is conservative compared to the study made by the North Carolina College of Agriculture of Pitt County farms in 1928. Here the interest rates ranged from *19.1 per cent for cash advances to 72.1 per cent for supplies advanced by merchants.* This tribute is exacted from the tenants on the basis of the planter's advance not only of his own capital but also of the capital he borrows from financial institutions. In 1934, for example, the interest rates on such borrowed capital ranged from 10.4 per cent, on government loans, to 16.4 per cent on merchant credit. But for the part of this "advanced" to cropper and tenant for subsistence, the landlord charged 37.1 per cent interest. (See T. J. Woofter, Jr., *Landlord and Tenant on the Cotton Plantation*, pp. 63, 64; William C. Holley, Ellen Winston, and T. J. Woofter, Jr., *The Plantation South, 1934-1937*, Research Monograph xxii, 1940, Government Printing Office, Washington, D. C.; Walter Wilson, *Forced Labor in the United States*, International Publishers, 1933, New York, p. 88.)

his word, or to ask to be shown the books, is considered a "personal insult to the landlord or credit merchant."[30]

Many of the South's lynchings have originated in landlord-tenant disputes over "accounting."[31] Attempts of the Negro croppers of southeast Arkansas to organize around the issue of "fair accounting" and for written contracts led to the bloody massacre of Phillips County, Arkansas (1919), in which approximately fifty Negroes were killed.[32]

Under such a system, cheating is a "normal" practice, fully consonant with the moral double-standard set by the planter's code. "A businessman in one of the counties . . . with a close knowledge of the credit dealings of most landlords and tenants . . . stated that 'practically all landlords' cheated their tenants in one way or another."[33] This is indicated by the prevalence of the so-called settlement jokes in the landlord's folklore. C. S. Johnson and associates in *The Collapse of Cotton Tenancy* tell the following:

> "A tenant offering five bales of cotton was told, after some owl-eyed figuring, that his cotton exactly balanced his debt. Delighted at the prospect of a profit this year, the tenant reported that he had one more bale which he hadn't yet brought in. 'Shucks,' shouted the boss, 'why didn't you tell me before? Now I'll have to figure the account all over again to make it come out even.' "[34]

The tenant in most cases cannot sell even his own share. Under property laws existing in most states, he cannot dispose of his crop until after the planter has been paid all rent due and "advances" received during the season. The planter is legally entitled to sell the crop without even consulting the cropper.[35]

In 1919 the Memphis *Commercial-Appeal* carried the following letter from a southerner:

> "In certain parts of the South, men who consider themselves men of honor and would exact a bloody expiation of the one who would characterize them as common cheats do not hesitate to boast that they rob the Negroes by purchasing their cotton at prices that are larcenous, by selling goods to them at extortionate figures, and even by padding their accounts with a view

of keeping them always in debt. A protest from a Negro against tactics of this kind is met with a threat of force. Justice at the hands of a white jury in sections where this practice obtains is inconceivable. Even an attempt to carry the matter into the courts is usually provocative of violence."[36]

As a result of these usurious extortions the cropper usually finds himself not only cheated out of every ounce of the surplus of his toil but left with his family below the level of bare subsistence. His plight fully justifies the observation of a former Agricultural Adjustment Administration official that "they live on the borderline of starvation."[37]

The vicious credit-debt circle in which the cropper finds himself trapped is rounded out by an edifice of legal measures designed to perpetuate it. Most notorious of these is the crop lien, which gives the landlord a prior claim on the crop of his sharecropper to the amount of the advances made to the latter in food, seed, fertilizer, etc.

Raper found that "in nine cotton states the landlord has the legal right to sell any and all property the tenant may have as payment of rent and furnishings."[38] The planter's word is law. Less than 2 per cent of all croppers have even the small protection of a written agreement.*

Peonage: Slavery for Debt

As defined by a U. S. Supreme Court decision, peonage is "a status or condition of compulsory service based upon the indebtedness of the peon to the master."

Modern vestiges of the infamous Black Codes, originally designed to restore forced labor conditions on the plantations after the Civil War,† continue to exist in the statutes of most

---

*Many legislative and judicial decisions have classed the cropper as a "tenant" for the purpose of making him liable for the "advances" and "furnishings." At the same time he has also been classed as a laborer who is paid partly in kind, thereby depriving him of title to any part of the crop, and serving as justification for the "oral and informal" nature of the cropper-landlord "agreement."

†During the first period of Reconstruction the southern states enacted

cotton states. Despite the fact that in recent times many of these laws have been held unconstitutional by higher courts, the planter's local courts and police have found a way to circumvent decisions of higher courts, if not by new laws then by extra-legal pressure and Jim-Crow sanctions.

Among these are the so-called false-pretense statutes which bind the cropper to the soil, and deprive him of freedom of movement. The tenant, under written—or in most cases verbal—"contract," is prevented from leaving his work against a landlord's wishes. Other laws make it "a criminal offense for a laborer or a tenant to accept 'advances' as part of a contract and then fail—for any reason—to perform that contract to the employer's satisfaction." [39]

Contract "jumping" is either a felony or a misdemeanor. Such was the import of the Georgia "Cheat and Swindle" statute of 1903, as well as the code of 1933. Under the former law, any tenant who jumps his contract or for any reason fails to perform the service contracted for, "to the loss and damage of the hirer . . . shall be deemed a common cheat and swindler and upon conviction shall be punished as for a misdemeanor."[40]

This law was finally declared unconstitutional by the U. S. Supreme Court decision of January 12, 1942.[41] But in 1946, according to a United Press release, a "Georgia legal leader expressed doubt that half of the state Justices of the Peace knew that the U. S. Supreme Court had overruled a 1903 Georgia 'Cheat and Swindle' statute which permitted virtual peonage here." This leader declared that Negroes still were being arrested "all the time" and forced to work out fines. His statement followed the Federal Bureau of Investigation's arrest of one Roswell P. Biggers, 65, charged with holding five Negro workers in peonage.[42]

legislation designed to continue the subordination of the Negro despite his technical emancipation. Eight states passed the famous Black Codes in a deliberate attempt to define the expected behavior of Negroes so as to coincide as nearly as possibly with that which characterized the Old South. These laws were enacted after the close of the Civil War and before either Reconstruction legislation or the ratification of the Fourteenth Amendment placed certain humane limitations upon state statutes. (Charles S. Johnson, *Pattern of Negro Segregation*, pp. 83, 159 *ff.*, 163 *ff.*, Harper, N. Y., 1943.)

The facts in the Biggers Case, according to Assistant U. S. District Attorney H. H. Tysinger, were as follows:

" . . . The plantation owner arranged the arrests of the men named on charges of obtaining money under false pretenses. Then 'buying up' their warrants, he returned them to his farm where they were to work off the debt. Biggers' tactics were to charge the underpaid men with defaulting debts to him. After they were jailed he paid their fines and cost of lodging, and obtained their release to him. The men were forced to work off the debts, or return to jail, a practice common to the community, according to Justice of the Peace J. R. Pirkle, before whom the warrants were sworn out.

"Biggers never gave receipts, so that men released to him never knew when their debts were paid. He was charged with working the Negroes at wages of 50 cents to one dollar per day, holding out all but one dollar a week 'on the debt!' "[43]

A similar pattern is followed in the so-called "vagrancy" laws operative in all southern states. These laws are used to obtain forced labor, especially on the plantations. It works out as follows: unemployed workers "having no visible means of support" are apprehended as vagrants. They are then given the dubious choice between accepting the employment offered by the planter or employer, or being sentenced to forced labor on the chain gang.[44]

The practice of employers getting Negro tenants or laborers by paying their fines in court has proved most tenacious and has by no means been stamped out. An accompanying practice is one which might be called the present-day version of ante-bellum slave trading, "whereby an employer pays a Negro's debt to a former employer or to a merchant, and, by taking over the debt, also takes over the worker."[45]

This practice has led to the "manufacture" of debts, and fines are levied for petty or fictitious offences upon the most flimsy accusations. Groups of Negroes often are "rounded up" and handed over for the price of the fine to an interested planter or employer who happens to be short of labor. In this manner, the police and courts act as enforcement agencies for debt peonage.

Another link in the chain binding the Negro debt-slave is the unwritten "gentlemen's agreement" among planters that *no* planter is supposed to accept a tenant who has not cleared with his previous employer. "Tenant stealing" is an infringement of southern Bourbon caste solidarity, a crime comparable to slave-stealing in the ante-bellum South.

"A typical case of this sort was reported in the press in 1929. The trouble started when J. T. Wilson, white manager of the Wirewood plantation in Greenwood, Mississippi, went to Macon in that state, signed up 23 families and chartered two freight cars to move them. When local business men and planters found out what was going on, a large posse was formed and Wilson was given ten minutes to leave the county—without 'his' families."[46]

It is in the plantation's system of legal and extra-legal controls that the tap root of modern peonage thrives. There has been no fundamental change in the whole legal system of the South in recent times.

The net results of debt thralldom are registered in the growing indebtedness and impoverishment of the Negro tenant. In a study of 700 Negro cropper families in Alabama, Harold Hoffsommer estimated that "they broke even during 45 per cent of the total years, lost money during 30 per cent, and cleared some profits above all expenses in 25 per cent." Of 3,000 current cropper families, Hoffsommer "found 40 per cent indebted to their present landlords with a debt of more than one year's standing averaging more than $80."[47]

Holding the Color Line

Here are the ropes binding the Negro to serfdom on the South's good earth. And they are tied with the Gordian knot of color caste. With the possible exception of South Africa, in no other country has "race" been made to play such a decisive role in the socio-economic oppression of a people. The racial differential finds its fullest expression in landlord-tenant relationships in the plantation regions. Here it operates to reinforce the social strictures imposed upon the Negro under the economic survivals of slavery, with the extra-economic element of racial coercion.

It has operated to hamper the free development of classes, and the process of class stratification becomes warped, distorted, and one-sided.

The great masses of Negroes are literally frozen at the lowest social levels (forming a rigid pariah caste). Movement up the ladder to the higher tenure groups is effectively barred.

A striking example of the race factor as a brake upon social advancement is given by Raper. Regarding the Negro's difficulties in the acquisition of land and the absence of "free competition," he writes as follows:

> "The Negro buys land only when some white man will sell it to *him*. Just because a white man has land for sale does not mean that a Negro, even the one most liked and respected by him, can buy it even if he has the money. Whether a particular Negro can buy a particular tract of land depends upon its location, its economic and emotional value to the white owner and other white people, the Negro's cash and credit resources, and, doubtless most important of all, his personal qualities in the light of local attitudes: He must be acceptable . . . safe . . . knows his place. . . ."[48]*

The same author reported that nearly one-tenth of the resident Negro land owners, by purchase, who had more than 25 acres, said that they had bought their land from white men. In three-fourths of these cases, the white man had taken the initiative, *i.e.*, approached the prospective Negro buyer and offered to assist him.

The net result of all this is that ownership by Negroes is

---

*Henderson states that "Almost no local credit agencies would lend money to a Negro to buy a farm, regardless of the security, if the transaction displeased any influential whites. The Negro would be eligible to buy a desirable tract only if it were located in an established Negro community. In many southern counties, the sheriff refuses to sell tax-forfeited state lands to a Negro if these are contiguous to land owned by whites." (J. Lewis Henderson, "In the Cotton Delta," *Survey Graphic*, January, 1947, p. 48.)

confined to the agriculturally least desirable land; and the Negro farms are much smaller than those of the whites. The average size of the Negro owner-operated farms was sixty acres in 1940, about the same as that of the white sharecropper (59 acres). The average value of land and buildings of the Negro farm ($1,443) was lower even than that of the white sharecropper ($1,908). The value of implements and machinery of the colored owner was given as $90 as compared with $322 for the white owner.[49]

Behind these planter-imposed difficulties of Negro land-owner-ship is one striking fact. Any encouragement given the Negro to move up the class ladder menaces the whole plantation tenure structure and its labor surplus.

Caste segregation enables the landlord to employ any number of sharp practices in regard to the prospective Negro land buyer. A scheme which amounts to thinly disguised robbery is the practice of planters in areas where nearly all tenants are colored. They "sell" land to Negro tenants in boom times and take it back without due process of law at the first opportunity in "hard times." Evidence of many such robberies was disclosed in 1934 by an investigator from the Department of the Interior.

Davis, Gardner, and Gardner report a large number of cases where tenants had attempted to buy second-grade land at $50 an acre during periods of inflation and had "lost" their farms during the period of deflation following 1929. "The arrange-ment had had this result: The landlord had received a rental of $50 per acre instead of $6 to $9, and in addition had had his taxes paid over a period of several years. In at least two cases, landlords 'sold' to colored tenants land they did not own."[50]

Flagrant cases of abuse of their rights as mortgagees by land-lords selling land to Negroes were reported by the same authors. Taking full advantage of the Negro mortgager who could obtain but little protection in courts, the landlord frequently sold land above its market price. In some instances, it went for as much as 40 per cent to 60 per cent higher!

In one case, the land sold was badly eroded. The 40 acres the tenants had "bought" were found to be no more than 30 and only about 10 of these were cultivable. "Upon the death of their landlord, after they had paid him $1,100, in addition to the taxes, the colored buyers were told by the landlord's heirs that he had not owned the land. The old colored man and his wife . . . began renting the farm again, for $100 a year."[51]

The Double Standard

The stifling effects of the race factor are most strikingly illustrated by the drastic differences in the economic and cultural status of Negroes and whites on the *same tenure levels*. This contrast which runs the whole scale of the agricultural ladder from landowner to the lowly cotton cropper is fully documented by Raper in his illuminating study of two of Georgia's Black Belt counties.[52]

Raper found that Negroes were concentrated in the lower tenure groups. But this is not all. *Within each group in each county* they were much weaker than the corresponding white group: the size of the farms, quality of the soil, amount of livestock and equipment, income, housing, and education.

In 1934 Negroes comprising 53 per cent of the population in Greene County and 68 per cent in Macon, owned less than 5 per cent of the land in both counties. One-seventh of the white owners held more than half of all the land.[53]

"Of the families studied, over a third of the white families and nearly three-fourths of the Negroes have no horse or mule; one-fourth of the families of each race have no hog or pig." One-third of the Negro families in Greene and over half of those in Macon had no cow or calf while among the whites only one-seventh had none.[54]

Cash incomes of families varying by race or tenure class averaged less than a dollar a day per family, and less than 20 cents a day per person. In 1934, in Greene County, the average cash income was $301.26 per rural white family and $150.74 per Negro family. In Macon County, the average cash income was $872.21 for the white family* and $299.56 for the Negro.[55]

---

*The relatively high incomes of the white families of Macon, Raper explains, were due to the operation of large acreage by subletting to tenants or by using wage labor, the expenses of which came out of the total expense reported.

In housing, the Negro dwellings were decidedly inferior. Approximately one-half were "unceiled as compared with one-eighth of the white dwellings. The white owners and renters had much better houses than the Negro owners and renters." In all, there was found to be "a greater difference between the dwellings of whites and Negroes within the same tenure group than between the tenure classes of the same race. A similar pattern was noted in the matter of leaking roofs, glassless windows, household furnishings, etc. In both groups the situation was bad, but the Negroes were decidedly the worse off."[56]

But the cultural superstructure arising from this economic cleft between Negro and white, and designed to preserve it, is most vividly revealed in the educational differential. Here was shown the most startling of all contrasts.

"In 1928, the white child of school age in Greene had $36.53 of public money spent upon his education, the Negro child, $3.11 —a ratio of twelve to one. In Macon the white child received $58.38 and the Negro $2.85—a ratio of eighteen to one."[57]

A sharp deterioration of educational standards was noted during the worst crisis years, with the miserable pittance of the Negro child reduced almost to the zero mark.

> "Between 1928 and 1934 the amount spent in Greene County upon the white child had decreased by 16 per cent, upon the Negro child by 40 per cent; in Macon, the white child's decrease was 12 per cent, the Negro's 36 per cent. Thus the racial differentials were even greater than in 1928; seventeen to one in Greene and twenty-five to one in Macon."[58]

In the war boom year, 1943-44, the ratio was still better than 4 to 1 in Greene County and 7 to 1 in Macon County.*

---

* In 1943-44, Greene County spent $80,953.40 for the education of 972 white pupils and only $31,519.93 for the education of 1,665 Negro pupils, while Macon County spent $77,803.78 for the education of 971 white pupils and only $27,964.62 for the education of 2,583 Negro pupils. This amounts in Greene County to $83.29 for each white child enrolled and $18.93 for each Negro child and in Macon County to $80.13 for each white child and $10.83 for each Negro child. (*Annual Report of the State Department of Education, 1943-44.*)

It is in the Bourbon-enforced cultural backwardness of the southern Negro that the key to the high ratio of Negro illiteracy in the nation generally is to be found. According to Professor Paul A. Witty, former major in charge of the army program for illiterates, and now Professor of Education at Northwestern University: of the estimated 10,000,000 adults in the United States whose illiteracy handicaps them as workers, as heads of families and as citizens, 3,000,000 are Negroes and 7,000,000 are whites.[59] Although Negroes constitute only one-tenth of the country, they comprise nearly one-third of the illiterates as reported (in the statistics one-half of the number of whites) by Professor Witty.

From the foregoing, the reader can readily see that any attempt to place the status of southern "poor whites" on a par with that of the Negroes is false. Beyond all doubt, the oppression of the Negro, which is the basis of the degradation of the "poor whites," is of a separate character demanding a special approach.

As early as 1913, V. I. Lenin, stressing the agrarian features of the Negro question, summed up the economic character of Negro sharecropping. In his study, *The Development of Capitalism in Agriculture in the United States,* based on the U. S. census of 1910, Lenin drew attention to the "remarkable" similarity between the economic position of the South's Negro tenantry and that of the former serfs in the agrarian centers of Russia prior to the 1860's:

> "The farmers we are discussing are not tenants in the European, civilized, modern capitalist sense; they are mainly semi-feudal or—what is the same in the economic sense—semi-slave *share tenants.*
>
> ". . . The sharecropping region . . . is the region of the greatest stagnation, where the toiling masses are subjected to the greatest degradation and oppression . . . Segregated, hidebound, a stifling atmosphere, a sort of prison for the 'emancipated' Negroes—this is what the American South is like."[60]

CHAPTER III

Big Business and the Plantation

THE PLANTATION is patently an outmoded struc-
ture in the country's economic life. Yet, it is not just a relic of
the past. If it has survived in defiance of social change and
progress, it is because it has been bolstered up and kept alive by
the dominant economic force of the country, finance capital.
Wall Street is the supreme usurer of the plantation. It is the secret
shrine revered by the Yankee-hating Bourbon landlords. It is the
great Moloch to which are offered up sacrifices soaked with the
blood, sweat, and tears of the Negro bondsmen and the great
propertyless mass of southern "poor whites." This entrenched
"big money" power of the North and East is the chief beneficiary
of Negro oppression, of southern distress and poverty. It
operates chiefly through the remote control of plantation credit.

This dependence of the plantation upon outside sources for
credit is nothing new. Even under slavery, the American plantation was never self-sustaining, for it was a hybrid of two systems, classic slave economy and modern capitalism, combining
the worst features of both. It was sired by a capitalist commod-
ity-producing society, developed under its wing and subjected
to its market relationships. Then, as now, the nature of the
planter's crop, its price and his returns were determined by
the capitalist market. His supplies and finances came from

outside. During slavery, the plantation was financed by big banking and commercial institutions in the North as well as in England.

But the really big invasion of the South and its agriculture by northern capital could come only with northern victory in the Civil War.

The bourgeois-democratic revolution of the Civil War and Reconstruction periods established the claim of the newly ascendent capitalist class of the North to dominance of the Southern market. The military defeat of the slaveholding oligarchy and the abolition of chattel slavery cleared the main obstacles to capitalist penetration of the South, for the rounding out of a national market under its complete and unchallenged dominance. The period of Reconstruction which followed coincided with the rapid economic and social growth of this class.

By the time of the Hayes-Tilden compromise of 1876, northern capitalists had grown beyond the stage when they had led the nation's victorious assault on the citadel of chattel slavery. As a result of the further concentration of economic and political power in their hands, they had been transformed into a fully developed exploiter class not only strong but corrupt as well, as evidenced by the Tweed Ring, Credit Mobilier, and Whiskey Scandals of the period. They were out to reap the full benefits of the new internal market that resulted from northern victory in the war. Inflated with war profits and power, the top capitalists had developed into a full-fledged financial and industrial oligarchy.

In the South, a direct product of northern victory was the new Bourbon middle class. Born during Reconstruction, this was an extension of ruling northern capitalist interests to the South and guaranteed the latter's supremacy in the former slave domain.

The new middle class consisted of cotton traders, merchants, and small manufacturers who had sprung up around the post-Civil War cotton exchange. It was, therefore, dependent upon large-scale cotton production—the plantation system to which it was tied by a thousand threads leading up to the big financial-industrial centers of the East. It was the "on the spot" intermediary between these centers and the planter interests of the South.

Northern capitalism—with its main economic and political aims achieved, and with control of the southern market and capitalist penetration of the region assured—had realized its main program for the revolution. It wanted "social peace" and a "return to normalcy," in order to reap the full harvest of plunder from a newly conquered market. It was also impelled by fear of the democratic movement from below, particularly in the South, with its continuous threat of overstepping the bounds set by narrow capitalist class interest. These are some of the main factors which led to the Reconstruction betrayal.[1]

From the Hayes-Tilden betrayal onward, the South's economy, its agriculture, industry, mining and transportation, was subjected to sustained and continuously accelerated penetration and development by northern capital. With respect to the plantation, this capital, following the classic pattern of all backward agricultural areas, flowed predominantly into the channels of trade. Here it functioned mainly as usurious loan capital, bolstering and preserving the economic and social survivals of the discarded chattel slave order. The infusion of "new blood" only strengthened the old plantation oligarchy which was not essentially disturbed in its monopoly of the land.

Slave survivals had become the social base for the new Bourbon landlordism. And these landowners were, in turn, the indispensable ally of northern capitalism, whose primary object was to hold exclusive monopoly of the world's greatest source of raw cotton, and to maintain its cheap production for northern textile manufacturers.

With the era of monopoly capitalism, all the economic and social trends of the preceding period were sharply accentuated.

The '80's and the '90's brought a new stage in the evolution of American capitalism. As a result of the constant and growing concentration of the nation's wealth and economic resources in the hands of an ever-narrowing circle of leading capitalists, the United States had reached the stage of monopoly and imperialism when big capitalist combines and trusts dominated the economic and political life of the country.

The power of the trusts and combines had become so great, that free competition, through which capitalism had developed, began to be transformed into its opposite, *i.e.*, monopoly.* Capitalist *laissez faire* had spawned its Frankenstein. A brand new type of financial oligarchy appeared, with tentacles reaching out to embrace and control all phases of the nation's life. By the first decade of the twentieth century, finance capital had succeeded in monopolizing the key points of American industry, transportation and trade, as well as raw material resources of the country. This became apparent with the founding of the Standard Oil Co. and U. S. Steel.

This new dynasty of entrenched greed was based upon the merging of large-scale industry with the capital of leading banks, the latter manipulating billions of dollars. The partitioning of the world among the great capitalist powers and the scramble for "unoccupied" areas for profitable investment of huge capitalist surpluses had begun.[2]

Significantly, in the United States this period opened with military aggression against Spain. The scramble for colonial spoils had already resulted in the division of the world among the great European powers. Young American imperialism, arriving late on the scene, was determined to secure its "share" and to emerge as the dominant power of the world.

Its vast internal market, which had not yet been fully utilized, provided a strong base for this new role. In this respect, the semi-feudal South, with its essentially colonial economic structure which assured to emerging American imperialism control of the world's cotton market, was a pillar of strength in the ensuing struggle for imperialist supremacy.

*In tracing the history of monopolies, Lenin says: "Thus, the principal results in the history of monopolies are: (1) In the 'sixties and 'seventies, the highest, furthermost stage of development of free competition with monopolies as barely discernible embryos. (2) After the crisis of 1873, a period of wide development of cartels; but they are still the exception. They are not yet durable. They are still a transitory phenomenon. (3) The boom at the end of the nineteenth century and the crisis of 1900-1903. Cartels become one of the foundations of all economic life. Capitalism has become transformed into imperialism." (V. I. Lenin, *Imperialism, the Highest Stage of Capitalism*, Little Lenin Library, No. 15, p. 22, International Publishers, New York, 1933.)

At the same time, the South itself was subjected to the full force of this new, highly concentrated power of United States finance capital, streamlined for better and more efficient plunder.

Imperialism—The Hidden Enemy

The Morgans, Rockefellers, duPonts, Mellons are today the real owners of the South. It is they who dominate the commanding heights of southern economic life, they who have underwritten the plantation system and its color-caste system. Their banks maintain the credit structure without which the plantation could not live. It is they who control the South's steel, coal, railroads, and utilities.

An investigation of Wall Street absentee control of southern economic life shows:

The region's vast coal resources are held by the Morgans, Mellons, Fords and Rockefellers.[3]

United States Steel Corporation, largest single steel producer in America, dominates the principal steel center of Birmingham. Republic Steel also has entered Alabama at Birmingham and Gadsden.

The Rockefellers have a huge stake in southern oil, which comprises two-thirds of the country's petroleum energy. So have the Mellons, owners of the Gulf Oil Corporation. Sixteen great oil companies listed as being among the two hundred largest non-banking corporations in America, have immense holdings in the South.[4]

Tobacco manufacture is likewise in the hands of non-southern interests and is controlled by several great concerns, four of which are among America's largest non-banking corporations.

All major southern railroad systems are owned and controlled elsewhere; all are more or less directly linked with the Morgan interests.[5]

"Most of the great electric holding company systems, whose operating companies furnish the light, heat, and power for southern homes and industries," the National Emergency Council's report tells us, "are directed, managed, and owned by outside interests. Likewise, the transmission and distribution of natural gas, one of the South's great assets, is almost completely in the hands of remote financial institutions."[6]

Commonwealth and Southern Corporation, a billion-dollar concern, is in the Morgan orbit.[7]

"For mining its mineral wealth and shipping it away in a raw or semifinished form," the National Emergency Council's report observes, "the South frequently receives nothing but the low wages of unskilled or semiskilled labor."[8]

The same picture is presented in the textile industry; many of the largest mills are in northern hands.[9] In Alabama 36 per cent of the spindles and 37 per cent of the looms were northern owned in the early thirties.[10]

Wall Street's Pro-Consuls

Through the domination of these key points in the South's economy, industry, trade and credit, the wealth of this region is drained off for the benefit of Wall Street. For example, the State of Georgia is 85 per cent absentee owned, "50 cents of every dollar on deposit in Georgia banks is owned in the North."[11] The "front men" in the South for the absentee Yankee overlords are the directors and managers of northern-owned southern industry. A. G. Mezerik effectively describes the role of these "pro-consuls" of imperial Wall Street.

"The manager," he writes, "who represents the absentee control of the North (or East), such as the power companies and the transportation system, is the simplest to understand. Whether Southern or Northern-born he lives to carry out the desires of his owners, and since the owners have placed investments in his hands for the purpose of profit, the motivation of each manager is to protect these profits, a chore which takes him into great activity on every front. Basically his corporation wants low wages, so the manager spearheads anti-union activities. His company interlocks with other Northern corporations who manufacture finished products sold in the South, so he has fought to keep the freight-rate differentials, since if the South developed its own industries they would cut into the Northern company's profits. The manager's Northern masters profit by the maintenance of a higher tariff, so he fights any attempt to bring the tariffs down.

"Increased taxes for education, health, and roads make costs higher for the absentee owner. They are not to be encouraged. Reforestation, soil conservation, crop diversification, all cost money, to no immediate benefit to the Northern corporate aristocrat. This manager, pushed by economic drives, is on principle against any and all of them, and it is fairly simple to follow his processes. He commands the colonial outposts for Northern overlords who have never been averse to the maintenance of the entire South as a slum area, a gigantic sweatshop dedicated to Northern profit."[12]

It is their job to maintain the southern lag and poverty as an essential condition for the extraction of super-profits from the starvation wages of the Negro and white masses. They desperately oppose all efforts to lift the South out of its lowly economic and cultural state. They are linked to the plantation owners not only by economic and class ties, but also often by blood relationship and intermarriage. These two groups, capitalists and planters, comprise Southern Bourbonry.

Wall Street Credit Structure

Finance capital's dominance of the plantation is exercised through its control of plantation credit. This control extends in an unbroken chain from the counting rooms of Wall Street through the regional and country banks to the local landlord and credit merchant. At the plantation end, it is anchored in the crop-lien system.

The key link in this chain is the country bank, to which is assigned the pivotal role of local intermediary, or agent, for the big northern financial institutions. It is through the network of these country banks that Wall Street has maintained control over cotton production and cotton marketing. W. Hustace

Hubbard, a member of a leading firm of cotton brokers, in 1923 described the system as follows:

> "These banks all have correspondents in the large cities, not alone in the South, but in the North as well. Through these channels filter down one way the financial opinions of the large cities and large banks, and up the other way, the views of the interior upon the state of trade and the condition of the crops.
>
> ". . . The crop notes, originally discounted by the country bank, will be found in the loan portfolios of the larger institutions of the cities, as the money to make and move the crop is sent out through the usual banking channels."[13]

Of the great power wielded by the banks, and their directing and supervisory role in the plantation economy Hubbard says:

> "It may be surmised that the country banks can exercise much influence upon the acreage in the spring and upon the marketing in the fall. It is the refusal of the country bank to advance additional funds with unpaid paper still on their books which has much to do with the curtailment of acreage in a year of stress, such as the spring of 1921 . . . Similarly in the fall they can exercise considerable influence upon the marketing of the crop."[14]

Plantation financing rests upon the crop-lien system. The whole Wall Street credit structure is based upon the maintenance of this relic of the infamous Black Codes. The landlord's prior lien upon the tenant's crop is the essential collateral for plantation credit. If he has also a lien upon livestock and other property of the tenant, as is the case in some states, so much the better. His credit facilities are thereby expanded. The crop-lien is the central cog in the system of legal controls, which sanction plantation landlordism and Negro serfdom.

Just as in ante-bellum times the chief consideration for a planter's loan was the number of slaves he owned, so now the extent of his credit is based upon the number of his tenant liens. Such holding of liens as collateral is an essential demand not only of private institutions but of the federal government as well.

Through this credit lien, the bulk of the returns from the plantation slavery is piped off into the coffers of the big financial interests of the North. Some indication of the tribute exacted can be gleaned from Woofter's plantation study. More than half (52 per cent) of the landowners had short term debts to meet current expenses on the crop. The average sum borrowed was $2,300, just half of the sum necessary to meet annual expenses. On these accounts the total· rate ran high: 10 per cent on governmental loans, 15 per cent on bank loans and 16 per cent on merchant accounts. Most of the credit was furnished by banks, governmental loans amounting to only 22 per cent of the short-term credit. Only landlords were eligible for governmental loans, since they held the only acceptable security—crop lien.[15]

"A check-up on 46 scattered counties in the South in 1934 showed that one-tenth of the farm land was in the hands of northern corporations, mostly banks and insurance companies," (headed by Metropolitan) which had foreclosed their mortgages.[16]

The tightening stranglehold of northern big money on southern agriculture is shown quite clearly. From 1910 to 1928, the amount of mortgage debt almost quadrupled in the seven southeastern states. Here the increases in mortgage debt from 1920 to 1928 were proportionately greater than in any other section of the country.[17] In 1935 it was estimated that 30 per cent of the cotton lands of various states were owned by insurance companies and banks.[18]

Finance capital in southern agriculture functions as a sort of oxygen tent preserving and continually reviving the aged and tottering plantation economy. Bulwarking its social, racial and legal controls with the might of the dollar, it helps to preserve pre-capitalist forms of exploitation, preventing rational scientific methods of farming and enforcing the ruinous single-crop system. Its role is artificially to retard and distort the South's modern development.

Finance Capital and the Southern Negro

The period of empire brought in its train a sharpening of political retrogression in the field of Negro rights. Repeal of the so-called "Force Bills"* by Congress in 1894 emphasized the refusal of the federal government to try any longer to protect the legal citizenship rights of the Negro. The "gentlemen's understanding" between the industrial-financial interests of the North and the Bourbon South was further strengthened.

The results were a manifold increase in the oppression of the main mass of the South's agricultural population, particularly Negroes. To their already onerous burden was added the weight of increased exactions by imperialist plunderers from the north. W. E. B. DuBois has described the effect of the development of finance capital on the Negro people within the nation:

> "The echo of industrial imperialism in America was the expulsion of black men from American democracy, their subjection to caste control and wage slavery. This ideology was triumphant in 1910."[19]

In the 1890's the southern states began to enact a series of disfranchising laws which were destined within the next sixteen years to abrogate completely the right of the Negro to the franchise in the South. DuBois points out "that between 1895 and 1909 the whole South disfranchised its Negro voters by unfair and illegal restrictions and passed a series of 'Jim Crow' laws which made the Negro citizen a subordinate caste."[20]

This political retrogression had its economic reflections. The trend toward increased Negro land ownership which had obtained since the Civil War, and upon which liberal hopes for the eventual emergence of the independent Negro yeomanry had been based, was suddenly reversed. In 1910, Negro land ownership in the south reached its peak—220,000 individual owners. Thereafter, it held fairly steady until 1920, when it began to decline generally, dropping to 173,000 by 1940.

The period also marked the defeat of the agrarian populist movement in the South with its promise of Negro-white unity

---

*To implement the Fifteenth Amendment to the Constitution, the Enforcement Acts were passed by Congress (1870-1871). The Act of 1870 penalized state officers and any person who attempted to deprive citizens of suffrage and their civil rights, and authorized the President to use armed force to this end. The Act of 1871 gave federal officers and courts control over registration and elections in Congressional Districts. (See W. E. B. DuBois, *Black Reconstruction*, Harcourt Brace, N. Y., 1935.)

against the growing encroachments of the Bourbon Wall Street bloc.* Southern populism was finally perverted by the treachery of such leaders as Tom Watson and Ben Tillman, who rode the crest of southern agrarian revolt, only to sell out to the "lily-white" Democrats.[21]

These years saw also a revival of the notorious Black Codes, a resurgence of the hooded terror of the Ku Klux Klan, and the defeat for re-election in 1905 of the last Negro congressman surviving the Reconstruction betrayal.

Thus the plantation, with its color caste and political controls, had become an integral part of American economic and political life, inextricably interwoven with the structure and substructure of American imperialism. The *status quo* of Negro inequality became a rigidly frozen pattern which could be broken only on the basis of anti-imperialist struggle.

The Economic Crisis

Big money's stake in the plantation system was most dramatically demonstrated during the early part of the 1929 crisis.

The world economic crisis marked the beginning of a decade of disaster for southern agriculture and its people. The collapse of agricultural prices following the 1929 stock market crash dealt a staggering blow to the South's cotton economy.

For years preceding the panic of 1929, the South's economic condition had been on the downgrade, and storm signals had been raised forecasting the inevitable disaster.

King Cotton, the sick man of American agriculture, had taken a turn for the worse. His ailment, a chronic case of "plantation-itis," coupled with the "boll weevil blues," had reached a critical stage which was rendered more acute by the uninterrupted

---

*The Populist movement expressed the revolt of laboring farm people at the end of the past century against the tightening grip of the trusts. Originating among the rebellious farmers of the West, this movement also acquired a large following in the South among small farmers, sharecroppers, and tenants. Revolt against the spreading hold of monopoly on southern cotton, and against the entrenchment of the single crop, formed the substance of the program of the southern Populist wing, which called for Negro and white co-operation around such issues as public ownership of railroads, Negro political equality, the fight to end lynching, and other radical reforms.

decline of world agriculture dating from the end of World War I. All nostrums of Dr. Hoover and, before him, those of Coolidge and Harding, had proved ineffective; the patient failed to respond.

During the 'twenties, the trend of cotton prices was mostly downward. Presaging the forthcoming crash, there was a continuous shrinkage of the world market for raw cotton and textiles. The situation became worse after 1929; both domestic and foreign demand for textiles dropped sharply.

Unemployment increased, reducing industrial income. Prices for cotton lint dropped off to half the pre-war level. More and more, the main cotton manufacturing countries other than the United States began to place purchasing contracts with producers elsewhere than in the United States.[22]

England and France, for example, began to rely upon cotton imports from their dominions and from Egypt and Brazil. Brazil's cotton production rose from an average of 492 million bales annually in 1925-29 to 1,856 millions in 1933-1937. The world's production of rayon fibers increased from 33 million pounds in 1920 to 1,948 million pounds in 1938. The production of these fibers was equivalent to 4,585,000 bales of cotton in 1938.[23]

The index number for gross cash income from cotton marketings showed a drop from 100 in 1925-29 to 41 in 1939.[24] Along with this catastrophic decline in the consumption of cotton was an increase in the carryover from 5 million to 13 million bales in the American crop between 1929-1930 and 1932-33.

In the five years following 1928, total farm returns from cotton and cotton seed fell by 70 per cent. The result was a sharp reduction in the average gross income of Southern farm families. The family income which had been $735 in 1928 was only $216 in 1932, in which year cotton fell to 4.6 cents a pound.[25]

This sharpening of the agrarian crisis was most startlingly revealed by the absolute drop in the area of cultivated land in the South. The area of harvested land declined from 43 million acres in 1929 to 36 million in 1932. As a result of the Agricultural Administration Act acreage reduction program, in 1933, it was down to 29 million. There was a further decline to 22 million in 1941, to 20 million in 1944 and to 17½ million in 1946.[26]

On the other hand, the decline in rural population was relatively slight. The number of Negroes in rural farm communities
declined in the ten years following 1930 by only 4.5 per cent—a
smaller decline than the 8.6 per cent of the previous ten years.[27]
The desperate plight of the farm Negro during this period is
shown most clearly by the fact that this "flight" from the land
could go on at all in spite of the lack of industrial outlets in the
cities.

The stark tragedy behind these figures, their meaning in
terms of human suffering and destitution, beggars imagination.
Although the census reveals a decrease of over 235,000 Negro
and white sharecropping families, large numbers remained in
agriculture, reduced to the sub-tenant status of casual wage
laborers.

The collapse of agricultural prices following the breakdown of
the 'twenties witnessed a "moving in" by the federal government
with measures to "save" southern agriculture.

The chief objective of the Hoover administration—through
these measures—was to prevent the threatened bankruptcy of
the large financial interests with heavy investments in southern
cotton and to preserve the plantation credit structure. To these
ends it directed the bulk of its emergency funds for agriculture;
46 per cent of these funds between 1929 and 1933 went to the
southern states.[28]

As early as 1928 the federal government had become a large-
scale investor in southern farm mortgages. In 1933, over one-
fourth of these mortgages was held by federal land banks in
which the federal government held 64 per cent of the total
capital stock.[29]

Nearly half (44 per cent) of the plantations covered in the
Woofter survey were mortgaged at an average of 40 per cent
of their value and 72 per cent of these were mortgaged through
government facilities.[30]

The first Hoover project allocating funds for direct loans to
farmers was the Regional Agricultural Credit Corporation.
Launched by the Reconstruction Finance Corporation, it was a
Wall Street-dominated agency, with most of its members holding
corporate directorships. Members leaving directory board meet-

ings of private big business reconvened as a government agency
to pass on the disbursements of federal finances.[31]

The numerous bank failures in the farm areas had resulted
in the drying up of the sources of short term credit; the Reconstruction Finance Corporation to a large extent replaced these
banks as sources of local credit. But only large-scale producers
benefited. The small cultivators, that is, the great mass of
tenants and small owners, were debarred from benefits by the
provision that the landlord's lien waiver must be obtained in
order to receive a loan, and by the fact that the average loan
was $1,000 and required heavy collateral.

The second source of federal aid was the feed crop loans,
organized presumably to provide short-term credit to small
farmers unable to get assistance from other institutions. Here
also the required security was either a lien on crops and livestock,
or first mortgage on personal property, requirements which effectively closed this avenue to the basic mass of small producers.
Even here, the landlords manipulated to cut in on a good chunk
of the federal crop loans by the simple device of waiving—tech-
nically—their first lien rights.

In 1933, Raper reported that Georgia Black Belt planters got
hold of many loans originally intended for their tenants through
verbal agreements with the latter. With nothing but the
landlord's verbal agreement, conveniently retracted upon the
receipt of the loan check, "the landlord virtually forced the
tenant to deliver the check to him."[32] He could not even cash
checks without the planter's authorization.*

Thus, the central theme of Hoover's so-called farm relief
measures was the protection of Wall Street and planters' investments, with the raiding of the public treasury to bolster the
feudal land system of the South, and to preserve its life-line,
Wall Street credit.

---

*This remained true under the New Deal. Stetson Kennedy relates
the following, reported by a twenty-four year old fugitive from peonage:
"When I received my first check from the A.A.A., Mr. ————— took me in
his car to get it cashed. On the way back he made me give the money to him,
letting me keep twenty-five cents." (Stetson Kennedy, *Southern Exposure*,
p. 56, Doubleday, N. Y., 1946.)

The obverse side of the coin was the increased impoverishment and dispossession of the masses of small cultivators, and here it was the Negro who bore the main burden. This basic pattern was carried over and accentuated in the Agricultural Administration Act.

A.A.A.—Another Pill for the Patient

In May, 1933, the Agricultural Adjustment Administration was created in the interest of the big planters and northern credit institutions. Its artificial pegging of cotton prices served to aggravate the social aspects of the crisis, and spurred on the process of economic deterioration and impoverishment of the lower strata.

The planter's interest was further safeguarded by his domination of local agencies administering the A.A.A. program, a domination based upon the Negro's political impotence which enabled the planter to grab the lion's share of the benefits.

Thus, the average A.A.A. benefit per plantation tenant family in 1937 was only $27 a year, that is, less than 10 per cent of the total income in cash of the tenant farmer, on 246 southern plantations.[33]

The Farm Security Administration program of social reforms, purporting to bring relief to the "little man in the farm business," brought no appreciable amelioration of the conditions of the great majority of cotton producers.

That appropriations for these programs were glaringly inadequate is shown by the following: while $5,328,800,000 was appropriated for A.A.A. policies during the period of 1934-41 (a disproportionate share of which went to the big landlords) the outlay for F.S.A. during the same period amounted to $1,120,-600,000—about one-fifth of the A.A.A. appropriations.[34]

Here again, we find accommodation to the landlord's Jim Crow code. F.S.A. programs were made to conform to dominant big-planter interests. Local administration was mainly in the hands of the planters and their friends, and possible F.S.A. clients had to be passed upon by local farmers' committees in which the Negro had practically no influence. This was notably true with regard to the so-called rehabilitation programs which included assistance of various kinds on an individual basis, and which took up the major part of the work and appropriations of the F.S.A.

What was the treatment of the Negro in the operation of this program? By January 1, 1940, there were in the South 154,381 white and 45,335 Negro "standard rehabilitation borrowers." Thus, while at least one-half of the southern rural population needing help was Negro, Negroes constituted less than a fourth of the total number of clients.[35]

Compared with the total estimated numbers of white and colored farm families which were either on relief or had an income of less than $500, those participating in the program amounted to 22 per cent of the whites and 11 per cent of the Negroes. A low-income white family had about twice the chance of a Negro family in the same circumstances of being accepted on the program. Higher average amounts of loan advances for whites than Negroes were also shown—$659 for whites and $606 for colored.[36]

Other F.S.A. programs such as resettlement and rental co-operatives were insignificant so far as the Negro was concerned. By the middle of 1940 there were only 1,393 Negro families on various types of F.S.A. resettlement projects—about one-fourth of all such families in the South.[37] Only 1,919 families were reached by the so-called tenant-purchase program. Four times as many whites were on this program. Thus there was nearly the same amount of discrimination in these cases as in the rehabilitation work.[38]

On the whole, New Deal social reforms in southern agriculture, while furnishing some relief to the totally destitute, proved woefully inadequate and did not even begin to repair the original damages suffered by the masses of Negro and white soil tillers as a result of the A.A.A.

Arthur F. Raper's appraisal of New Deal reforms in the South's agricultural structure still holds good. Writing in 1936, before the 1940 Census, he saw in his field studies the main facts later verified by census returns, and summarized them thus:

> "The New Deal with its cotton restriction program, its relief expenditures, and its loan services . . . has rejuvenated the decaying plantation economy. Those who control the plantations are now experiencing relative

prosperity. On the other hand the landless farmers . . . are not only failing to escape their chronic dependence but are actually losing status. Many tenants are being pushed off the land while many others are being pushed down the tenure ladder, especially from cropper to wage-hand status."[39]

The F.S.A. foundered on the jagged reef of Dixie landlordism, and a similar fate awaits all programs having for their aim the benefit of the "common man" in Southern agriculture, *unless they are planned as a part of a basic attack upon racial discrimination, plantation feudalism, and the forces of monopoly capital which profit from such exploitation.*

CHAPTER IV

The Shadow of the Plantation

THE SOUTH contains one-half of the country's land which is arable for six months of the year, two-thirds of the land having more than 40 inches of rainfall annually. It has abundant resources: oil, natural gas, limestone, and water power, and possesses 40 per cent of the nation's forests. More than one-third of the nation's good farms are in the South. Half the nation's marble output comes from this section, 97 per cent of its phosphates, 99 per cent of its sulphur, and two-thirds of its crude oil. It is a section which leads the world in the production of cotton, tobacco, and corn.[1]

It is the social position of the Negro in the South and his serf-like oppression on the Black Belt plantations that furnish the clue to southern backwardness and poverty, to the economic, social, cultural, and political inequality of the overwhelming mass of the South's white folk as compared with that of the rest of the country.

Degradation of the Whites

It is not accidental then, that where the Negroes are most oppressed, the position of the whites is also most degraded. Facts unearthed and widely publicized, including the Report of the National Emergency Council to the late President Roosevelt, have thrown vivid light on the "paradise" of racial bigotry below the Mason-Dixon Line. They expose the staggering price of "white supremacy" in terms of health, living and cultural standards of the great masses of southern whites. They show "white supremacy"—the shibboleth of Bourbon overlords—to be synonymous with the most outrageous poverty and misery of the southern white people. They show that "keeping the Negro down" spells for the entire South the nation's lowest wage and living standards.

"White supremacy" means the nation's greatest proportion of tenants and sharecroppers, its highest rate of child labor, its most degrading and widespread exploitation of women, its poorest health and housing record, its highest illiteracy and lowest proportion of students in high schools and colleges, its highest death and disease rates, its lowest level of union organization and its least democracy.

Sharecropping has drawn into its orbit tens of thousands of poor white farmers. Woofter says that " . . . while the vast majority of white agricultural workers were owners in 1860, by 1930 over three-quarters of a million white families in the Southeast had joined the tenant or laborer class."[2] In 1930, 5 per cent of the plantations were operated exclusively by white tenants and 42 per cent by white and Negro tenants.[3]

Nearly 45 per cent of sharecroppers were white in 1940.*

The widespread exploitation of children inherent in the plantation sharecropping system is why the South leads the nation in child labor. The National Emergency Council reported that about three-fourths of all gainfully employed children between the ages of ten and fifteen worked in the southern states, although these states contained less than one-third of these children of the nation.[4] In other words, child labor was more than nine times as prevalent in the South as in the rest of the country.

It is but natural that the poll-tax bloc in Congress, representing the Dixie planter interest, has paced the drive against application of child labor laws to agriculture.

The stultifying influence of plantation economy in the Black Belt on economic and political conditions in the entire South explains also the degrading plight of southern women, subject to an even more intensive exploitation than that suffered by the

*The percentage of white sharecroppers dropped during the war years but still stood at 38 per cent in 1945.

men. As late as 1938, only one of the southern states had established an eight-hour day for women in any industry.[5]

Wages in 1938 were anywhere from 30 to 50 per cent below those of the rest of the country.[6] In 1940 the per capita income of the southeast* was only $309. Compare this with a national per capita income of $573. Containing 14 per cent of the nation's population, the region received only 7.3 per cent of the nation's wage total.[7] Even in the war boom years, wages of skilled workers in some industries ran as much as 30-57 per cent below the national average.[8]

What Price White Supremacy?

Political controls which are aimed primarily at the disfranchisement of the Negro have also resulted in depriving the mass of the poor whites of their right to the ballot. In 1942, 6,000,000 southern whites were disfranchised as compared to 4,000,000 Negroes.[9]

Lynching, a device of the Bourbon ruling classes designed to keep the Negro in "his place," is turned against the white worker whenever he attempts to improve his conditions or to join forces with the Negro in the struggle for his rights. Raper, covering the six years following the coming of the New Deal, reports:

> "In 1934 and 1935, there were 42 deaths in the South from labor strife. In 1936 and 1937 the number had dropped to 5, while for 1938 and 1939 there were 14. . . . It is significant that for each year between 1934 and 1940 nearly one half the labor fatalities in America occurred in the South, with scarcely one fourth of the nation's population and less than one fourth of its industrial workers."[10]

In fact, every measure passed to curb the Negro has resulted in destroying the civil rights of the poor whites. At the bottom of the cultural backwardness and impoverishment of the southern white is the position of his black neighbor. America's Tobacco Road begins in the Black Belt.

---

*The Southeast includes Tennessee, Alabama, Florida, Georgia, Mississippi, North Carolina, and South Carolina.

White illiteracy in thirteen southern states is *twice* that of the rest of the country. Half the southern boys were unable to meet the minimum requirements for military service. The rest of the nation furnished 65 eligible soldiers from every hundred called in for examination by the draft boards. The proportion of men rejected was 40 per cent higher in the South than in the rest of the country.[11]

The Bilbonic Plague

In Bilbo's Mississippi, A. G. Mezerik points out, forty-five out of every one hundred Mississippians between the ages of five and twenty-four are not even enrolled in a school. Three hundred thousand people are crippled or incapacitated by venereal disease. Two hundred thousand are chronic malaria carriers. Ten thousand are slowly dying of tuberculosis.[12]

With 28 per cent of the nation's population, the South receives only nine per cent of the nation's income and has less than one billion of the nation's twenty-eight billion dollars insurance assets. The total endowment of all colleges and universities in thirteen southern states equals the endowment of only two New England universities. And this situation obtains in a section whose material resources are among the richest in the nation.[13]

These facts give the lie to the myth of a "Solid South," so assiduously cultivated by the professional besmirchers of the Negro.

The fable of a united white South, standing firm and solid against the "menace" of "Black Domination" in defense of "white womanhood," was exposed long ago by that notable southerner, George W. Cable:

> "The struggle in the Southern States has never been by the blacks for, and by the whites against, a black supremacy, but only for and against an arbitrary pure white supremacy. From the very first until this day, in all the freedman's intellectual crudity, he has held fast to the one true, National doctrine of the absence of privilege and the rule of all by all."[14]

The hokum of southern Bourbonry is now unmasked for what it is: a cunning lie of a minority governing caste calculated to hide the deep social fissures in southern life. It is the peculiar Dixie version of the stratagem, "divide and rule."

"It is . . . apparent," comments Woofter, "that in excluding the Negro the South is, in a way, politically dominated by the Negro question. Before all others it looms as the bulwark of the one-party system. It was a determining factor in the prohibition vote. It affected the South's stand on woman suffrage and it ramifies into hundreds of questions of public policy, it influences the South's position on child labor, it is a stumbling block in the administration of compulsory school laws, standing as an ever-present shadow across the door of political councils."[15]

Plainly the South can progress only by breaking the oppression of the Negro. "A people which enslaves another people forges its own chains," said Karl Marx.[16] The same idea was expressed in colloquial language by Booker T. Washington: You can't hold the Negro in the ditch without staying in it with him.

This liberating truth shatters all artificial race lines and points up the objective base for the alliance of the Negro people and southern white workers and poor farmers in the struggle for a "solid" South of genuine democracy.

That this truth is being understood by an ever-widening sector of white southern labor and progressive intellectuals is seen in the advance of labor unity below the Mason-Dixon line and in the struggle of both Negro and white against poll-tax disfranchisement and the renewed rampages of fascist hate organizations such as the Ku Klux Klan and Columbians, Inc.

But it is not only in the South that the corroding effects of the plantation are manifested. It is a national blight and it pursues its chief victim, the Negro, wherever he may seek refuge.

Color Line in Industry

The shadow of the plantation falls upon the Negro in Harlem, in Chicago's South Side, in the hundreds of urban "Black Belts" throughout the country, frustrating his efforts toward economic and social betterment. The twin evils of poverty and Jim Crow dog his heels, setting the pattern for his new urban life.

The "color line," which in the agricultural regions of the South freezes the Negro at the bottom rungs of the economic ladder, operates in industry to achieve the same end. The net result is the establishment of a "job ceiling" above which a Negro can rise only rarely and under which the great mass of urban wage earners are forced into the categories of lowest paid and least skilled jobs in industry or into the menial drudgery of domestic and personal services.

As the Bureau of the Census reported in 1940:

> "Striking differences between the occupations of whites and Negroes were shown in 1940 census statistics. Farmers, farm laborers, and other laborers constituted 62.2 per cent of all employed Negro men and only 28.5 per cent of all employed white men. Only about 5 per cent of all employed Negro men, compared with approximately 30 per cent of employed white men, were engaged in professional, semi-professional, proprietary, managerial, and clerical or sales occupations. Skilled craftsmen represented 15.6 per cent of employed white men and only 4.4 per cent of employed Negro men. More than half of the Negro craftsmen were mechanics, carpenters, painters, plasterers and cement finishers, and masons."[17]

Of the three million (3,032,061) Negro wage earners employed outside agriculture in 1940, more than half were service workers. One million (1,003,508) were in domestic service. Another half million (522,229) were engaged in other "service" jobs such as hotel and restaurant, laundry and building service, etc. In addition, more than half a million (636,600) were unskilled laborers. Half a million (464,195) were classified as "operatives," that is, employed in manufacture, mining, trucking, communications, and transportation. Thus there were less than 380,000 individuals to make up the manager, proprietor, professional, clerical, sales, foremen, and craftsmen groups.

Nearly a million (910,123) were unemployed or were working on emergency projects in 1940.[18] In the same year, seven out of every ten employed Negroes were engaged in unskilled work, and ninety-four out of every hundred in "manual" occupations. The proportion of unskilled workers among Negroes was three hundred and fifty per cent greater than among whites![19]

A breakdown of the United States Census of 1940 for Chicago revealed the following racial differential for that midwestern metropolis: 74.3 per cent of the Negro male workers as compared with 39.3 of white were engaged in the lowest three occupational categories—semi-skilled, unskilled, and servants. The disproportion between Negro and white was nearly two to one.[20]

And this in Chicago, the mecca of Negro migrations from the Cotton South, a city which contains the world's largest concentration of Negro industrial workers and which boasts of the prog- line," the great midwest melting pot has failed signally to blend ress of its colored citizenry. Thanks to the workings of the "color this important segment of its multi-ethnic population into the assimilated whole. And the story of Chicago is the story of all northern industrial communities.

The starting point of job discrimination against the Negro is the labor market. Here he is denied the right freely to compete for the kind of jobs to which he aspires and for which he is qualified.

The second stage is within industry itself where through various devices, such as discrimination in applying seniority rules, in opportunities for "in plant" training as well as in private industrial courses, and finally as the result of Jim Crow bars still operative in many craft unions,* the door is closed to the advancement of any significant number of his group beyond the level of the semi-skilled.

A temporary breach in the bastion of job Jim Crow was forced by the industrial boom of World War II. In 1942 the federal government established a Fair Employment Practice policy, designed to sweep aside Jim Crow barriers for the speedy mobilization of the country's industrial might. This, together with the rapid advance of progressive unionism, symbolized mainly in the

*At least fourteen trade unions specifically excluded Negroes from membership in 1944 by provisions in their constitutions or by-rules; five excluded them by tacit consent, and nine unions afforded them only segregated auxiliary status. Typical of the first category is the constitution of the Locomotive Firemen, which limits membership to "white born, of good moral character." (Herbert R. Northrup, *Organized Labor and the Negro*, pp. 2-3, Harper, N. Y., 1944; see also Florence Murray, ed., *The Negro Handbook, 1946-1947*, p. 112.)

Congress of Industrial Organizations, created a favorable interlude for the Negro people in which their long cherished hopes for economic and social betterment were brightened. The precarious beachhead to industrial opportunity was widened. The "job ceiling" was slightly raised, with the entrance of thousands of Negro men and women into areas of skilled employment from which they had been traditionally barred.

But the pattern was not broken. The final report of the Fair Employment Practice Committee (FEPC) revealed that of the "total job orders received by the United States Employment Service offices in eleven selected areas during the period of February 1-15, 1946, 24 per cent of the orders were discriminatory."[21] Although the Negroes in skilled and semi-skilled occupations had doubled between 1940 and April, 1944, nearly two-thirds of all Negro women workers (62.5 per cent) remained in service occupations and close to half (44.5 per cent) still held domestic service jobs. Nearly half the Negro men still worked on farms or as unskilled laborers (28 per cent on farms and 20.3 per cent in other unskilled jobs). Although more than a third of all white women were clerical workers or salespeople, less than one Negro woman out of thirty was able to get such a job.[22]

Indisputably the present trend is toward re-establishment of the pre-war status quo. The employer policy which decrees the Negro to be the "last hired and first fired"—a rule which has been made to operate with the precision of an economic law—is still in force. This fact was brought to the fore by the mass lay-offs and downgrading after V-J Day in which a disproportionately high percentage of Negro workers was affected. A United States Census Bureau survey, cited by the *Report of the President's Committee on Civil Rights,* disclosed that "from July, 1945, to April, 1946, unemployment among whites increased about one and one-half times while unemployment among non-whites [chiefly Negro], more than tripled."[23]

To sum up. While it cannot be denied that over the years beginning with World War I, Negro labor has gained a foothold in the industrial plant of the North, this foothold has always been a precarious one. By and large Negroes are still living on the fringe of the country's industrial economy. From the standpoint of the policy of big business they are the expendables of our country's industrial labor force.

The foregoing points up the over-all strategy of U.S. monopoly capitalism in regard to the Negro people. It is a strategy designed to hold them in perpetuity as a special reserve of cheap and underprivileged labor, an instrument with which to undercut the standards of their white brothers—a deterrent to working-class unity, a ball and chain to hold back the advances of organized labor.*

The central pivot in that policy is to preserve by all means, legal and illegal, the social isolation of the Negro, to hem him round with an unbreachable wall of Jim Crow, re-enforced by artificially fostered racial prejudices. And the prime condition for the continuance of this policy in the North is the preservation of the system of medieval torture of the black peasantry of the South, from whose degraded and poverty-ridden ranks the "special reserve" is constantly replenished, to threaten with the direness of plantation hunger the living standard of the entire nation.

Jim Crow in the North and West is premised on the maintenance of this fear of the northern worker for his living standard.

The northern textile worker has seen the southern runaway mills lower his wage and rob him of his job. He has been hit by the plantation standard of living which sets the standard for southern textile wages, the lowest of any major American industry.

It has been the traditional tactic of the employing class to use the migrant Negro sharecroppers of the South and the poorest peasantry of Europe, Mexico, and Asia as wage-cutters and strikebreakers and to utilize the resulting resentment of white workers to foster prejudice against these groups, splitting them from the main body of American labor and persuading white workers to accept for these "inferior" groups, wages and living standards which undercut their own.

The preservation of the plantation system with its annual crop of half-starved, uneducated fugitives to the North is essential to

*In later years, the C.I.O. particularly began to see through this strategy, as shown by the fight of some unions for anti-discrimination clauses in employer-labor contracts.

the continuance of the dividing tactic, which is basic to the dominance of monopoly capital.

Such, in brief, are the underlying economic factors behind the continued social proscription of the Negro in the North.

Northern Pattern

In the North, segregation generally lacks the sanction of law. Here it is enforced rather by custom and extra-legal practice, by formal and informal social pressures. Its mainstay is residential segregation, epitomized in the notorious Negro ghetto, where the great mass of colored urban dwellers are corralled in a state of permanent social quarantine.

Take the Negro community of any of a dozen large northern industrial centers. A social diagnosis of the evils afflicting the inmates of these ghettos reveals a common pattern. Invariably, the Negro district is located in the most dilapidated, run-down slum section—the city's blighted area. Its population lives in the most frightful squalor in ramshackle, vermin-ridden shacks and firetrap tenements. Buildings remain unrepaired year after year, with garbage disposal and street cleaning neglected. A survey of one Harlem block in 1946 revealed more than 1,400 violations of the buildings and sanitary codes in some 700 apartments.

The lack of elementary sanitary conditions prevailing in these slums is intensified by overcrowding, with families literally piled on top of each other. In Chicago's Black Belt, in 1944, Negroes were "living 90,000 to the square mile as compared with 20,000 to the square mile in adjacent white" neighborhoods.[24] The same picture was reproduced in other Negro urban centers such as Harlem, Detroit, and more recently, Los Angeles. In the latter city 30,000 Negroes were reported, in 1944, to be living in the area formerly inhabited by 7,000 Japanese.

Residential Jim Crow means exorbitant and oppressive rents. In Detroit, for example, Lester Velie found that:

> "For his crowded flat or room in blighted Black Bottom or Paradise Valley, the Negro pays 30 to 50 per cent more than whites pay for better quarters. A family jammed into a single room, sharing toilet facilities with six other

families (the legal limit in Detroit is two, but is unenforceable), will pay from $11 to $16 weekly or $47 to $69 per month. Before rent ceilings came, landlords tripled and quadrupled monthly incomes by evicting white families and renting to Negroes; easy pickings."[25]

Jim Crow also means shoddy and inferior merchandise and food sold in neighborhood stores at higher prices. It means overcrowded schools. In 1938, 13 of the 15 Chicago schools running on double and triple "shifts" were in Negro neighborhoods.[26] Similar conditions prevail in Harlem and other congested Negro communities.

What are the effects of these conditions on the health of the population? "In 1925 Chicago had the lowest death rate for any American city of 1,000,000 and over, but the Negro death rate was twice that for the white!"[27] "The average death rate for the years 1928-32 was 9.2 for native whites, 10.4 for foreign whites, and 20.0 for Negroes."[28] In 1940, the death rate for non-whites in Illinois was still 15.7 per 1000 population and 10.9 for the white population.[29]*

But the substandard health conditions of Negroes in northern urban communities are most glaringly revealed in the high tuberculosis morbidity and mortality rates among them. In Chicago death rates for tuberculosis were 250.1 per 100,000 population for the Negroes as against 45.4 for the whites in 1939-41; in New York it was 213 for the Negroes as compared to 40.4 for the whites; in Newark, N. J., 275.5 for the Negroes and 39.9 for the whites; in Detroit, 189 for the Negro and 55.6 for the white.[30]

A central device for maintaining residential Jim Crow is the

---

*Chicago was no exception to conditions in the North immediately following World War I. In 1920 the death rate for whites in Indiana was 13.2, for non-whites, 22.2; in Michigan 13.8 for whites and 25.7 for non-whites; in New York 13.8 for whites and 19.6 for non-whites; in Rhode Island 14.2 for whites and 26.3 for non-whites. Though New Deal policies reduced the differential, the death rate remained higher for non-whites than for whites everywhere in 1940. In 1943, the Negro death rate for the United States was 12.8 and the white death rate 10.7. (*Sixteenth Census, Vital Statistics of the U. S., 1900-40;* and *Vital Statistics of the U. S., 1944.*)

"Restrictive Covenant," an agreement among property owners of adjacent white neighborhoods not to rent or sell property to Negroes. Though obviously unconstitutional, the legality of such agreements has been upheld by court decisions.[31]* Even the Federal Housing Administration tacitly sanctions such agreements by underwriting the mortgages on privately-built houses subject to restrictive covenant.[32]

Legislative and judicial acquiescence in the exclusion of Negroes from publicly aided projects, as in the case of the Metropolitan Life Insurance Company's vast Stuyvesant Town Project in New York, is a variation of court sanction of the restrictive covenant. It constitutes a dangerous precedent for similar projects in at least 22 other states. As Charles Abrams, New York housing expert, points out in the *New York Post,* July 30, 1947: "On the claim that it will promote slum clearance, the establishment of the ghetto and the 'restricted community' receives not only legal blessing but public aid."

In Chicago, it was estimated that 75 per cent† of the residential area was involved in such agreements by 1930.[33] These covenants, supported by continuous anti Negro agitation of real estate boards and property owners' associations, operate to keep the Negro population penned up and congested in an area that is but a fraction of the size needed by their growing numbers. It is not surprising, therefore, that the territory fringing the Black Belt has been converted into a virtual no-man's land, where "racial" tension is at the highest, often flaring up into ugly riots between Negro and white.

Intimidation, terror, including incendiary vandalism, are among the weapons used to "hold the line" against the continu-

*For example the N. Y. Supreme Court decision in 1947 of *Kemp vs. Rubin* in suburban St. Albans, upholding the restrictive covenant.

The U. S. Supreme Court in June, 1945, refused to review the decision of the Washington, D. C., District Court of Appeals upholding such a covenant. On May 3, 1948, however, the U. S. Supreme Court decided that while there is nothing in law which prevents restrictive covenants between private individuals, the state courts may not enforce deeds containing such restrictive covenants.

†*To Secure These Rights: Reports of the President's Committee on Civil Rights* (p. 68) places its estimate at 80 per cent.

ous efforts of Negroes to extend their living space or to break out of the iron ring of Jim Crow and establish residence in better neighborhoods. An editorial of the Chicago *Defender* entitled "Danger: Dynamite at Large," says in part:

> "Hate-crazed incendiaries carrying the faggots of intolerance have in the past several months attacked some 30 homes occupied by Negroes on the fringes of the Black Belt, solely because these colored citizens have desperately crossed the unwritten boundary in their search for a hovel to live in. Buildings have been set afire, bombed, stoned, and razed. Their occupants have been shot and slugged.
>
> "To date, the Chicago Police Department has done virtually nothing to apprehend the guilty."[34]

These are the bitter facts of life of the Negro people in the North. Fitted into the over-all picture they add up to the angry indictment of America's rulers contained in the petition of the National Negro Congress to the United Nations (June 6, 1946).

Among the items in this petition the following are most striking:

> "Family Income: As of 1940, two-thirds of the Negro families earned less than $750 a year,* and this was true notwithstanding the fact that about 2 in every 5 Negro women were in the labor force, in contrast to 2 in every 8 white women. Here, too, it is important to note that the government, itself, declared that a city family of three needed, in 1941, an income of $1,475 'to cover current living expenditures,' almost exactly twice that actually obtained by most of its urban Negro citizens.
>
> "Housing: . . . In the United States, in 1940, there were 3,293,406 dwelling units for Negroes. Of these over one million (1,082,128) 'needed major repairs,' and almost two million (1,908,100) had no running water. Over twice as many Negro homes as white (35.1 per cent

---

*The average income of Negro families in the United States is $1,043, as compared with the average income of $3,062 for white families. *Seventy-five per cent of Negro families make less than $1,000 a year*, while the income of nearly one-third of these families (30.8 per cent) was less than $500 per annum. (Elmo Roper, *New York Herald Tribune*, Dec. 25, 1947. His data were based on a sample survey taken by *Fortune* magazine in Aug., 1947.)

and 16.3 per cent) needed major repairs and almost three times as many Negro homes as white (62 per cent and 26.6 per cent) had no running water. Twice as many white homes as Negro homes (82.9 per cent and 43 per cent) had electricity. All these figures are, of course, very much worse in the South, where the bulk of the Negro citizens live. Thus, to illustrate, it may be mentioned that well over 70 per cent of all *Negro homes in that area have neither electricity nor running water.*

"Health: This oppression cripples and kills. Sickness, which incapacitates for a minimum of one week, is 40 per cent more common to the Negro than to the white. In 1940, while 46 out of every 1,000 white children born alive did not live to reach their first birthdays, 85 Negro children died during the same period. And the proportion of deaths for children from one to four years of age is almost twice as high for the Negro as for the white, while the maternal death rate is more than twice as high. Finally, while a white man could expect, in 1940, to reach almost 63 years, the Negro man's life expectancy was 52; and the figures for white and Negro women were 67 and 55 respectively."[35]

The net results of this poverty were most startlingly registered in educational deficiencies (illiteracy and semi-literacy), among Negro draft registrants in the recent war. The percentage of draft registrants deferred for this reason between May 15, 1941, and September 14, 1941, was eleven times greater for Negroes than for white.

The guilt for these conditions lies in the plantation slave pens of the southern Black Belt, with its feudal-minded Bourbon lords and its Yankee monopolist sponsors. They alone bear the responsibility for the evils afflicting the Negro people. Behind Negro urban poverty lie the ruin and destitution of five million Negroes living in conditions of semi-slavery in the plantation regions of the South.

The plantation is the generator, continually reproducing Negro inequality in all walks of life, condemning America's colored tenth to a Jim-Crow subjugation throughout the country.

"Gentlemen's Agreement"

The unsolved Negro agrarian question in the South is the springboard for the fascist salient into the heart of our country's democracy. The two most viciously reactionary currents in the country today merge in the tie-up between the parasitic and predatory sections of northern big business and the feudal agrarian interests of the South.

Here, in this unholy alliance of the nation's most rabidly anti-democratic forces, we have the modern version of the old "gentlemen's agreement" through which northern reaction sold democracy and the Negro down the river to the slave-driving interests of the South at the end of Reconstruction. It is this legacy of reaction, bequeathed by the betrayers of freedom in 1877, which has consistently served as a main pillar of the political domination of American monopoly capital and now serves as a bulwark of its postwar drive towards fascism and world supremacy.

As far back as March, 1938, Franklin Delano Roosevelt exposed these forces in the South who "believe in their hearts that the feudal system is still the best system." Linking the representatives of the southern lynchocrats and their Yankee backers with fascism, Roosevelt condemned the whole foul breed, pointing out that "there is little difference between the feudal system and the Fascist system."[36]

The truth of this observation by the late President was confirmed in an editorial of the *Charleston News and Courier,* household organ of South Carolina's ruling clique. In a spirit reminiscent of that state's leadership in the secessionist plot of 1861, the newspaper defiantly proclaims the political credo of southern Bourbonry:

> "Again let it be . . . clearly understood that were the *News and Courier* a democratic newspaper, if it believed in democracy as President Roosevelt believes in it . . . it would demand that every white man and woman and every black man and woman in the South be

protected in the right to vote. It would demand the abolition of all 'Jim Crow' cars, of all drawing of the color line by law. That is democracy. But the *News and Courier* is not a democrat. It fears and hates democratic government. . . ."

"In South Carolina, the Democratic party has been, so far as the Negro vote is concerned, a *Fascist* party, and that is why the *News and Courier* 'cooperates' with it." (My emphasis—*H.H.*)[37]

The political instrument of this sinister combination is the bloc of southern poll-tax Senators and Congressmen allied with the northern reactionaries of both the Democratic and Republican parties. Through the disfranchisement of two-thirds of the voting potential of the South, the Bourbons have managed to return to office year after year. And as a result of the seniority rules of the House and Senate, they have succeeded in dominating a majority of the key committees of both houses in Congress. They are responsible to no one but themselves and their backstair friends from up North.

Parading a phony regional patriotism, they are nevertheless owned "body and breeches" by the Wall Street corporations. Invariably their effort is directed to whittling down the democracy of the whole country to the level demanded by their own feudal interests and those of their Wall Street mentors.

Over the years, they have built up a consistently reactionary group in Congress ready, at a nod from the tories of high finance, to do battle against all progressive measures which would benefit labor, Negroes, and the common people generally. These "regional Quislings" of Yankee financial greed, led by Rankin, Bilbo, and Eastland of Mississippi, Smith and Byrd of Virginia, Cox and Russell of Georgia, Ellender of Louisiana, and Connally and O'Daniel of Texas, have been the most persistent Negro and labor baiters in the country, the implacable foes of all democracy.*

*The "secession" of the southern bourbons from the 1948 Democratic National Convention, under the fraudulent banner of states' rights, dramatized this, without in any way abolishing the "gentlemen's agreement" in relation to the Negro question. The incorporation of Truman's "civil rights"

Under Roosevelt's leadership of the Democratic Party, this angry poll-tax pack was held at bay. But with the post-war offensive of monopoly capital at home and abroad, it was again unleashed. The Truman Administration, pursuing the Wall Street policy of world domination, inevitably opened the door to the most backward anti-democratic elements in American life—the feudal agrarian interests of the South. It transferred some of the most important political offices from the northern liberal and urban wing of the Democratic Party to the southern "white-supremacy" wing, and thereby increased the influence of southern Bourbonry in the political councils of the nation.* It remained for the border-state "liberal" Truman, professing to continue the Roosevelt program (shades of Andrew Johnson!) to elevate this democracy-hating pro-fascist clique to new prominence. Together with the Republican Tafts, Vandenbergs, and Bridges, the Dixie poll-taxers formed a bi-partisan battering ram to scuttle the New Deal social legislation, to impose upon the country the odious Taft-Hartley union-busting law and to undermine the cause of world peace.

program in the 1948 Democratic platform was essentially no more than an election maneuver designed to stem the mass shift of the decisive Negro and progressive vote towards the Progressive Party led by Henry Wallace.

*Another step in this direction was the changing of convention rules by the Democratic National Committee in 1947, by giving to each state that went Democratic in the last election a bonus of two delegates to the national convention of the party.

"Liberal Remedies"

THERE IS A STARTLING PARADOX in the Negro land problem in the United States. Existing in the very midst of the world's most highly industrialized country which ostensibly long ago abolished all pre-capitalist economic relations, it is nevertheless a type of problem customarily associated only with backward, industrially retarded lands which have still to complete their bourgeois-democratic revolutions. And because of this, the real nature of this problem in the United States, as well as the conditions of its solution, have been more easily obscured.

The Size of the Problem

Simply put, the issue is the transfer of the land from the monopoly of a small, semi-feudal class of big landed proprietors to the mass of the landless peasantry. It is this issue which today is at the root of the titanic conflict raging throughout the colonial and semi-colonial world, and which only yesterday was so dramatically solved by the peoples of central Europe and most of the Balkans. In countries like China, India, Indonesia, and Korea, it is no longer possible to deny the necessity and inevitability of agrarian revolution, for the simple reason that scores of millions of these peoples have made this issue their own.

Agrarian revolution is the indispensable condition for democracy and progress for over half the world's population aspiring to national independence and freedom. And it is a condition which can be realized only in struggle against the renewed attempts at enslavement by finance capital and pre-eminently American monopoly capital which has emerged in the postwar world as the chief aspirant to world domination and the bulwark sustaining all the reactionary, semi-feudal remnants striving frantically to hold back the advance of democracy.

Serious students of the South, by acknowledging the plantation evil, recognize that behind southern backwardness and poverty is this same semi-feudal enslavement of the masses of tillers of the soil. But in most cases they point out the evil only to shy away from the simple and obvious conclusion—land redivision. And yet, the necessity for this solution has continued to exist since the end of the Civil War when the confiscation of the land of the rebel planters and its redistribution among the Negroes and landless whites was cynically rejected by the dominant political powers of the country, even though land redivision was demanded by the Negro freedmen and ardently advocated by the most consistent democrats of the day.

The bitter indictment which the great Frederick Douglass pronounced in 1880 against this betrayal of the Negro freedman and of democracy sums up the very essence of the question as it stands to this day.

"To the freedmen was given the machinery of liberty," he declared bitterly, "but there was denied to them the steam to put it in motion. They were given the uniform of soldiers, but no arms; they were called citizens, but left subjects; they were called free, but left almost slaves. The old master class was not deprived of the power of life and death, which was the soul of the relation of master and slave. They could not, of course, sell their former slaves, but they retained the power to starve them to death, and wherever this power is held there is the power of slavery. He who can say to his fellow-man, 'You shall serve me or starve,' is a master and his subject is a slave. This was seen and felt by Thaddeus Stevens, Charles Sumner, and leading stalwart Republicans; and had their counsels prevailed the terrible evils from which we now suffer would have been averted. The Negro today would not be on his knees, as he is, abjectly supplicating the old master class to give him leave to toil. Nor would he now be leaving the South as from a doomed city, and seeking a home in the uncongenial North, but tilling his native soil in comparative independence."[1]

Thaddeus Stevens, the great strategist of Radical Reconstruction, had sought to give legislative form to this primary condition for the independence of the Negro freedmen and the creation of a truly democratic South. In March, 1867, he had introduced his famous land division bill into the House of Representatives, calling for the confiscation of the landed estates of the leading Confederates, with exemption only for holdings under 200 acres, while each freedman was to receive 40 acres and $50 cash for a homestead. To those who sought to stigmatize his measure by calling it revolutionary, he replied boldly: "It is revolutionary . . . It is intended to revolutionize. . . . This may startle feeble minds and shake weak nerves. . . . So do all great improvements in the political and moral world."

It was beyond his power to sway the final vote on his measure but his argument was irrefutable.

"How," he demanded, "can republican institutions, free schools, free churches, free social intercourse, exist in a mingled community of nabobs and serfs; of the owners of 20,000 acre manors with lordly palaces and the occupants of narrow huts inhabited by 'low white trash'? If the South is ever to be made a safe republic, let her lands be cultivated by the toil of the owners or the free labor of intelligent citizens. . . . The country would be well rid of the proud, bloated and defiant rebels. . . . The foundation of their institutions must be broken up and relaid, or all our blood and treasure have been spent in vain."[2]

By refusing to break up and relay these foundations, to carry through the democratic revolution on the land, northern capital, which doomed Stevens' land division measure, not only deprived the masses of Negro freedmen of any solid economic basis for their newly won liberty and laid the basis for their speedy re-enslavement, but actually condemned the entire South to its subsequent one-sided development and dependent status. The path outlined by Stevens and Douglass, entirely consistent with the capitalist expansion of the country, would have created a new and truly democratic sector of American development. But the ruling capitalist circles not only regarded the expropriation of the planters as a threat to capitalist property in general, but understood that it would have meant the creation of a class of independent producers essentially hostile to big capitalist domination. This path, therefore, was not taken. But in rejecting this solution of land redivision, the ruling powers automatically retained the conditions that continued to make this solution necessary. The need and desire for the land by the landless masses of Negro and white tillers of the South remained.

At the same time, the fear of a truly democratic solution of the land question in the South also remained. In fact, with the growth of monopoly capital, this fear has become even more pervasive. But oddly enough, the very abandonment of fundamental land reform during Reconstruction is being used today as evidence of its impracticability. In a logic which regards such a necessary solution as historically outmoded because it failed of adoption when· first advanced, it must indeed be as dead as its original proponents.

It Isn't Painless

Plainly, breaking up the plantation through land redivision, giving the land to the actual tillers of the soil, is basic to any genuine agrarian reform. A radical democratic formulation of the land problem must challenge the present monopoly of the landlords.

It is precisely ·here that most liberal theorists balk. Their efforts are reduced at most to a pitiful, futile attempt to carry through a gradual, painless transformation of semi-feudal land-ownership into capitalist ownership.

Gunnar Myrdal, the Swedish Social-Democrat imported by the Carnegie Foundation to make an "objective" analysis of the American Negro problem, offers in two huge volumes what has been hailed as the very last word in scientific thought on the question. His findings, on which a veritable army of American scholars and investigators were employed, are appropriately summed up in the title of the book: *An American Dilemma*.

How does Myrdal treat the pivotal question of land reform in the South? He begins by rejecting the sound observation of DuBois that "to have given each one of the million Negro free families [during Reconstruction] a forty-acre freehold would have made a basis of real democracy in the United States. . . ."[3]

Myrdal will have none of such radical interpretations of the job of Reconstruction. "This may be true enough," he says, "but it should be kept clear that the historical setting would hardly have allowed it."[4] Clamping down on any hopes or ideas that the modern plantation serfs may harbor as regards access to the land, he warns that "it is even more Utopian to think through anew the Reconstruction problem in terms of modern social engineering."[5]

Myrdal does not say exactly why "the historical setting would hardly have allowed" the transfer of the land to the Negro freedmen. But the reason can easily be seen from his criticism of Reconstruction. At first glance, Myrdal appears critical of Reconstruction's failure to expropriate without compensation the big estates of the rebel slaveholders in favor of the freedmen. But only at first glance. Actually, Myrdal's criticism is based on different grounds: the failure of the government to remunerate the ex-slaveholders for *their property losses in human beings!* Myrdal actually bemoans the fact that "the North obviously did not hesitate to expropriate the slave property and let it loose on the region. . . . The owners must have felt this to be a grave injustice inflicted upon them, and even Northerners must have reflected that this property was acquired under the law. . . ."[6]

In other words, depriving the slaveowners of their slaves

without compensation was not only a moral injustice, but also an unlawful act. Whether Myrdal likes it or not, the fact is that it happened! How, then, does this demonstrate that the "historical setting" would not allow the redistribution of the slaveowners' land? Actually it does not and cannot demonstrate this. What it does show is Myrdal's reason for rejecting such redistribution. And that reason has nothing to do with what was *historically possible* in the United States immediately after the Civil War. According to Myrdal the uncompensated emancipation of the slaves was a violation of the slaveowners' individual property rights. Also to have taken their land without compensation would, in his opinion, have only compounded the injustice to the slaveowning oligarchy, since it would obviously have been a further violation of property rights! Ostensibly this second step was not taken because such violations would have been in direct contradiction to individual capitalist property rights and it was the capitalists who controlled the economic and political power of the country at the time.

Myrdal does not himself add this last term to the syllogism; he merely implies it. But here apparently is the "reason" why "the historical setting would hardly have allowed" confiscation of the land by Congressional enactment and its redistribution among the emancipated slaves. According to Myrdal's logic, therefore, if it was *historically impossible to confiscate* the land from the ex-slaveowners because that would have meant a violation of individual property rights which the capitalists could not and did not tolerate, it should also have been historically impossible for the government to emancipate the slaves, since that was most certainly a violation of property rights. The trouble with Myrdal's logic is that the slaves *were* emancipated without compensation. His entire reasoning rests upon an ethical injunction rather than upon the historical fact that there was a slaveholders' rebellion, that the Civil War was a revolution, in which political power was transferred to a new class, and that emancipation was a distinctly revolutionary act, sanctioned by Congress and the people, contemptuous of the property rights of slave traders. The confiscation of the land of the rebel traitors as proposed by Thaddeus Stevens would have been no more and no less revolutionary, and was just as possible "in the historical setting" of the Civil War and Reconstruction, as emancipation itself.

If it did not happen, it was not because it was historically impossible or inconsistent with capitalist development at the time. It was because the big bourgeoisie which took the political leadership firmly into its own hands abandoned the completion of the bourgeois-democratic revolution, and there were no independent popular forces strong enough, even where they were willing, to compel it to complete the revolution. In this sense the historical setting did not allow the Negro freedman to receive the land. But all that this establishes is the fact that he did not get the land and the relation of forces which kept the land from him. In no way does it disprove the historical necessity or possibility of land redistribution at the time. There is a vast difference between an historical event that did not happen because there was no objective need for it or no possibility of its realization and one that did not happen despite the need and possibility. To ignore this difference is to eliminate from consideration the actual content of human history, to abandon the scientific approach in the study of history, and especially in the formulation of policy in the living struggle for human progress.

Thad Stevens, at least, was consistent. He argued that since the government had taken the revolutionary step of emancipation and given the slave his freedom, it should complete this revolutionary act by also giving him the land as a material means for enjoying that freedom. By comparison, Myrdal's consistency is reactionary and utterly unrelated to historical reality. It takes the twisted form of arguing that there should have been neither confiscation of the land nor emancipation of the laborer without compensation, and therefore that there *could* have been no revolutionary land redistribution—although there was revolutionary emancipation—because it would have been a revolutionary violation of individual property rights. All that Myrdal achieves here is to condemn what was done, namely, emancipation, and justify what was not done, namely, failure to redistribute the land.

Myrdal's Proposals

Myrdal is unquestionably dissatisfied with the course history actually took. He would have preferred a "rational reform" of southern economy, one which "would preserve individual property rights to the maximum," which rights he insists are "always of greatest importance for a smooth readjustment."[7] The rational reforms which Myrdal considered possible during Reconstruction are:

> " (1) Remunerating fully the slave owners out of federal funds. (2) Expropriating the slave plantations or a larger part of them and remunerating fully their owners out of federal funds. (3) Distributing this land in small parcels to those cultivators who wished it, against mortgaged claims on their new property, and requiring them to pay for the land in yearly installments over a long period. . . . (5) Instituting a scheme of taxation to pay off the former slave- and land-owners. . . ."[8]

The substance of this "rational reform" is remuneration of the slaveholders for both land and slaves. It is quite possible that the ex-slaveholders, after the military defeat of their rebellion, would have been content to settle for Myrdal's "rational economic reform." In any case, the "Lost Cause" has found in Myrdal a new pleader! But in his great concern for the property rights of the slaveholders, the rights of the Negro freedmen completely vanish. Myrdal's reforms would not only have compelled them, as a condition for access to the land, to reimburse their parasitic former masters whom they had already enriched by three centuries of unrequited labor, but would have produced the conditions for their speedy re-enslavement. Under his plan for Reconstruction, the former traffickers in human beings whom he would have so generously remunerated out of public funds would have used those very funds to regain the land. They would have done so by buying it back at cheap prices from the tax-ridden, mortgaged, indebted Negroes! The outcome would have been the rise of a type of Junkerism hardly distinguishable from that which at present holds sway below the Mason-Dixon line. But in reality, not even this method of "securing" land to the Negro was adopted. And, as far as northern capital was concerned, it obviously did not prefer Myrdal's type of "rational reform."

The fact is that history did not pick Myrdal's solution. His "rational reforms" simply did not happen. The actual course of events showed that the class forces involved in the historical process move along other lines than the "smooth readjustment" of Myrdal's reformist blueprint. Indeed, history is so irrational and extravagant that it even dismisssed Myrdal's argument, so decisive in bourgeois considerations, that the cost of his program "would have been trifling compared with what Reconstruction and Restoration, not to speak of the Civil War, actually cost the nation."[9]

In real history it is an established fact, confirmed by accumulated world experience on the agrarian problem, that only where the formal abolition of feudalism was accompanied by the complete breakup of the landed estates did the mass of peasants achieve economic and political emancipation. And wherever the formal abolition of slavery or serfdom was *not* accompanied by the extirpation of landlordism, there political power either remained in the hands of the former landholding class, or was speedily regained by them. Such was the case in Italy, Prussia, Poland, Hungary, Romania, right up to World War II, and in Russia prior to the socialist revolution of 1917.

The Lesson of History

Reform approximating the Myrdal scheme, the form designed to disturb least the inviolable property rights of the big feudal landlords and hence their political power, was carried through in the Russia of the tsars. The "Great Reform" of 1861, which was supposed to free the serfs and provide them with land, while compensating the nobility, was summed up by Lenin four decades later: "The peasant, 'emancipated' from serf labor, emerged from the hands of the reformers a crushed, plundered, degraded man. . . . Nothing was left for him to do except 'voluntarily' accept serf labor."[10]

Of course, after the Socialist Revolution of 1917 the Soviet

Union, that pioneer of modern twentieth-century democracy, solved the land question once and for all, furnishing the pattern for the fundamental solution of the agrarian question under socialism. And as a result, in less than twenty years, the peasantry passed rapidly from a miserable impoverishment under tsarism, through the abolition of landlord holdings and redistribution, to well-to-do collective farmers.

The classic precedent for thoroughgoing land reform *under capitalism* was the great French Revolution of 1789. The radical reforms instituted by the Jacobins uprooted the feudal order in old France, cleared its soil of all incumbrances to progress, laid the rock foundation upon which was eventually erected the modern French republic. Because these land reforms reached down into the very roots of the feudal order and tore them up, the French people were able to withstand and eventually beat off all attempts at permanent restoration of reaction. The counter-revolution, Bonapartism, the temporary restoration of the monarchy—none of these was able to shake the grip of the French peasant on the land which he had won in the Revolution of 1792.

In this same context of radical land reforms obtained under capitalism must be cited the achievements of Mexico. In the Mexican revolution the political power of the haciendados (landlords) was undermined by expropriations effected under the Cardenas government. These reforms were put through against the bitter opposition of Wall Street, attesting to the revolutionary groundswell which had embraced Mexico and its people, who were determined to break the age-old oppressive yoke of the landlords and their absentee Yankee supporters. These gains, however, are once more seriously threatened.

Also carrying forward this great tradition of the French revolution into modern times and under contemporary conditions are the sweeping land reforms initiated by the new people's governments of the liberated countries of Eastern and Central Europe—Yugoslavia, Czechoslovakia, Poland, Hungary, Bulgaria.[11]

In Asia there are examples of the Communist-led democratic region of China where sweeping land reforms have been carried out for the benefit of the Chinese peasantry, and that of the

Soviet zone of Korea, where the estates of the big landowners were confiscated outright. These are a few instances of fundamental agrarian reforms, the only kind which truly benefit the actual tiller of the soil. Myrdal would hide from the Negro people these liberating lessons of world experience, shunting them off into a blind alley with a stop sign marked "Dilemma!"

Of a similar pattern is Myrdal's attempt to deal with the question of agrarian overcrowding in the South, which he regards as a basic problem but which he divorces from its fundamental cause, the plantation system.

"It is true," he says, "that countries like Denmark have a much higher population density in their agricultural areas." But he explains this on the basis that "both the objective market conditions and the rural culture are incomparably more favorable than they can be in the surveyable future in Southern agriculture."[12]

Myrdal conveniently overlooks one small point: The "higher market conditions" and higher "culture" which the Danish farmer enjoys are the fruits of an agrarian revolution which was long ago achieved in that country, a revolution which Myrdal and his enlightened imperialist sponsors of the multi-million dollar Carnegie Foundation would deny to the Negro of the South.

Having thus closed all avenues to a solution of the problem, Myrdal quite logically rejects any change of the status quo through organized mass effort such as the building of organizations among the agricultural masses and collective bargaining with the planters. "... *Any success in raising the earnings and living levels for farm labor on Southern plantations will accentuate, or rather make explicit in the form of unemployment, the basic over-population of Southern agriculture.*"[13] This is a rejection of even the minimal program of the New Deal!

What then is Myrdal's solution? He has none. He has only a dilemma!*

---

*It is indeed a sad commentary on American liberal scholarship that Mr. Myrdal's reactionary bias and long-winded effusions on the Negro question should be so universally and uncritically acclaimed among scholars, Negro

Other Panaceas

Myrdal, however, is not the only one seeking a "smooth readjustment" of the economic and social problems of the South. There is an entire school of liberal writers who profess to see such a solution in its "industrialization." Their thinking starts from the premise that capitalism has a workable check and balance system, that somehow it keeps watch upon itself and can divest itself of obnoxious social features, and that in response to a natural law the Wall Street leopard will change his spots.

It is not surprising, therefore, that World War II and its temporary industrial boom were accompanied by a sudden rash of optimism in liberal circles, both in the North and South, an optimism which found its most ardent exponents among southern regionalists.

The establishment of government-subsidized war industries in the South, the increased industrial activity of that region, and its resultant higher wages, higher cotton prices, greater profits—all were greeted as evidence of the beginning of the long overdue "technical and industrial revolution" in the South, the opening of a "new era" of industry and modern mechanized farming. The liberal reformers went all out in optimistic expectation. At long last, they thought they saw fulfilment of their cherished dreams of an industrialized South, freed from economic and political vassalage to northern corporate ownership.

In rural districts, they hopefully claimed that the "revolution" was pulling southern agriculture out of its ancient back-

and white, as the latest word on the Negro-white relationships in the U.S.A. In a poll conducted by the *Negro Digest* and purported to represent a cross-section of outstanding opinion, including foremost educators, book critics, authors, and race relations specialists, 15 out of 19 who replied chose Gunnar Myrdal's *American Dilemma* as giving the most "complete, well-rounded picture of American race relations." (*Negro Digest*, Nov., 1946.) A notable exception, worthy of serious study, is the critique of Myrdal by Oliver Cromwell Cox in *Caste, Class, and Race*, pp. 507-38, N. Y., 1948. For a detailed criticism of Myrdal's ideological approach to Negro problems, his crass historical distortions, see Herbert Aptheker, *The Negro People in America*, International Publishers, N. Y., 1946.

wardness and decadence. The semi-feudal sharecropper was being supplanted by the modern agricultural wage laborer. Accordingly, they insisted, the oppressive yoke of Negro serfdom was being progressively lifted. The complicated Negro problem and the "racial" antagonism it engendered were being automatically disentangled. All this was to be brought about presumably as the natural result of the workings of blind economic forces. And there were going to be no attendant social upheavals!

Perhaps the most sanguine expression of this great daydream was expressed by former governor of Louisiana, Sam H. Jones, and his collaborator, James Aswell, in an article in *Liberty* magazine:

> "The changes afoot in this region," they wrote, "are comparable to England's industrial revolution which began in the latter half of the eighteenth century. That other revolution was spark-plugged, moreover, by an identical industrial factor: the machine . . . Widespread adoption of agricultural machines *already perfected* will keep the Negro moving out—along with sizeable numbers of white farm laborers—and will swell the exodus to a flood unless counter measures of daring and imagination are taken."

These counter measures can be summed up, we are told, in "industrialization—the perfect complement to machine agriculture." Further stressing the fact that economic and cultural retardation has been a "national policy" ever since "the War Between the States," Jones and Aswell conclude that:

> ". . . the picture is changing . . . A definite feeling exists, all the way to Washington, that the South should now be encouraged to process its own vast natural resources with its own labor in its own plants."

Upon this flimsy premise of half-truth and wishful thinking, a glowing picture is painted of the new South which was to emerge during the war years and the decade following:

> "Forty-acre farms supplanted by the 200 to 250 acre pattern. Hand labor largely replaced by machinery. The one-crop system replaced by diversification.

"Pasture lands and feed crops paving the way for a vast livestock industry—with the day of importing meat, dairy and poultry products at an end.

"Marginal lands planted to forests, replenishing the rich primeval growths. Two hundred million sterile acres can thus produce wealth.

"The 300 minerals, including great assets of coal and oil and gas, used to build new industries employing black man and white man by the thousands.

"Incomes, Negro and white alike, up. Living standards up. Malnourished sharecroppers and 'cheap laborers' gone from the face of the land.

"Education brought to all the people, its cultural phases supplemented by practical courses geared to the economic needs of the region. *Health standards and population trends—up.*"[14]

War and Post-War Industrialization

But neither the premise nor the expectations of this idyllic picture has any serious relation to the actual line of development in the South. Unquestionably, as a result of World War II, finance capital and the government were compelled to expand industry in that region. In fact, the government spent seven billion dollars in the South. War industries (chemicals, rubber, iron and steel, airplanes, ship building) increased 279 per cent. The non-war industries (food, tobacco, textiles, paper, leather, lumber, furniture, petroleum, stone, clay, glass) increased 40 per cent. The biggest factors in the war industry increase were shipbuilding and aircraft plants. As a result, by 1943 employment of wage and salaried workers in the South increased about 70 per cent over 1939 (from 1,637,000 to 2,772,000), employment in the war industries increasing more rapidly than in the non-war industries. More than one-third of the total increased employment was in government-owned, privately operated plants.

Furthermore, despite some shut-downs and drastic cutbacks in the war industries V-J Day was followed by a post-war boom, and as a result a certain amount of industrial expansion continued in the South. As the *Wall Street Journal* phrased it in its

New Year, 1948, forecast for the South, "You can hear industry boom from Virginia to the Gulf."[15]

Describing this post-war expansion in more general terms, the *Wall Street Journal* writes:

"A host of new factories will sprout in the ten south-east states this year. Louisiana, for instance, has over 260 new businesses signed up. Many a plant that had the last brick laid in '47 will whirr into full speed. Others will be blown up to new capacity. They'll pour out tons of textiles, foods, and chemicals, the south's key factory goods. And more tons of paper cups and cotton pickers, cheese and cars and cellophane, potato chips, and prefab houses . . . A year ago North Carolina reported 406 new plants about to go up and 262 in line for expansion, to the tune of $146 million. Many of these plants in the Tarheel State will start rolling or hit full output this year. Atlanta expects six new industries 'in the $1 million or more class' this year. Ground was dug for some 455 new plants in 140 of Georgia's 159 counties in the first ten months of 1947. In Tennessee, the Memphis area alone added 70 new manufacturing firms to its rolls last year."[16]

For the year 1948, southern capital professed to be particularly optimistic. Summarizing the situation for the New York *Journal of Commerce,* in its New Year, 1948, survey, Legh R. Powell, Jr., president of the Seaboard Air Lines Railroad Co., wrote:

"Two years after the close of World War II, the South is emerging from the commercial uncertainties of the reconversion period with a vigor which holds promise for continuing prosperity in 1948. Industrial activity has continued at a high level throughout 1947, and figures on total production for the year will probably exceed any peacetime year in history. Power sales, always an accurate index of industrial activity, have broken all previous records. Expansion of power producing capacity continues over systems of the major power companies of the South and many new large projects are contemplated

for 1948 and the next few years. Another accurate criterion for gauging the industrial activity of a region is
found in iron and steel. The iron and steel industry,
vastly expanded in the South during the war, continues
to operate at record peacetime level and every indication
points to a continued demand considerably in excess of
supply for several years to come. It is the concensus that
the years immediately ahead will be the most productive
in the history of our economic life."[17]

On the face of things, all this war and post-war activity would
appear to be no mere temporary development, but part of a
broad and successful trend which must culminate in the complete
industrialization of the South. And this is how the new year
prophets of an even brighter future for the South prefer to see
it. Thus, according to Powell, in the *Journal of Commerce,*
"although industrilization of this area has been proceeding at
a rapid pace during the past two decades, the competitive demands of the next few years will accelerate this development."[18]
Similarly, the *Wall Street Journal* writes:

"This expansion is no sudden spurt of new year energy.
It's part of a long-time drive to put more factories on
the south's farm-dotted horizon. Pioneers of the movement were the textile mills that came south and moved in
like boll weevils to be near the cotton fields. Other
factories sprouted near the source of their raw materials
—chemical plants, food factories, steel mills. The war
speeded the process. The post-war boom kept it rolling."[19]

Here again, for the southern toilers, Negro and white, this
war and post-war industrial development has undoubtedly
eased the noose of poverty around their necks. The southern war
industries in particular furnished some outlet for agrarian labor
seeking to flee the Black Belt plantations. The pressure on the
agrarian economy of the South was somewhat relaxed. And
in this process there was clearly a growth of the Negro proletariat in the South, with accompanying trade union organization.
The shift of tens of thousands of Negroes from the farms and
agricultural communities to industrial production was one of
the striking developments of the war period.

Likewise, as far as capital is concerned, this industrialization has undoubtedly resulted in a considerable accumulation of local capital, and the growth of the local middle class, together with pride in the "new industry," the desire for the development of a "balanced economy" and a greater willingness to invest in the industries needed for such an economy.[20] It has even encouraged speculation about the possibility of making the South a prosperous place to live in for the exploited masses.[21]

But one need only stop to examine the character and limits of this industrialization to realize immediately the absurdity of the suggestion that it is taking place or can take place on the basis of the South's own accumulated capital resources, or that the South is either free to develop or in the process of rapidly developing an all-sided industrial economy which will transform the economic, social, and political character of that region. The evidence warrants a no more sweeping conclusion than that contained in the opening words of the New Year's forecast in the New York *Journal of Commerce* by C. McD. Davis, president of the Atlantic Coast Line R. R. Co.:

> "The South has long been thought of as primarily an agricultural region and as a producer of raw materials. What is not yet entirely realized in other regions is that the South, within recent years, has made important strides industrially."[22]

Basically, as the *Monthly Labor Review* of the U. S. Department of Labor pointed out in its special issue on labor in the South, October 1946:

> ". . . From the colonial period to the present the South has remained predominantly agrarian. To agriculture must be added the economic activities that depend directly upon the forest resources of the region and upon the wealth, including petroleum, under the earth. The South has been primarily an exporter of raw and semi-finished products; its industrial development began relatively late and under severe initial handicaps. The ante-bellum South, for various reasons, did not encourage the growth of industrial enterprise; and even as late as 1930 a group of Southern intellectuals could argue (in

I'll Take My Stand) that the social cost of industrialism outweighed its benefits. Industrialization, however, has increased significantly. In 1880, less than 8 per cent of the wage earners employed in manufacturing in the United States were in the 13 Southern states. By 1939 this percentage had risen to 17.2. . . . Manufacturing employment in the South increased sharply during the war years. . . . The manufacturing base in the South has been comparatively narrow, resting largely upon the textile industries (principally cotton textiles and hosiery), lumber, furniture, and tobacco, with petroleum refining in the Southwest. Other industries (iron and steel, machinery, apparel, and a host of others) have been rather thinly represented. However, the war apparently has strengthened a tendency for the industrial structure of the South to broaden, partly as a result of the rise of essentially new industries, and partly from decentralizing tendencies elsewhere. Texas is a conspicuous example, and the Southeast is vibrant with new industrial undertakings."[23]

But despite this "broadening," textiles, food, and chemicals have remained the south's key factory goods. The effect of the war production did not alter the basic patterns of southern economy, and nothing has happened during the postwar boom even to suggest that the South was developing a machine-tool industry, without which the talk of an independent, "balanced" industrial development in the South is meaningless, let alone to indicate that there were any prospects for such an extensive and all-sided industrialization as to involve a radical, structural transformation of the region's economy. On the contrary, the same optimistic forecasts for 1948 in the *Wall Street Journal* and the *Journal of Commerce* which joyfully point to the South's own capital resources provide the evidence of the complete dependence of the South's expansion on northern monopoly capital, are compelled to note the shadows of coming crisis which herald the collapse of this industrial expansion, and actually base their hopes for a "bright promise for the South" on the self-defeating prospect of complete domination of the world market by American monopolies.

Thus, on the first point, despite the big talk about the South's own capital resources, and the availability of this capital for further industrialization, the actual list of new enterprises cited by the *Wall Street Journal's* New Year's survey reads like a register of some of the biggest northern trusts. Says the author of this survey, speaking of the industrial boom that is heard from Virginia to the Gulf:

"It might be Louisiana's giant Standard Oil of Jersey plant that's expanding into one of the world's largest refineries or Mississippi's new million dollar Sterling Drug Co. plant that will soon start pouring out milk of magnesia. In Tennessee it may be International Harvester's new $30 million factory that will hire 3,000 workers and roll out an army of mechanical cotton pickers. Or the $50,000 expansion at Kelly Foods Co. that keeps 25 people busy cooking up salad dressing and Brunswick stew. Or Du Pont's $20 million nylon plant going up in Chattanooga. To a southerner 'expansion' may mean Alabama's new B. F. Goodrich and Goodyear Tire and Rubber plants, both swinging into peak production, or the Welch Grape Juice Co. plant in Arkansas that's been equipped to crush more local grapes into more juice. Part of the picture are Georgia's Ford and General Motors assembly plants that will roll full force this year and its new Lily Tulip Cup plant that hopes to become largest of Lily's paper cup chain. And reflecting all this is the huge Sears-Roebuck retail store in Winston-Salem, N. C., now in the ground clearing stage. It will boast the longest sales floor in the southeast."[24]

This is hardly surprising in view of the fact that the war only served to strengthen the stranglehold of monopoly on the economic life of the country, particularly of the South. Before the war one hundred large corporations accounted for about 30 per cent of the nation's manufacturing output. Now they put out 70 per cent of it. More than 500,000 independent business concerns went out of existence during the war.[25] That the war strengthened Wall Street's grip on the nation's economy is so obvious that even an official of the Justice Department had to admit: "The concentration of economic power in the hands of a few small vested groups is today higher than ever before in our history."[26]

It is these few groups, the big financial interests of Wall Street, Boston, Cleveland, and Chicago that also command in the domain of southern economic life, and whatever significant industrialization there has been is associated primarily with the firms they own or dominate. Even a partial itemization of these firms, which the reader will find in the appendix to this book, demonstrates the complete dependence of southern economy on the masters of the national economy as a whole, and it is, in general, in the nature of monopoly capital to restrict production rather than to permit it to expand freely, not to speak of the limitations imposed by the condition of the world market today. This means that it is idle to talk of the industrialization of the South without reference to the line or conditions of development of the entire economy of the country. And the national economy, because it is so highly monopolized by a few groups of big capital, and because of the general crisis of world capitalism, is no longer capable of expansion except on the basis of production for war. From this viewpoint alone, therefore, the further industrialization of the South would find an insurmountable barrier in the domination of monopoly capital.

A specific example is provided by the *Wall Street Journal* itself when it cites a "sour note" from Alabama which throws sharp light on the obstructive and dominating role of the giant monopolies and the extent to which the industrialization of the South is at their mercy. The *Wall Street Journal* writes:

"The southeast's biggest iron and steel producer—still nicknamed the Cotton State—can't get enough of these vital items to feed its factories. Its iron, steel and coal companies have order books bulging far into the future; its cast iron pipe plants are booked well into 1949. . . . Many steel short plants have been forced to lay off men. Practically no iron and steel users are operating at capacity."[27]

The steel trust's refusal to produce at capacity in order to maintain monopoly prices by an artificial scarcity of steel and out of fear of postwar overproduction and crisis was a public scandal throughout 1947. This in itself would be sufficient to demonstrate how utterly utopian is the idea that the South will industralize itself out of its present position. But aside from this, the national economy is moving towards a major cyclical crisis, which brings us to the second point.

Warning signals of this crisis are already visible in the South as they are in the North. The same *Wall Street Journal* which made such bright predictions for the South for 1948 could not avoid noting these signs.

"Yet the new year," it wrote, "won't bring all sunshine and flowers to the southland . . . Cautious observers in Atlanta say today's boom may start to slump in the coming months, with non-durable goods hit first. One sign: Department store sales in this section showed less dollar gain over '46 in the first nine months of '47 than other areas. North Carolina retailers report a buying slump in some fields. More consumers are balking at high prices. Unit sales at Christmas showed little or no gain over a year ago. Here and there an oversupply of labor crops through. For instance, two war-swollen Georgia cities, Brunswick and Savannah, haven't enough jobs to go around since war plants and shipyards closed. It shows up sharply in the sagging sales figures on merchants' ledgers."[28]

The fact is that American capital, North and South, is today and for the next period basing all its hopes upon the artificial continuation of a war economy and the economic domination of the world with the help of the Marshall plan, so ardently supported by the southern poll-tax bloc in Congress. And it is doing so both as a means of achieving that world economic hegemony and of avoiding the major economic crash inherent in the capitalist economic system. The adventurist and self-defeating character of such an orientation may not be immediately evident to everyone, but, and this is our third point, there can be no doubt that there can be no solid or enduring future for the industrialization of the South on the basis of such prospects.

But, aside from this, the dream of the uninterrupted and

all-sided industrialization of the South fails to reckon with another, and in a way, the most decisive barrier. That barrier is the deliberate policy of finance capital of artificially retarding the economic development of the South and preventing the rise of such a "balanced economy" as southern liberals dream about. The Wall Street overlords have ruled that the industry of this region shall be confined to the minimum needs of the extraction of its natural resources on the basis of the super-exploitation of its cheap substandard labor. They do not invest capital in the south in order to create a "balanced economy" in that region. They do so only to secure needed raw materials, cheap labor, and a profitable market, in short, to extract the super-profits made possible by the agrarian hinterland character of the South. As the *Wall Street Journal* points out:

> "Industries have come south to find more than handy raw materials. Some want cheap, abundant fuel like Louisiana's natural gas—she's the second biggest producer in the U.S. Others have an eye on the mild weather or the comparatively cheaper and 'more amicable' labor that is still largely unorganized. Some industries are coming south as part of their drive to scatter factories and cut distribution costs. Says an official of Westinghouse Corp., which will complete a new lamp plant in Little Rock, Ark., next summer: 'We make a 10-cent article and the nearer we are to our markets, the more cheaply we can sell it.' "[29]

Donald V. Fraser, president of the Missouri-Kansas-Texas Railroad Co., contributing to the New Year's review of the New York *Journal of Commerce,* and pointing to six major factors favorable to continued industrial expansion in the Southwest—the fuel, labor, market, minerals, climate, and agriculture—says that "as to labor, the Southwest is a source of keen, intelligent, native workers—men and women who are individualists at heart."[30] In a large advertisement right beneath Mr. Fraser's article, the Tide Water Power Co. of Wilmington, North Carolina, inquires: "Are you looking for a Southern location?" And, as its first inducement to the northern capitalist to locate in some small town of eastern North Carolina, it says: "In many of Eastern North Carolina's excellent small towns, where there are at present no large industries, you will find an ample supply of intelligent, adaptable, friendly workers." Other inducements to the northern manufacturer, besides "intelligent, native labor," are "cooperative local government," and "a rich agricultural background." The *Monthly Labor Review*, in its October, 1946, issue on labor in the South, explains the reason for the low-wage level which is what the southern "ads" mean by "intelligent, adaptable, friendly labor."

"The low-wage level of the South," the *Monthly Labor Review* declares, "is accounted for in large measure by the predominance of agriculture and the relatively large supply of unskilled labor competing for jobs in comparatively few industries. Other important factors include a large population relative to employment opportunities, decentralization of industry, comparative lack of unionization, and limited degree of protective-labor legislation by the States."[31]

There can be no question that northern capital is determined to maintain this situation in the South, and hence the conditions that make it possible. Whatever industrialization it promotes, therefore, is kept strictly within the limits of maintaining monopoly advantages, control, and super-profits.

This is shown not only in its labor policy. It is also demonstrated in the fact that side by side with the investment of capital in southern industry goes the effort to prevent the development of local enterprise, especially through the operation of patent control and cartel restrictions.

"Time after time," writes A. G. Mezerik, "Southern and Western communities have fallen hard for the idea that they should establish locally owned industries. They have raised money, built plants—and failed. The reasons for the broken dreams were, more times than not, patents and cartels which operated to keep the local group from efficient production or from finding a market for their completed product. All through the South and the West are these monuments to dead hopes—run-down, deserted buildings with shattered windows. These grim reminders of the penalty for challenging Eastern supremacy have killed the initiative of community after community. They have opened the way for giving concessions to the same Eastern interests who throttled the local endeavor. In desperation these Eastern industries have been invited to build a branch plant. Dallas, Texas, has 2,900 branch operations and almost no locally owned manufacturing plants. All through the South and the West, desperate municipalities, unable to compete with the East, have succumbed and offered tax exemption, money benefits, and guaranteed low-wage labor to Eastern interests . . ."[32]

The character of the relation of monopoly capital to the South is shown further in its struggle to maintain the North-South freight differential, higher interest rates in the South with the accompanying higher cost of living,* and generally the status of debtor for the South in relation to Northern capital. In a word, the relations are suggestive of those of imperialists to a colony from which they are able to draw super-profits.

It is these realities in the South that account for the steady movement of population out of that region, notwithstanding the war and post-war boom, a fact which shows what the people think of all the talk about a coming industrial utopia in the South. Thus, the *Wall Street Journal* complains that "many southerners have moved elsewhere to hunt better jobs and more opportunities. Half the southeast's 10 states have watched their population slip back since 1940, although the area as a whole gained 3.9 per cent. More than 100,000 Missis-

---

*"From the outbreak of war in Europe until June 1946, retail prices of goods and services used by moderate-income families rose more rapidly in most large cities in the South than the national average for large cities in the United States." (U. S. Dept. of Labor, "Labor in the South," *Monthly Labor Review*, Oct., 1946, p. 526.)

The average increase in the cost of living in 34 large cities of the country as a whole between August, 1939, and June, 1946, was 35.2 per cent. However, in Savannah, Ga., the increase for the same period was 41.6 per cent; in Jacksonville, Fla., it was 40.5 per cent; in Birmingham, Ala., it was 38.8 per cent, and in New Orleans, La., it was 38.4 per cent. (*Ibid*, p. 527.)

sippians have left the state; Arkansas' nose count has dropped 9 per cent since pre-war."[33]

Or, as Mezerik puts it:

> "All through the South the low level of education, the high cost of living, and every other factor which goes into making life difficult can be, in part, traced back to the hold of the North. The waste of human material is reflected in an Army survey which reveals that thirty-five percent of white Southerners in service had no intention of returning to the South after the war."[34]

To keep the South an economic hinterland of the nation's industrial establishment, and to use the oppressed Negro people as a tool for holding down the living standards of the whole South—such is the program of the absentee Wall Street rulers. And it is with this key strategy of finance capital, not to speak of the limitations inherent in the present monopolist stage of capitalism engulfed in a general crisis, that the liberal theorists failed to reckon in building their air castles of an industrialized South.

The result of this strategy of northern financiers is that industrial development in the South is distorted and lopsided, geared as it is to the expediency of its absentee rulers, rather than to the necessities of the region and its people.

The South's industrial development has been deliberately guided to avoid disturbing the plantation and its semi-feudal labor force. It is not accidental that the South's largest industry, textiles, has been developed as a "white" industry. As James S. Allen points out:

> "The principle of industrial development in the South . . . was to leave the black labor supply of the plantation untouched, to find a solution of the problem of the labor supply which would not need to overcome the restrictions of the semi-feudal agrarian economy upon which cotton production is based."[35]

It is significant that even the war industries in the South, financed as they were by the Federal government, could do nothing to undermine the semi-feudal patterns of southern life. And it was the industries engaged in war production that absorbed most of the Negro labor from the plantations and agricultural communities. The shutdown of these temporary war industries has blocked the only significant outlet in the urban South for the Negro agrarian "over-population." Moreover, as the President's Committee on Civil Rights testified in 1947, the shut-downs and drastic cut-backs reproduced the established patterns of discrimination against the Negroes.[36] Those Negro workers who had become skilled or semi-skilled workers as a result of the war boom soon found that they would have to return to their pre-war status of common labor or the menial drudgery of domestic and personal service. There simply were no prospects of jobs in the trades in which they had been employed during the war.

Furthermore, the Negroes' hope for industrial employment was further shattered by the reversal of New Deal trends, with the scuttling of the government's Fair Employment Practice policy and the return to state control of the U. S. Employment Service.

Summed up, the outlook for continuing the war and post-war industrialization of the South is far from promising. Even if there were every reason to suppose that the present economic boom must continue for a long time, and there would be no crisis to interrupt the whole process, the further development of this industrialization would soon find a barrier in the program and restrictions of monopoly capital upon which it is essentially dependent. At best, industrialization in the South has been and can only be strictly limited. There has been some increase in the proletarianization of the laboring population and some development of a white middle class. The latter, which is particularly weak, has been the main source of the dreams about a peaceful economic and social transformation of the region. But whatever industrialization there has been has in no way involved such basic reshaping of the South as to exclude the semi-feudal relations and slave survivals characteristic of southern economy. It could not have involved any such change because American economy, North and South, is dominated by monopoly capital, and monopoly capital is not pursuing and cannot pursue a policy of economic progress, let alone social and political progress, in the South.

Prospects of Post-War Agriculture

What are the prospects for post-war agriculture in the South? Here the picture is even more clear. The basic factors of chronic crisis which had plagued southern agriculture since the end of World War I, though hidden in recent years behind the facade of an industrial war boom, have by no means been resolved. On the contrary, they have again been unleashed in the economic life of the post-war South, portending social disaster for its people. Not only are the basic problems posed by the agricultural collapse of the 1930's not solved; in some instances they were further aggravated by the war. Signs now point to a return of the old unbalanced "normalcy" that has always been the bane of Dixie's people. The warning signals of a new and more devastating crisis have been raised. One symptom is the instability of the cotton market.

The parity price of cotton in 1946 was from 5 to 8 cents above the world price. This presages eventual loss of markets for American cotton. Then, too, cotton has not recovered its place on the world market. It faces stiffer competition than ever. The Labor Research Association, pointing up this sobering fact, states:

> "In general, the demand for . . . American cotton has been sharply cut by the development of rayon and other artificial fibers and by increased production of cotton in other countries. In the foreign markets, which have been important for American cotton, this can no longer compete successfully at American prices with cotton from less developed countries having lower standards of living and lower money costs."[37]*

The inflationary character of present cotton prices was brought sharply into focus by the cotton panic of the fall of 1946. Although the market soon made up most of the initial loss,

*America's share of raw cotton production has fallen from about 80 per cent in 1880 to 55 per cent in 1924 and 43 per cent in 1944.

this "break" in cotton, accompanied by similar slumps in other commodity markets such as wheat, hides, etc., was nevertheless a storm signal of what lies ahead for the South's working farmer.

The above factors, taken together with the maturing new cyclical crisis, with its inevitable curtailment of the cotton market, are straws in the wind, heralding a new agricultural collapse in the South.

Big business and its policy makers, fully aware of these portents, are already proceeding with plans to shunt the burden of the coming catastrophe onto the shoulders of the mass of working farmers. In a report published in March, 1945, under the title *Variations in Farm Incomes and Their Relation to Agricultural Policies,* the experts of the National Association of Manufacturers and the U. S. Chamber of Commerce baldly proposed that, of the six million farm families in this country, one-fourth should be immediately eliminated from agriculture and that eventually as many as two-thirds (four million) should be pushed out. What groups of farm families are to be eliminated? On this score, the report leaves no doubt. It proposes that government policy should now be directed toward encouraging production "on those farms which are capable of providing the largest average returns per unit of labor and capital expended."[38] Clearly this is the proposal for the mass elimination of middle and small farmers in the South.

This theme was carried further by the *Wall Street Journal* of September 24, 1946, in which appeared a front page article under the title, "Crop Quotas Spurred War Output; Now the Plan Is for Curtailment." The Wall Street advocates of big business insist that no voluntary plan would work because "too many loopholes" would be left "for the independently-minded farmer."

The same point was made by Rep. Clifford Hope of Kansas, a G. O. P. "farm-bloc" Congressman, writing in the December, 1946, issue of Joseph Pews' *Farm Journal.* Says Hope: "Agriculture is faced with the fact that the demand for many of its products is less than during war time, and adjustments must be made as to volume and nature of production."[39] The proposal here is to disregard the wartime promises made to farmers that prices would be pegged at no less than 90 per cent of parity. It calls for a revision of parity and the use of price support payments as a level to force reduction.[40]

Needless to say, with such perspectives, the outlook for a "smooth" development of agriculture is as bleak as the outlook for such a development in industry. For the masses of the South's farm people there is only suffering and struggle ahead. The domination of the entire economy by parasitic, predatory monopoly capital excludes any possibility of a smooth and easy solution of the agrarian problems in the South on the basis of mechanization and scientific progress. Even for the country as a whole, an increase of 55 per cent in the number of tractors in use during the war still left two-thirds of all the census-listed farms, nearly four million, without tractors, and of these one and a half million, or one-fourth of the total, do not even own a horse or mule.[41] Similarly in the South, mechanization has taken place mainly on the big plantations. This can be seen from the most recent census data.

The dominant figure in the mechanization of agriculture in the South—as throughout the rest of the country during the past quarter century—is the tractor. The development of tractorization in Mississippi, for example, is marked by (1) The rapid proportionate increase in the number of enterprises using tractors, and in the number of tractors; (2) The small proportion of census "farms" in the state that have tractor power, despite the rapid proportionate increase.

The figures for the past quarter century show:[42]

TABLE I

	1920	1925	1930	1940	1945	Per cent increase 1940 to 1945
Farms with tractors		598	1,674	4,818	7,905	14,611	85
Number of tractors		667	1,871	5,542	10,577	21,077	99

Despite this rapid growth only a small percentage of Mississippi's acreage is farmed by tractor power, because in the South the tractor is plowing soil where the roots of chattel slavery are still deeply imbedded. The situation in 1945 was (*Multiple Unit* report):

TABLE II

	Without tractors	With tractors	Per cent of units with tractors	Total
Single units	111,695	5,326	4.5	117,021
Multiple units	19,358	9,028	31.8	28,386
	131,053	14,354	11.0	145,407

Thus, nearly 70 per cent of the multiple units, and 95 per cent of the single units and 89 per cent of all units—have no tractors.

The retardation of mechanization by the sharecropper system of production is evident in still another set of figures. If we divide the total number of multiple units (28,386) in four quartiles (of 7,096 multiple units each) according to size of unit, we get the following:

TABLE III

Quartile	Per cent of units with tractors
First	11
(smallest multiple units)	
Second	19
Third	32
Fourth	64
(largest multiple units)	
Average	32

Thus among the largest multiple units more than one-third of all units (36 per cent) are *without tractors*. On one-third of the largest units, therefore, the mule and horse are still the sole source of traction power.*

The naive contention of the liberal gradualists that the feudal-like agrarian economy of the South is being transformed into modern mechanized capitalistic farming through the automatic

*Within this quartile group the percentage of multiple units with tractors varies, with the one-third figure as the average for all the 7,097 units in this group.

workings of economic factors alone is belied by any serious examination of the above facts.

To be sure, these tables are based solely upon 1945 data from Mississippi. This state, however, is the banner cotton state of the old South, embracing the super-plantation area of the Yazoo Valley, in which are centered the largest plantations of the region. From the standpoint of terrain, as well as the greater size of plantation units in this state, more than in any other of the old South, there exist the most favorable factors for mechanization. Therefore, an examination of the statistics of mechanization of Mississippi should furnish the acid test for the theory of the "new technical revolution" which, according to its protagonists, is now sweeping the southern countryside. But what do we find?

In this state, there has been a rapid increase in the ratio of tractors in use, that is, a high ratio of tractors purchased in relation to those already in use. But the total number of census farms with tractors is an extremely small per cent of all farms. And most existing farms, particularly the smallest ones, will never be able to afford a tractor under the existing tenure conditions. The more that tractors increase on the bigger operations, the worse it will be for the smaller ones. The big plantations will be able to produce cotton at prices that do not allow for the subsistence of smaller ones, not to speak of the small marginal farms.

Even in the domain of economics, the theory of "gradual" solution of the South's agrarian ills runs counter to reality. It is true that the attempt to reduce the cost of production is inherent in agriculture producing for the market under capitalism, and that mechanization is the main means for achieving this end. It is indisputable, therefore, that the tendency toward lower producing cost, mechanization, and the resulting increase in capital investment is characteristic of agriculture under capitalism. The International Harvester, which for decades has been working on a cotton picker, the tractor companies, the experiment stations and the big planners are doing their utmost to cut costs.

But here it is a question of conflict between two contradictory trends and methods of reducing costs; that of mechanization and that of cutting the croppers' subsistence. For, it must not be forgotten that in the South, mechanization proceeds within the framework of a semi-feudal agrarian set-up, controlled by finance capital which, along with capitalistic forms, tends to promote and perpetuate the old and out-moded relics of slavery in the exploitation of the mass of the basic soil tillers. Here, as in the colonies and other backward areas, mechanization meets the obstacle of extra cheap labor. The presence in abundance of cheap and unfree labor in the plantation regions tends to make mechanization unprofitable. Cheap labor lowers the cost of production level at which mechanization is profitable, as compared with other farm areas. In short, the lower the cost of labor, the more efficient must the mechanized equipment be in order to compete with hand labor.

Of course, a crisis with its attendant market restrictions, price collapse, and unemployment, would cut the "costs" of croppers, and might deter the planter from putting in a tractor or another tractor, and induce him to stick to the cropper and the mule. On the big, partly mechanized plantations, these same factors would tend to offset the advantages of a small labor force and induce the landlord of such establishments to fall back on sharecropper labor throughout the entire pre-harvest period.

Table 1 shows a marked slowing down of mechanization on Mississippi farms for the decade 1930-40, which embraces the crisis years. However, toward the latter part of this decade, the AAA reform helped to ease the credit situation by adding to the supply of cash the planters could put into machines. But the most significant fact in increasing mechanization during this period was the premium AAA "benefits" offered in effect for reducing the number of tenants.[43]

The backward, feudal-like character of plantation economy, which ensures the greatest intensity of exploitation for the least capital investment, is an essential feature of finance capital's control, guaranteeing the absentee Wall Street rulers and coupon clippers their lion's share of the plunder of the South's plantation serfs. High interest rates and the difficulty of obtaining credit are one of the features of agriculture under capitalism, retarding the development of agricultural technique. This phenomenon operates with particular force in the South.

This is borne out by the fact that a great obstacle to mechanization has been the higher rate for planters' credit charged by banks and financial institutions. In a sample poll of the Southeast regarding factors retarding mechanization, half of the informants revealed the difficulties of financing the purchase of machines.[44]

In summation: mechanization, along with capitalistic forms of labor, will continue to increase in southern agriculture. But to assume that this development will proceed at such a tempo as radically to change the existing semi-feudal agrarian pattern of the region is but wishful thinking. Mechanization, proceeding against the backdrop of southern agrarian relationships, can lead only to the intensification of the permanent agrarian crisis which has plagued the South and its people for over a generation. It can lead only to the speeding up of the pauperization of the mass of southern soil tillers and their displacement in increasing numbers from productive labor on the land.

Such would be the inevitable results of the increasing inequality in competition between the huge mechanized estates and the smaller plantations which the process of mechanization entails. It is these elements of southern agricultural collapse which will come more and more to the fore as the crisis of southern cotton deepens.

The crisis will accelerate the displacement of sharecroppers, tenants, laborers, and small farmers from the land. Where are these American D.P.s to go? They cannot escape by flight to the city where the South's restricted industrial plant provides no place for their absorption. They can therefore only swell the ranks of the unemployed. And, in the case of the Negro, he faces new barriers as a result of the scrapping of the wartime measures against job discrimination. To remain on the farm means starvation and sinking to a squatters' poverty and misery. In either case, it means masses of people thrown out of the productive process. The only alternative is one of struggle against the exploiters and it is precisely this conclusion that the theorists of gradualist economics seek to evade.

CHAPTER VI

Land and Freedom

THERE IS NO ESCAPE from the conclusion that freedom and prosperity for the people of the South, Negro and white, can be won only through drastic overhauling of the present system of land ownership and agrarian relations of the region. The fight for such radical change must be placed in the very heart of any effective program.

The plantation system which stifles the development of the South's productive forces and warps the lives of its people must be swept away. This foul relic of the chattel slave past, subsidized from the North, can have no place in a fully democratic America. It must be relegated to the limbo of historical monstrosities.

Along with the plantation must go its odious increments of sharecropping, debt-slavery, riding-boss supervision; its outmoded methods of soil usage; its one-crop system, and finally the barbarous institution of color-caste, which freezes the Negroes in permanence at the bottom of the social pyramid. This democratic, agrarian revolution, which Reconstruction passed up in default, has been long overdue. It is a task which must be assumed now by the modern forces of progressive democracy as an integral part of the struggle for progress and democracy in the country as a whole.

The abolition of the plantation system means, first of all, land redivision, the starting point of any agrarian revolution in the South. The big plantations must be broken up and land redistributed in favor of those who work it, Negro and white. Sharecroppers, tenants, and other laborers must have ownership of the land they till. The thousands of small, mortgage-ridden, subsistence farmers who live on the fringes of the plantation belt and are excluded by planter monopoly from the best land must be given access to the good land at the expense of the big estates.

Land to Those Who Work It

At the same time, the one-third of the South's eroded soil must be reclaimed and made accessible to the actual working farmers. This extension of the area of cultivable land will serve a twofold purpose: it will enhance the possibilities of developing economically sound holdings and it will relieve the frightful overcrowding endemic to the region.

Redistribution alone, however, is not enough. The new class of independent small holders must be made secure in their tenure. Here two measures are necessary: (1) The backlog of poor-farmer debt must be wiped out through a drastic scaling down of such debts or through complete cancellation. Usury must be abolished. (2) The new owners must be furnished with the essential tools of production—seeds, fertilizer, livestock, machinery—by means of cheap, long-range government credit. Land is useless without tools, and cheap government credit is essential to check the restoration of landlordism once it has been abolished.

Furthermore, the new class of independent farmers must be helped by federal funds in the co-operative purchase and operation of mechanized equipment. In a modern system there can be set up tractor pools, repair shops, groups of technical advisers, and training courses for handling the heavy machinery under government aegis. Located in each southern farm county, such technical centers and specialists would make possible the changing of the poorly equipped family farms into efficient, productive units.

In this respect, the progressive people's democracies of central and eastern Europe afford valuable lessons. The governments of these countries, representing and fighting for the interests of the workers and peasantry, have found the answer to agrarian progress on the basis of small, independent holdings to be the encouragement of co-operative enterprise, such as collective credit organizations, co-operatives for the sale and purchase of essential manufactures, and horse and tractor stations. In Poland, for example, even though agriculture continues on the basis of individual farming, modern machinery is being made available even to the smallest farms. The Polish government is supporting "Peasant Self-Help Unions" which secure implements that serve entire villages.[1]

In short, land redivision plus co-operative farming—that is the key to the agricultural rehabilitation of the South. It would abolish the conditions which condemn the masses of soil tillers to landlessness, and at the same time assure the technical progress of agriculture by promoting the widest use of machinery and the application of science. In this way it would raise the antiquated agricultural technique of the South to modern levels, enhance the living and cultural standards of the masses of working farmers, and open the way to the ultimate development of large-scale production. In other words, this is the road towards overcoming the lag of technical development in agriculture behind that of industry which is the material basis of agricultural poverty under capitalism, and is accentuated in the South by the monopoly-nourished survivals of slavery.

Electrification and Industrialization

The modernization of southern farming methods means rural electrification together with the industrialization of the South. Cheap electric power must be made available to every farm family. This can be achieved only through a comprehensive program designed to develop the region's tremendous power resources. Rampaging rivers that have hitherto brought disaster to the South's countryside must be harnessed to useful purpose. An idea of the tremendous possibilities for rapid technical development of the South can be gleaned from the Tennessee Valley project initiated under the Roosevelt New Deal.

Despite restraints placed upon the full development of this

project by the bitter opposition of reactionaries, the power trust, the railroad corporations, and their political hatchet men such as the notorious Senator McKellar, the net result of the project has been the reclamation of a large eroded and wasted area of southern soil. Here new industries have sprouted and tens of thousands of formerly backward people have received a higher standard of living.*

Any serious program of rehabilitation of the South's agrarian economy must include the fullest extension of such projects as the TVA to every suitable site in the region, providing a basis for its all-sided industrial development. The failure to develop such a project in the much larger Missouri basin, for example, is condemning the Missouri Valley to a steady decline. Only a Missouri Valley Act with full control over irrigation, flood prevention, power development, and the rational exploitation of natural resources could save that area. As one of the editors of the St. Louis *Star-Times* wrote, "the late President Roosevelt was an ardent supporter of the MVA idea, but his successor has given it only lip-service. Even the latest floods were not enough to move him beyond that."[2]

The chief opponents of the MVA idea, this writer explained, "are the private power interests, the railroads, cattlemen with their eyes on public lands, and such old-line pressure groups as the Mississippi Valley Association, the National Reclamation Association, and the National Rivers and Harbors Congress," whose chief "stocks in trade are (a) the silly argument that MVA is 'communistic'—though even the New York *Daily News* favors it; (b) that methods successful in the Tennessee Valley cannot be used in that of Missouri; and (c) that there *is* no MVA plan . . . "[3] Despite this opposition, such projects provide the basis for effective flood control, soil reclamation, cheap rural electrification and power for local industries capable of producing cheaply the means of production and consumption for southern agriculture, and helping to relieve the agrarian overcrowding.

*In 1933 the average Tennessee Valley farmer paid $35 a year for 600 kilowatt hours of electricity. In 1946 the same family paid $34 but had more than tripled the amount of electricity used, a total of 2,000 kilowatt hours. (See *Daily Worker*, February 23, 1947.)

Rebuilding the South's Soil

Along with the above, concrete measures must be taken to
end the ruinous single-crop system and rebuild and restore to
productive use the eroded, damaged, or abandoned soil wasted
through the deadening influence of the plantation which prevents
the application of new methods. The single-crop system which
ties the South's farmers to a monopolistic market and makes
the region dependent upon the outside for essential manufactured articles, must be replaced by a rational system of farming.
This would include scientifically planned crop rotation and
diversified farming, with emphasis on the production of food
and dairy products, vegetables, fruits, and new industrial crops.

The rebuilding of the soil would require federal outlays
for such measures as the grading, ditching, and terracing of
fields, and a big scale program of protective planting and
reforesting of damaged hillsides, as well as an elaborate fertilizer
program to supply fertilizer to all farms, especially the smallest,
which need it most.

White Supremacy Must Go

The abolition of the plantation system means, finally, the
complete destruction of the Jim-Crow color caste institution
whereby the big planters oppress and exploit the Negro people.
This institution has served both as a "moral" justification and
as an effective means for maintaining and continuing plantation
slavery in modern life. Without the abolition of all forms of
white supremacy, it is impossible to save the land or the people
who work it. Since the entire Jim-Crow system has its roots
in the plantation, only the abolition of the plantation can
permanently remove the soil which has produced and sustained
this barbarous system. But "white supremacy" is the plantation
lords' chief line of defense, the bulwark of the Bourbon exploiters' rule. Basic land reform, therefore, is unthinkable
without the destruction of the entire system of Negro oppression.

Plainly, these far-reaching changes are necessary if the Negro
is to be free, if the South is to rise out of the quagmire of
economic and cultural blight, and if the malignant sore eating

at the very heart of our country's democracy is to be cauterized and healed. They comprise the basic ingredients of the long delayed agrarian revolution in the South. If successfully prosecuted, these measures would release the imprisoned productive forces of the region, requite the gnawing land hunger of the southern tillers of the soil, Negro and white, create the conditions for the rise of a class of independent and prosperous small owners and for the further development of the class struggle for the democratic reconstruction of the South. They would strike the manacles of semi-serf bondage from the Negro people, destroy the most important material base of Jim-Crow oppression, and lay the groundwork for destroying the whole system of "color caste" which dictates inequality for America's colored citizenry throughout the country and in all walks of life.

These changes would break the backbone of Junkerism, Dixie style, whose representatives in Congress are hell-bent on essaying a role in contemporary American life similar to that of their dethroned feudalist counterparts in central and eastern Europe, as the torchbearers of native fascism. It would shake loose the putrid soil which nourishes the whole foul breed of fascist Negrophobes of the stripe of Bilbo, Ellender, Rankin, and Talmadge.

Is It Practical?

Is there any prospect for the achievement of such drastic changes within the frame of existing conditions, of a state dominated economically and politically by finance capital?

The bourgeoisie, which would not carry through this land reform during the Civil War and Reconstruction, when capitalism was comparatively youthful and waging a progressive struggle against slavery, will surely not carry it out today, when capitalism is in its decadent, imperialist era, and monopoly capital seeks to make use of the most backward feudal elements in the interests of untrammeled exploitation. The transformation of the agrarian structure of the South will not come from above. On the contrary, the real economic rulers of the South and a federal government which represents the concentrated power of big capital rather than the interests of the people can be counted on to use their maximum strength to crush any attempt at fundamental land reform in the South.

At the same time, co-operative farming, difficult at best under capitalism, is an idle dream in the South without land redivision. This was amply demonstrated by the experience of the New Deal which showed the complete futility of co-operatives for the mass of poor farmers under conditions of southern landlordism. As J. Lewis Henderson pointed out in a comparatively recent survey of the semi-feudal plantation system, the very principle of co-operation means sharing of benefits and democratic control, and this would obviously be an immediate threat to the entire white-supremacy pattern. The attempts of the Farm Security Administration to organize small farmer co-ops in the South, therefore, met with resistance and essential failure. The few existing ones are manipulated so that benefits and savings do not extend to the mass of small farmers, and Negro tenants "seldom receive the benefits of such co-ops, as any patronage dividends usually stop when they reach the landlord."[4]

Moreover, as long as the economy of the country as a whole is dominated by monopoly capital, there is no possibility of any far-reaching change in the technical basis of southern agriculture. It is "normal" under capitalism for the technical development of agriculture to lag behind that of industry, and as long as capitalism prevails there can be no real prospect for all-around mechanization of agriculture in a backward area like the South, and without such comprehensive mechanization there is no way out of agricultural poverty. Indeed, under southern plantation conditions, the "normal" gap between agriculture and industry characteristic of capitalism is highly accentuated. Where mechanization does proceed in the South, tenants and farmers are tractored off the land. On non-mechanized plantations, the labor force is even more exploited as a consequence. It also means the more intensive exploitation of the hard-driven "independent" farmers who, with their "one row, one mule system," are unable to compete and survive.

The development of power projects in the South is also kept in check and obstructed, and, with the government at this time more firmly in the hands of the trusts and corporations than ever, there can be no doubt that anything done along this line will be subordinated entirely to the profit needs and military plans of big capital. With the South, the nation's so-called "economic problem number 1," virtually occupying a semi-colonial position within the country, there can be no talk of any extensive development of the productive forces there, even if other conditions were favorable.

Altogether, therefore, the conclusion is inescapable that the liberation of the Negro people and the transformation of the agrarian relations in the South cannot be achieved through the further economic evolution of capitalism in that region. They can be achieved, on the one hand, only through the development and organization of the economic and political struggle of the landless masses, Negro and white, aimed against the entire "Southern system," and supported by the working class and other progressive forces of the country as a whole. On the other hand, they can be achieved only when the government is free from the influence of the monopolies, in short, is a truly people's government, firmly rooted in the public ownership of the economy, and whose first concern is the welfare of the masses and the progress of the country, and not the profits of the trusts and corporations. Only under the aegis of a genuine people's government in the United States can the status quo in southern land relationships be radically altered in favor of the great bulk of the agricultural population, Negro and white. Only such a government will be capable of instituting the all-embracing social, economic, and political reforms so urgently needed by the mass of southern common folk. But whatever one may think of the conditions necessary for the realization of the foregoing measures, there can be no question that the adoption of these measures is indispensable for progress in the South and for the democratic development of the country as a whole. There is no other way to improve the conditions of the southern masses.

Liberal Objections

To most liberals this is tantamount to socialism and just as reprehensible. They may advocate the separate proposals advanced here, short of land redivision, or in isolated cases even admit the necessity of giving the land to the landless. But when the conditions for realizing all those proposals are clearly set forth, they see red. The fact is that every time the people have tried to improve their conditions fundamentally or have attempted to take their destinies into their own hands, or put the stamp of their needs and interests on the course of development, their action was immediately condemned as communism. But what is involved here is not communism, although the people cannot introduce fundamental measures today in their interest without removing the stranglehold of monopoly capital and consequently taking the road to a classless, socialist society. The type of measures involved is in its nature purely democratic; measures, consequently, which historically should and could have been adopted by the bourgeois revolutions. The fact that the bourgeoisie has refused to adopt them and the need for them has continued into the era when the next major stage of historical development will be socialism, and their adoption consequently becomes part of the over-all historical movement and struggle for socialism, does not alter the nature of these measures. The fact that only the masses have an inexorable interest in fighting for them, and that these measures can be achieved only if the power of monopoly capital is broken, proves neither that they are socialist nor that the struggle for them can be postponed until the advent of socialism.

In themselves, these measures represent no more than the abolition of conditions characteristic of the feudal stage of historical development. To abandon or postpone the struggle for these measures because of the conditions necessary for their realization is tantamount to abandoning the struggle for democracy and progress. As far as the masses are concerned, they cannot cease aspiring for the realization of these measures, even though this realization may be in the comparatively distant future, without entirely losing the spirit of resistance and struggle even for the smallest gains in the present. Without these bigger things, democracy is an empty shell, a fraud, and a mockery.

"*Left*" *Objections*

If the liberal, confusing the nature of these measures with the conditions for their realization, rejects radical land reform on the ground that these conditions mean socialism, the ultra-left critic rejects them *in the name of* socialism. To him the whole idea of land redivision is reactionary, ostensibly because technical progress depends upon large-scale production, and land redivision would mean encouraging small, individual property as against large-scale property. As far as he is concerned the question of land and freedom for the Negro will be solved automatically with the coming of socialism, and there is consequently no need for a special struggle for these demands.

Actually, while neither the measures presented here nor the conditions of their achievement necessarily mean socialism, neither do they mean a departure from the path to socialism. On the one hand, therefore, to maintain that a people's government is an indispensable prerequisite for the realization of the foregoing measures is not equivalent to arguing that they can be achieved only under socialism. For, while it is possible that the establishment of a truly people's government in the United States might not be achieved until such a government would necessarily be a socialist government, it is also possible for a people's government to come into office which is not yet directly socialist. On the other hand, it is idle to talk of socialism in the United States without the development of the broadest struggle for the solution of precisely such democratic questions as are represented by the liberation of the Negro people and fundamental land reform in the South.

The trouble with the ultra-left argument is that it fails to understand either the conditions for the achievement of socialism or the character of the Negro liberation question. In effect it means the abandonment of the fight for both. To speak of socialism while disregarding the conditions of achieving it is to assume an end result without the process or the elements producing it. Scientifically, such an approach is intolerable; practically, it is absurd. The social character of modern production and the welfare of the people have long made socialism both necessary and possible. But it is axiomatic by now that the necessary and possible will not be transformed into living reality until the exploiters are unable and the exploited are unwilling to continue in the old way. This means that the industrial working class must not only be prepared to fight for the new way of life, but it must have as its allies in the struggle the other exploited and oppressed strata of the population suffering, directly or indirectly, from the domination of monopoly capital and that these strata, therefore, must be drawn into the struggle, which can be done only on the basis of their own demands.

In this struggle, the landless soil tillers of the South, Negro and white, are historically on the side of the industrial proletariat. But their basic aim is to be rid of landlordism and the semi-feudal conditions which keep them in bondage and poverty. While socialist agriculture could solve this problem most thoroughly, the masses of sharecroppers, as yet in the stage of aspiring to individual land holdings in the face of the feudal monopoly of the land, could hardly be mobilized to fight for a purely socialist solution. At the same time, the fight for land division is a fight for a democratic aim which cannot be waged today without hitting at one of the main bulwarks of monopoly capital and consequently at the chief barrier to the establishment of socialism. Land redivision, therefore, is progressive not only in relation to the semi-feudal plantation system, but also in relation to the task of winning fighting allies against monopoly capital among the exploited and oppressed population generally.[5] In fact, under conditions where the government is truly a people's government, land redivision serves to advance, and not retard, technical progress in agriculture, and to prepare the necessary basis for higher forms of agricultural production.

Like the land question in the South, the question of Negro freedom is a democratic demand, the struggle for which is one of the major conditions for the ultimate achievement of socialism in the United States. At the same time, it is obvious that only under socialism will the Negro people in the United States be completely free from exploitation and oppression in any form. In this sense, therefore, socialism is the major condition for

Negro freedom. But since it can actually become such only if the Negro people, supported by the white toilers, also wage an active struggle against the source of their oppression, it is absurd to talk about winning socialism first and Negro freedom will automatically follow. Actually this means telling the Negro people not to fight for land and freedom, but for socialism. This not only ignores the special features of the Negro question, but cancels out the very element which establishes the inter-relationship between it and socialism, namely, the active involvement of the Negro people in the struggle for their own freedom. It does so by presenting the question of freedom as something which will be brought to the Negro people as a gift by socialism. This is an invitation not only to the Negro people, but also to the white working class to abandon the actual struggle for Negro freedom.

Immediate Demands

We shall discuss the special features of this question in the next chapter, especially as they bear upon the fight for basic agrarian reform in the South. Meanwhile, it should be evident that in this fight it is imperative not to neglect the immediate needs of the agricultural population. The following are some of the points towards which immediate struggle should be directed:

Reforms directed to the abolition of the sharecropping system, its economic and legal supports; lower percentage of crop yield for rentals; abolition of crop-lien laws; for the legal right of the sharecropper and share tenant to the crop, his right to sell it on the open market at his own will; for written contracts between landlord and tenant; abolition of usurious credit rates; the right of the tenant to buy where he pleases; abolition of all laws and practices supporting peonage, such as the vagrancy laws, the "jumping contract" laws and the "enticing labor" laws; allocation of adequate acreage to each tenant for the raising of essential food crops for home consumption.

Some of the most urgent needs of all tenants and small farmers can be met by: reduction of land rents, the placing of land purchasing services within the reach of small owners and of tenants; revival, extension, and liberalization of the Farm Security program, and its rehabilitation, settlement and rental co-operative programs; increased federal appropriations for the Farm Security Administration with a liberalization of loan services by reduction of collateral and interest rates so as to bring these loans within the reach of the masses of small farmers and tenants; a democratic reorganization of all local administrations, free from landlord control, with proportional representation of Negroes on all local FSA boards; the use of idle land for settlement of displaced farm families; extension of social security to include small farmers; free access to the land, and the removal of all privileges protecting the planters' land monopoly.

Farm laborers require: the removal of all semi-feudal conditions; a living cash wage and application of the Federal Wages and Hours Law; extension of Federal Unemployment Insurance to compensate for the seasonal character of the work; placing unemployment insurance once more in the hands of the federal government; abolition of all vagrancy laws and all practices enforcing peonage; the establishment of the right to organize, bargain collectively, and strike.

The needs of the Black Belt in housing, education, health, and public works can be partially met by federal and state support for adequate educational, housing, health and public works programs; equal allocation of the educational funds, equal facilities, and abolition of the Jim-Crow school system.

In the field of political democracy, demands include the abolition of the Jim-Crow caste system, abolition of the Jim-Crow laws, and establishment of full equality for Negroes in all spheres; electoral reforms, the right to vote and hold office, abolition of white primaries, the immediate passage of federal anti-poll tax legislation; the enactment of a federal anti-lynching bill, federal prosecution of lynchers, death penalty for lynching, the banning of the Ku Klux Klan, and other such extra-legal terrorist organizations; enforcement of the principle of the right of self-defense, the organization of mass joint defense committees, Negro and white, for active resistance to lynch terror; enforcement of freedom of speech, press, and assembly, and the right of all farming people to organize.

Lessons from Experience

The struggle for these demands has an important background of living experience to draw upon as a guide. In the deep South, from the time of chattel slavery to the present, this urge for the land has been the driving motor of the Negro's fight for human rights and justice—his ever-insistent and unceasing demand. The right to the soil he tills, to the ownership of a plot of earth of his own, has always constituted the hard core of his ideal of freedom.

This quest for the land was the turgid undercurrent of the hundreds of slave insurrections and conspiracies of ante-bellum times. It was the throbbing heartbeat of the epochal battle of Reconstruction. And today the land question, still unsolved, is the hub on which the fight of the bitterly oppressed but restive Negro people is bound to turn in the Black Belt for equality and freedom.

Aside from the migration led by Moses Singleton in 1879 and the almost legendary "Wheel and Alliance" which in the 'eighties organized Negro and white farmers and miners in Alabama, the first widespread movement of Negro sharecroppers in the present century seems to have been the one organized in eastern Arkansas in 1919. The United States Department of Labor explains the impetus behind this movement:

> "During the period of prosperity and labor scarcity in World War I the Negro sharecroppers had shared in the profits from high cotton prices. In the postwar deflation they bore a major part of the burden. Planters attempted to shift some of their losses to tenants by manipulating accounts and in some cases practicing outright fraud."[6]

To these reasons must be added the nationwide unrest among Negroes as a result of the broken promises of World War I. This movement was weak in that it was isolated from white sharecroppers in the region; also, it lacked the support of an organized labor movement in the urban centers. It was quickly and ruthlessly crushed. While the details of these experiences from the end of Reconstruction to the second decade of the twentieth century have yet to be pieced together by historians, the struggles of the 'thirties are still part of living memory and the material about them is more extensive and accessible. These struggles of the early 'thirties resumed the thread of the share-croppers' movement that had been broken in 1919. They began with the organization of the Negro Farm Workers, Tenants, and Sharecroppers Union, which got off to a favorable start. It was conceived under conditions of a more matured labor movement and the presence of an active Communist Party.

As the U. S. Department of Labor study, *Labor Unionism in Agriculture,* describes it (while disparagingly referring to the historic Scottsboro case and other southern frame-ups as mere "incidents" initiated from the "outside"):

> "The most dramatic rural organization in Alabama dur-
> ing the thirties was the Negro farm workers' and tenants'
> Sharecroppers Union. This was one result of the Com-
> munist Party's organization campaign among southern
> Negroes, which also gave rise to such incidents as the
> celebrated Scottsboro case, the Angelo Herndon trial,
> and the numerous mine 'disorders' in the Birmingham
> area. Although initiated by 'outside' white radical in-
> fluences, these incidents were, nevertheless, symptomatic
> of underlying unrest and antipathy in the established
> relationships between the whites and Negroes . . . The
> doctrines of unionism found ready response among Ne-
> gro tenants, sharecroppers, and laborers, who were un-
> dergoing severe hardships during the years of depression.
> It is difficult to judge whether the burden of depression
> which fell so heavily on the cotton-growing areas of the
> South were especially severe in Alabama, and whether
> sharecroppers suffered more in this state than in others.
> Prof. Harold Hoffsommer in the study of 1,022 Alabama
> farm households receiving relief during 1933 estimated
> that in 89 per cent of the years spent at sharecropping,
> the net economic outcome for this group was either to
> break even or to suffer a loss. He concluded that the
> so-called financial loss to the sharecropper was largely
> a decline of social or occupational status and an increased

dependence upon landlords, since in most instances the sharecroppers had no finances to lose."[7]

The first local of the Sharecroppers Union (S.C.U.) was organized in Tallapoosa County, Alabama, in 1931, in the worst period of the depression, before the government had begun any measures whatever for relief. The organization was at first more successful among Negro tenants of the upper brackets—that is, cash and standing renters, and Negro small farm owners facing loss of their land through mortgage foreclosures.

From its inception, the union faced violent attempts at suppression on the part of the plantation owners and their local agents. The fight first broke into the open on July 16, 1931, at Camp Hill. The occasion was the breaking up, by local sheriffs and deputies, of a meeting held by sharecroppers to protest the Scottsboro frame-up. On July 17, a Negro member standing guard was alleged to have shot and wounded the local sheriff. When officers came to arrest the Negro, his house was found to be barricaded by armed unionists. In the battle that resulted, one Negro was killed and five wounded.

The local movement was not killed by suppression. During the next year, the S.C.U. continued to grow and by the spring of 1932 it claimed a membership of 500.

The next outbreak took place in Reeltown in December, 1932. On that occasion the union came to the defense of one of its members, Cliff James. The whole affair was a frame-up by the local authorities, a plain effort to provoke the union. James had been denied the usual credit by merchants and by his landlord. The landlord served a writ of attachment on James' livestock, which James refused to give up when the writ was served. The sheriff and his deputies, attempting to seize the cattle, were confronted with armed union members who had barricaded the house. The sheriff and two deputies were wounded, one union member was killed, and several others were wounded.

Now began a manhunt accompanied by terror and violence. A mob of more than 500 tracked down Negroes in the woods. There is no account of the number of Negroes killed during those days.

Reeltown pointed up also the deep unrest among the white farmers. The officials could not get together a posse from the same county. The farmers began to see through the barrage of racist incitement, their common interests with the Negroes.

The determination of the croppers themselves was shown in the manner in which the union members packed the courtroom at Dadeville at the trial. Although the judge postponed the case and the next day the highways were blocked, the Negroes managed to get to the court, by paths which they alone knew. Sentences of several years were given to the convicted members.

However, by the following spring, the union had gained a membership of about 3,000, among which a few white sharecroppers were included. Its influence had extended to counties other than Tallapoosa.

After Reeltown, the program of the union began to make use of collective bargaining methods, attempting to enforce federal government programs for rural relief against the landlords who sought to control and, in most cases, to block that relief. In 1934, the union organized a strike of Tallapoosa county cotton workers asking 75 cents a hundredweight. In some areas, demands were won.

By 1935, the organization claimed a membership of 10,000. By this time its emphasis was more on the organization of plantation laborers and on displaced croppers and tenants driven out by mechanization and the crop restriction program.

Why did the union eventually decline? Chiefly, there was the question involved in organizing different strata of agricultural masses into one organization—small owners, tenants, sharecroppers, and wage laborers. The leaders decided that it was impractical to conduct simultaneous activities in the interests of wage workers, tenants and small owners, ostensibly because of the divergence of interest among these groups. In an attempt to solve this question, the S.C.U. was finally dissolved, with the tenants and small owners transferred into the Farmers Union of Alabama. The wageworkers formerly in the S.C.U. entered the Alabama Agricultural Workers Union. Later, in 1937, through an A. F. of L. charter, the Agricultural Workers Union was converted into the Farm Laborers and Cotton Cultivators Union. This union was finally absorbed in the United Cannery, Agricultural, Packing, and Allied Workers of America, C.I.O.

In the big plantation area of eastern Arkansas, meanwhile, a movement was developing that was to lead to one of the most dramatic and powerful organizations of the 'thirties. With the reduced demand for cotton came a reduced demand for labor on these plantations, most of which were absentee owned. A wholesale dispossession of tenants and sharecroppers took place, due to decreased buying power in the depression, to government crop-reduction programs, and to mechanization. Planters who dispossessed sharecroppers and replaced them with wage workers gained for themselves all the government's benefit payments.

It was in this situation that the Southern Tenant Farmers Union had its origins. It began in Poinsett County, Arkansas, in July 1934, interracial from the outset. Men like Claude Williams, a minister, were prominent in it. In 1937, it became affiliated with the United Cannery, Agricultural, Packing and Allied Workers.

The Southern Tenant Farmers Union conducted a series of strikes, some of which met with minor successes. The action dramatizing the plight of the South's sharecroppers and wage workers came in January, 1939, when 1,300 evicted croppers camped on the main highways of Missouri. Planters had evicted a greater number of croppers than usual in order to keep all crop-reduction checks. On January 6, evicted croppers met in Sikeston, Mo. Under the leadership of a Negro preacher, Reverend Owen Whitfield, vice-president of the S.T.F.U., the croppers marched through U. S. highways. As a result of pressure, the National Guard in Missouri was forced to supply tents and blankets to the highway campers. Declaring the camps a health menace, county and state officers broke them up. Evicted croppers were forced to scatter so that their conditions would not become a matter of public attention. Through the S.T.F.U., most of the families gained emergency relief grants from the F.S.A. Even the F.B.I. was forced to agree to the claims of the demonstrators that they were protesting conditions of poverty. Unfortunately, the F.B.I. also absolved the landlords.

What the S.T.F.U. accomplished was best summarized by a union bulletin in 1940:

> "The union has succeeded in exposing certain brutal-
> izing aspects of the plantation system, and has brought
> to light many cases of peonage and forced labor. It has
> caused governmental investigations, both State and Na-
> tional, to be made into conditions in the cotton industry.
> No lynchings have occurred in the areas where these
> people have organized, and constitutional guarantees
> of freedom of speech and assemblage have been recog-
> nized for the first time in many decades. Wages have
> been raised and hundreds of thousands of dollars in
> Government benefits and grants were secured for the
> sharecroppers through the union's efforts. Better contracts
> with planters have been effected. Members of the union
> had been elected to local A.A.A. committees, and for the
> first time the sharecroppers have had representation on
> some of the policy-making agricultural bodies."[8]

Some Conclusions

This brief resumé of modern agrarian struggles in the South emphasizes a number of points which should never be lost sight of in the struggle for Negro freedom. These points may be thus summarized:

The Negro tiller of the land is the focal point around which the democratic transformation of the South turns. In this strug-gle, Negro and white tillers are interdependent, having a com-munity of interests against those of the landlords.

The history of agrarian struggle in the South emphasizes the important role of the Communist Party and indicates the neces-sity of support from city workers, trade unions, and liberal groups in the building of the land struggles.

This history emphasizes also the highly *political* character of the fight for southern agrarian reform, and the inseparable link between economic and political changes in that region. The fight for the most elementary demands in the sphere of agrarian re-form immediately runs afoul of the political power of the landlords, entrenched in the plantation system with its anti-Negro social and legal sanctions.

In the South, as nowhere else in the country, the fight for the smallest demands to relieve the suffering of the people assumes almost at once a political character. This essentially revolutionary character of the demands of the Negro soil cultivator arises from the semi-slave economic and political setup in the region. There every demand leading in the direction of democracy becomes at once a challenge to the feudal privileges of the Bourbon ruling caste and is immediately countered by terror and the wildest racist provocation.

The observation of Lenin regarding the struggles of the Russian peasantry against feudal tsarism applies fully to the fight of their Negro American counterparts, the sharecroppers. Their partial demands, he observed, are more revolutionary than the partial demands of the city industrial workers because they represent the belated and unfinished struggle against serfdom and feudalism.[9]

The Negro Nation

IN THE STRUGGLE against the plantation system of the South, the Negro people are necessarily the chief driving force. The liberal "remedies" which shy away from the fundamental economic changes indispensable for the democratic transformation of the South, ignore this crucial fact and, with it, they ignore the special character of the social and political struggle of the Negroes.

The Myth of Race

The "white supremacists" insist on presenting the Negro question as one of race. This makes it possible for them to "justify" the notorious color-caste system in the name of spurious race dogmas which depict the Negro's servile status in American life, not as the result of man-imposed prescription, but as a condition fixed by nature. Negro inequality is supposedly due to natural inherent differences. In this credo, Negroes presumably are a lower form of organism, mentally primitive and emotionally undeveloped. "Keeping the Negro in his place" is thus allegedly prescribed by nature and fixed by Holy Writ. Color of skin is made an index to social position. Race, a strictly limited biological concept, becomes a social factor and is used as an instrument for perpetuating and intensifying Negro subjugation. The Negro problem is explained in terms of natural conflict between races, the result of inborn peculiarities.

This hideous distortion, whose roots go back into ante-bellum times and beyond, permeates the entire cultural pattern of the South; this vile calumny is fixed in the South's folkways, mores and customs, sanctioned in its laws, and, in the last analysis, buttressed by violence and lynch terror.

The lie of the natural, innate and eternal backwardness of the Negro and other dark-skinned peoples is the theoretical foundation upon which rests the whole noxious system of Negro segregation and its corollary, "white supremacy."

Formerly a rationalization of chattel slavery, it is used to justify the Negro's present-day vassalage. Held down by an all-pervasive and absolute system of Jim Crow based on color of skin and curl of hair—whose myriad taboos hound him from the cradle to the grave—the Negro is America's "untouchable."

Buell G. Gallagher observes in *Color and Conscience:*

> "Slavery as ownership of chattel is gone: as a caste system it remains. Its purpose is to keep non-whites in a position which, in one way or another, is inferior or subordinate to that of whites. Its devices range from lynchings and mob violence, at one extreme, through legal enactment and extra-legal manipulations of courts and police, to custom and etiquette as instruments of caste control."[1]

From its tap root in the semi-feudal plantation system, anti-Negro racism has spread throughout the country, shaping the pattern of Negro-white relationships in the North as well. With the clandestine encouragement of Yankee financial power and its controlled agencies of public opinion, art, literature, education, press, and radio, the dogma of the Negroes' "inherent inferiority" has been cunningly infiltrated into the national consciousness of the American people. Woven into the national fabric, it has become an integral part of the "American way of life," despite repeated refutation by authoritative science.

In reality, the so-called racial persecution of the Negro in the United States is a particular form and device of national oppression. The use by an oppressor nation's ruling class of such social differences as language and religion to preserve the isolation (and thus the economic and social inequality) of a subject people is common knowledge.

Everywhere in the world, a study of the national question reveals the use of these differences by the ruling bourgeoisie as the foundation for its strategy of "divide and rule," of fomenting strife and friction between the toilers of various nationalities. In Hitler's Germany with its slogan of "one race, one culture, one nation," racism reached a high peak making the cult of race the cornerstone of state and world policy. Bloody pogroms, artificially created almost overnight against Jews, became the openly declared official program of Nazi rule.

In America, the roots of racism are deeper, sunk as they are in the unsolved land question of the Black Belt. The current upswing of racism in the United States is utilized by monopoly capital in the drive toward fascism and its by-product, war. In the United States, perhaps more than anywhere else in the world, a far-flung system of racial persecution, springing from the mire of chattel slavery—with strong survivals up to the present day—provides an even more fertile soil than Hitler had.

Racism, always the game of a reactionary governing class, is being played for much higher stakes today.

Among American Negroes, physical difference becomes almost the sole characteristic whereby the subject race can be distinguished from the oppressor nation. In the absence of such socio-cultural distinctions between white and Negro as language and religion, the "racial visibility" of the Negro enables the Anglo-Saxon ruling clique to set him apart from all others among the population as a permanent object of scorn and oppression.

Effect on the Negro

In the ideology of race, the dominant classes have a much more potent weapon at their disposal than even religion and language. The latter, as social phenomena, are historically transient; whereas race, a physical category, persists. And once a people has been smeared with the stigma of "racial inferiority" they are *ipso facto* ruled out as unworthy of nationhood and its inherent right of self government—a right which in itself is presumed to be the special privilege of "superior" races.

This deliberately cultivated emphasis on the racial factor, particularly on the aspect of color differences, has not been without its adverse effect upon the Negro. It has indeed acted as a retardation on the growth of political self-assertion. The fog of racist obscurantism, thrown up by his oppressors, has made difficult clear political orientation, *i.e.*, the job of locating and thus confronting the real enemy—the forces of monopoly capitalism. It is therefore not surprising that until quite recently Negro protest has been shunted off into the blind alley of a defensive "racialism." What is in reality an aspiration for identity as a nation has sought expression through false symbols of "race" foisted on him by white rulers. He has perforce defined his fight for freedom as a fight for "racial equality," "racial opportunity."

Manifestly, the Negro problem cannot be defined by any racial formulae. Ideologically, they obscure the economic and political conditions for the achievement of Negro equality, and impede the full and necessary clarity as to the nature of the issue. They are tank-traps to block the road to the understanding of the profound revolutionary implications of the struggle of the Negro people for liberation.

The maintenance of the pariah status of Negro Americans, their lack of equality, is an integral part of the policy of American finance capital. That policy has for its objective the achievement of the following:

1. The artificial and forcible stifling of the free economic and cultural development of the Negro through racist persecution as a basic condition for maintaining his super-exploitation and for maintaining the degradation of the great mass of southern white folks;

2. The infection of the organism of American democracy with the virus of race hatred as a deterrent to the formation of a common front of labor and democratic people against the common enemy—monopoly capitalism.

The fulcrum of that policy is the retention by monopoly of the slave survivals in the Black Belt as an essential economic and social base for its allies—the decadent, Bourbon squirearchy of the South. And now, this policy has led to the conversion of the entire South into a bulwark behind which the most noxious forms of native fascism are rallying for a full-scale sortie against the democracy of the whole country and the world.

Real Nature of the Problem

The secret to unraveling the tangled skein of America's Negro question lies in its consideration as the issue of an oppressed nation. Within the borders of the United States, and under the jurisdiction of a single central government, there exist not one, but two nations: a dominant white nation, with its Anglo-Saxon hierarchy, and a subject black one.

Unlike the white immigrant minorities, the Negro, wearing his badge of color, which sets the seal of permanency on his inferior status, cannot, under contemporary economic and social conditions, be absorbed into the American community as a full-fledged citizen, limited as this absorption is in practice even for large sections of the white minorities. He cannot hope to escape as long as the status quo remains unchanged in the South. True, there are colored minorities, such as the colored Latin Americans —Mexicans, Puerto Ricans and others; there are Orientals, and remnants of the American Indians. But these also are tarred with the brush of color—and are in the main relegated to the category of "unassimilables," outside the limits of majority democratic tradition.

But the classification of the Negro as a "minority" leaves unanswered the question posed long ago by George W. Cable, a foremost champion of Negro rights: why one-tenth of the population, all natives of the United States, and by law an inseparable part of the nation, do not have the same full measure of citizenship that they would have were they entirely of European rather than of partially African descent. For really, as Cable put it, the Negro remains in America a "perpetual alien."[2]

The policy of Jim-Crow proscription of America's black folk has resulted over the years in the shaping of the Negro as a distinct economic, historical, cultural, and, in the South, geographical entity in American life. The Negro is American. He is the product of every social and economic struggle that has made America. But the Negro is a special kind of American, to the extent that his oppression has set him apart from the dominant white nation. Under the pressure of these circumstances, he has generated all the objective attributes of nationhood.

The history of the Negro people in the United States is unquestionably intertwined with the history of the rest of the American people. But to say no more than this would be to falsify both the special story of the Negro people and to befog the history of American capitalism. For, on the one hand there were the dominant whites, and among them existed from the beginning the division into economic classes. The Negroes, on the other hand, were forced into the stream of American history in a special manner—as oppressed slaves whose present position as a whole people still bears the marks of the slave lash.

The Negro was not freed by the Revolution of 1776, nor was he fully freed by the Second American Revolution of 1861-77— the Civil War and Reconstruction. The fact is that the first American republic contained a glaring flaw—the institution of chattel slavery. This despite the aims so proudly proclaimed by the Declaration of Independence of man's inalienable right to life, liberty, and the pursuit of happiness. Excluded from these "inalienable rights" was an important segment of the American people—the Negro slave who, at the time, comprised one-fifth of the country's population.

Thus, the new American national state created as a result of revolution got off to a false start. This "omission" was to prove almost fatal. The glaring ambiguity of a nation half free and half slave was recognized by the most advanced statesmen of the period, by Paine, Jefferson, Franklin, Samuel Adams, and others.

It was the belief of the Founding Fathers that slavery would soon die out. Slavery was not particularly profitable, except in a very few areas. The tide of history turned with the industrial revolution in England and the various inventions, topped by the cotton gin, which created a world-wide demand for cotton. In 1789, when the Constitution was adopted, no one doubted that there would soon be an end of slavery. By 1818, when the debate began on the admission of Missouri, a new slavocracy had arisen which was demanding expansion into new lands.

The compromises which the Constitution contained on the

issue of slavery precluded the participation of the Negro in the first American republic. It prevented his democratic integration into the new national state. He was thus cheated of the fruits of the victory to which he had contributed in terms of 5,000 of his people in the revolutionary armed forces.

But the constitutional compromises only postponed the issue of slavery. This issue was to flare up anew in the second decade of the nineteenth century and was to occupy the spotlight in American politics up to the end of the Civil War.

The question of slavery, as Marx observed, was for half a century the moving power of American history.[3] The issue was finally resolved only by the Second American Revolution—the Civil War and Reconstruction.

Here again, for the second time, hope was held for the full integration of the Negro into American life as a free and equal citizen, for the consolidation of Americans, black and white, into one nation. But again the revolution was aborted, again the Negro was left outside the portals of full citizenship. The great betrayal of 1877, sealed by the Hayes-Tilden gentlemen's agreement, turned over the management of the South to the new Bourbon classes, who were given the chance to reconstruct that region "in their own way."

Again the Negro was denied the fruits of the victory which he had helped to win. Deserted by his erstwhile allies, he was left landless and at the tender mercy of the former slaveholders. Again, as in the Revolution of 1776, he was placed at the doorstep of full freedom only to have the door slammed in his face—an unwelcome intruder. This second great defeat blasted his hopes for democratic absorption into American national life.

But a qualitative change had taken place in his status. Freed from chattel slavery by the uncompleted revolution, he was now ready for the appearance of economic classes within his group, which under the conditions of segregation and imperialist oppression, necessarily served as driving forces for a movement of national liberation. The process of class stratification among Negroes was of necessity a slow and tortuous one, taking place as it did against the overwhelming odds of post-Reconstruction reaction. But proceed it did, so that the Negroes, who at the time of their release from chattel bondage comprised an almost undifferentiated peasant mass, had by the beginning of the twentieth century become transformed into a people manifesting among themselves the class groupings peculiar to modern capitalist society. Along with an increasing mass of wage laborers, there began to appear a class of small business people, with more or less well-defined capitalist aspirations. This class was to find its spokesmen among the educated middle class. The rise of a Negro bourgeoisie marked the appearance of a class which, striving to defend its own interests under American conditions, was destined to initiate an historical movement which could only develop in the direction of national freedom. The process of class differentiation developing against the background of Jim-Crow oppression, and in conditions of continued majority concentration of Negroes in the Black Belt, thus formed the main objective conditions for their emergence as an oppressed nation.

The advent of imperialism, the epoch of the trusts and monopolies, at the turn of the century, riveted the yoke of white ruling-class tyranny still tighter, with the result that the Negro was thrust still further out of the pale of American democracy into deeper isolation within his own group. The rise of a finance-capitalist oligarchy to dominant position in American economic and political life precluded the possibility of peaceful democratic fusion of the Negro into a single American nation along with whites. Thenceforth the issue of Negro equality could be solved only via the path of the Negro's full development as a nation. The Negro question had now definitely become the problem of an oppressed nation striving for national freedom against the main enemy, imperialism.*

*The uniqueness of the Negro problem in the United States lies in the fact that the Negro was left out of the country's general democratic transformation. Quite the reverse was the development in France. Pre-revolutionary France was what Mirabeau aptly called a "formless heap of disunited peoples." These peoples were welded into one united French nation as a result of the revolution. For example, in France all ethnic groups, without exception, Bretons, Normans, Basques, Alsatians, etc., shared equally in the "liberty, equality, and fraternity" achieved by the great French Revolution. They were therefore all welded into one French nation on the basis of this

Objective Conditions for Nationhood

Geographically, the Negroes are scattered throughout the United States, but almost one-third of their number (five million) are still massed in the Black Belt area, including its peripheral counties. Despite the migrations of the last eighty years, they exist as a stable community and form a majority of the population over a broad area.

We defined the Black Belt in Chapter I as an area girding the heart of the South, encompassing its central cotton-growing states and 180 counties in which the Negroes constitute more than half (50 to 85.5 per cent) of the population. From this core, the Black Belt Negro community overflows into 290 or more neighboring counties, whose populations are from 30 to 50 per cent Negro. In the whole of this area, then, in a total of approximately 470 counties, live five million Negroes.

This Black Belt region is the heartland of the American Negro. Here he has lived from generation to generation. It was upon its Atlantic Seaboard that his forefathers landed in Jamestown, Virginia, over 300 years ago. As a chattel slave, the black man followed the trek of King Cotton and the plantation across the face of the South. He planted and raised the South's chief cash crops, tobacco and cotton. His unrequited labor as a slave formed an essential part of the primary accumulation of wealth upon which the towering edifice of American industrial civilization was founded. Yet, eighty-five years after "emancipation" he is still denied his share. He remains a disinherited pauper, a social leper in his own homeland, groaning under the burden of absentee rulers and their regional henchmen, forced to obey laws which he has had no part in making.

democratic transition. Had any one of these ethnic groups been excluded from the benefits of that revolution, as were the Negroes from the American revolution, a national problem similar to that of the present-day Negroes would have survived in France. Similarly in Britain, although the democratic transition followed its own peculiar pattern, the Welch, the Scottish, the English all shared in its benefits. The Irish, who were excluded from this process of democratic transformation, remained an oppressed nation within the geographic configuration of the British Isles.

Any serious examination will show that the Negro population of the Black Belt is tied together by myriad internal bonds, by all facets and agencies of modern capitalism, has all the prerequisites for existence as a nation. In the Black Belt, there is a division of labor between city and country typical of our capitalist era. Though it is primarily an agricultural community, this area has its cities, serving as commercial and industrial outlets for the agrarian hinterland, cities such as New Orleans, Savannah, Mobile, Memphis, Charleston, Atlanta, Norfolk, Winston-Salem, all lying within the Black Belt or at its periphery. These cities are economically and historically part of that region. This is so notwithstanding the fact that Negroes comprise roughly only thirty to forty per cent of the populations of these centers.

As elsewhere in the modern world, town and country are linked by a unified system of transportation and communication, by monetary unity, by a common banking and credit structure, by all media essential to modern capitalist market relationships.

Among the Negro people of the area, there exist all class groupings peculiar to capitalism, which historically provided the basis for the emergence of modern nations. Not only do Negroes work as laborers in the cotton and tobacco fields; they work also in the coal mines, steel mills, saw and planing mills, ginning and cotton seed oil mills, in furniture, turpentine refining, in processing of tobacco, in chemical industries and in pulp and paper, in longshore and logging, on railroads, etc.

There is a Negro upper class or bourgeoisie, living in both urban and rural communities, striving as do all bourgeois classes for the extension of its markets. Its most influential segment resides in the cities, functioning mainly in the fields of insurance, small-scale banking, real estate, undertaking and other services for the Negro community. There is also a sprinkling of well-to-do Negro farm owners in the rural areas. This Negro bourgeoisie has its ideologists in the educated middle classes, striving for the modern development of their people. There is the thin stratum of professional people, including doctors, lawyers, teachers, ministers (the largest group), and social workers.* The development of all these classes is artificially retarded by American monopoly capitalism and its Bourbon cohorts. All classes suffer from the ferocious national oppression. The people as a whole find their interests running counter to this stifling Jim Crow. The Negro workers want modern conditions of labor; the sharecroppers, poor farmers, and plantation hands want land and freedom from the yoke of peonage; the town middle classes and intellectuals want equal opportunities in businesses and professions.

Although the Negro community in this area has all these economic and social elements of capitalism welding it together, we must not lose sight of the decisive fact, that the region's economy remains backward, mainly agrarian in character. The full development of modern capitalism has been arbitrarily arrested. In this respect the region's economy is typical of that of colonial and other retarded nations. One can say that the Black Belt is a kind of "internal colony" of American imperialism, made to function mainly as the raw material appendage of the latter. The character of the oppression of the Negro people in no sense differs from that of colonial peoples. The economy of the region is not controlled by the Negro capitalists. Its immediate direction is in the hands of white local capitalists and landlords, who act as the outpost command for the real rulers, the financial dynasty of Wall Street.

This only emphasizes the fact that the economy of the Black Belt is typical of that of an oppressed nation, whose full development is artificially and forcibly retarded by imperialism.

Negro Culture

A common tradition and culture, native to Negro America, has been in the making since the first Negroes were landed at Jamestown. The special history of the Negro people in the United States is the history of oppression and the struggle against it. It is the history of the misery of the chattel slave

---

*Most Negro institutions of higher learning are situated in the South, at Atlanta, Nashville, Washington, D.C., etc. The largest Negro insurance company is at Durham, N.C. The only Negro daily newspaper is published in Atlanta.

sold from the holds of the slaveships into bondage where an unknown tongue prevailed. It is the history of more than two hundred heroic slave revolts and insurrectionary plots, all of them foredoomed and ruthlessly suppressed. The history of the Negro people has infused the Negro with hopes, ideals, customs, and traits which are blended in a psychology whose activities and aims move in a thousand ways toward freedom and equality. This psychology has been evidenced in slave revolts, in participation in the democratic wars of this country and in its political life, especially during Reconstruction, and in the various organizations which developed the liberation movement of modern times.

The entire development of Negro music, literature, poetry, and painting, of churches, fraternal groups, and social societies, bears the imprint of this struggle for liberation. The psychological as well as the economic need for continuous struggle to gain equal democratic status, to throw off the oppressive chains and assume the upright posture of a free people—this is and has been the dynamic of Negro culture.

This fact was pointed out by Dr. W. E. B. DuBois in his introduction to the appeal to the United Nations, submitted by the National Association for the Advancement of Colored People, in February, 1947:

> "The so-called American Negro group, therefore, while it is in no sense absolutely set off physically from its fellow Americans, has nevertheless a strong, hereditary cultural unity, born of slavery, of common suffering, prolonged proscription and curtailment of political and civil rights; and especially because of economic and social disabilities. Largely from this fact have arisen their cultural gifts to America—their rhythm, music and folk-song; their religious faith and customs; their contributions to American art and literature; their defense of their country in every war, on land, sea and in the air; and especially the hard, continuous toil upon which the prosperity and wealth of this continent has largely been built."

The Negro people are a separate folk, a people with distinct interests, feelings and attitudes built upon their common history of suffering and oppression.

"The result," continues the statement, "has been to make American Negroes to a wide extent provincial, introvertive, self-conscious and narrowly race-loyal; but it has also inspired them to frantic and often successful effort to achieve, to deserve, to show the world their capacity to share modern civilization. As a result there is almost no area of American civilization in which the Negro has not made creditable showing in the face of all his handicaps."[4]

Notwithstanding its many points of contact with the culture of the dominant white nation, this Negro culture has its own distinctive features. Thus there has arisen within the Negro community a socio-cultural structure corresponding to the status of fixed inequality forced upon him by the dominant white nation. There is among the Negro community a multiplicity of organizations, national and local, devoted to every field of human interest and endeavor: to education, to civil rights, to the special interest of various professional groups and of women, youth, veterans, and business enterprises. There is a Negro church which in many parts of the country is a social rallying point of the Negro community.

The authors Drake and Cayton, describing Bronzeville, Chicago's Negro community, observed that:

"The people of Bronzeville have, through the years, crystallized certain distinctive patterns of thought and behavior . . .

"While Bronzeville's institutions differ little in form from those in other Midwest Metropolis communities, they differ considerably in content. The dissimilarity springs primarily from two facts: Because the community is spiritually isolated from the larger world, the development of its families, churches, schools and voluntary associations has proceeded quite differently from the course taken by analogous white institutions; and, second, Bronzeville's 'culture' is but a part of a larger, national Negro culture, its people being tied to thirteen million other Negroes by innumerable bonds of kinship, associational and church membership, and a common minority status. The customs inherited by Bronzeville have been slowly growing up among American Negroes in the eighty years since slavery."[5]

The cultural pattern of Chicago's Bronzeville has its replica in Harlem, in Detroit's "Paradise Valley," in the Pittsburgh Hill section, in Los Angeles' Central Avenue, indeed in every Black ghetto in America, the greatest of which is the Black Belt itself. National Negro culture finds expression in a rich folk lore, in music, in the dance, in an expanding and virile theatre movement and in a highly developed literature. It is voiced in a rapidly growing press. (In 1946 the combined circulation for 137 Negro newspapers was almost two millions.[6]) But, through whatever medium it manifests itself, this culture is built around themes of distinctly Negro life and Negro problems.

Coming from the heart of the masses of people welded together by like yearnings, stirred by the same causes, this culture expresses the deep-felt aspirations of the Negro people, their strivings to break through the walls of the Jim-Crow ghetto and to achieve recognized status as a free people.

The present great Negro political awakening is finding expression in a new resurgence of Negro literature and art. Langston Hughes, outstanding Negro folk poet, has hailed this new cultural "renaissance" as transcending in depth and scope the vast wave of Negro cultural activity following World War I, which found in Alain Locke its foremost interpreter.[7]

To the glory of poetry, it may be said that in literature Negro poets raised most clearly and feelingly the ringing tones of struggle for liberation. Standing highest among these bell-like singers are such contemporary poets as Langston Hughes, Countee Cullen, and Sterling Brown. Among the younger poets are Owen Dodson, Gwendolyn Brooks and Margaret Walker. The interpretative writings of Alain Locke, the novels of Arna Bontemps, Richard Wright, Ann Petry, the poetry of James Weldon Johnson, the biographical work of Shirley Graham, the plays of Theodore Ward, the dramatic interpretations of Canada Lee, have enhanced the treasury of American and world literature and art. The great people's artist and leader, Paul Robeson, is a towering example of the magnificent contributions of the Negro people in the world of music and drama. William Grant Still, outstanding contemporary Negro composer; Marian Anderson, world famous contralto; Richard Barthé, foremost Negro sculptor; Ernest Crichlow, prominent illustrator and caricaturist, and Hale Woodruff, prize-winning muralist, are only a few of the many creative Negro talents in these fields. In the roster of creative writers who have dealt and deal now with Negro life are names of Negroes who vie for top honors with all other writers in the United States.

To the literary expressions of a resurgent Negro people must be added the increasing numbers of works by Negro scholars and scientists which represent, on the whole, a deeper probing of the problem. Outstanding among these are the works of that sterling Negro scholar and fighter, W. E. B. DuBois, and of the eminent historian Carter Woodson. The late George Washington Carver, one of the world's great scientists, is an example of their outstanding achievements in the sciences.

Progressive scholars have done yeoman work in unearthing the Negro's pre-American past, in piecing together that broken line of Negro history and the contribution the black man has made throughout time and throughout the world. They have refuted the spurious race stereotypes depicting the Negro as a man without a past, without a history, and, therefore, unworthy of an equal place at the table of civilization.

The myth of the Negro's past as only a "drawer of water and a hewer of wood" is now exploded. And in the shattering of this myth, the Negro has seen himself emerge as the inheritor of a rich historical tradition with antecedents reaching back into the dawn of civilization itself. This literature has brought to the consciousness of Negro America and to an ever growing segment of whites the missing pages of American and African history, the great contribution made by the Negro to civilization and democracy.

The trends which Alain Locke noted in the 'twenties have

become more fully matured. What he said then can more emphatically be stated today:

> "The day of 'Aunties,' 'Uncles' and 'Mammies' is . . . gone. Uncle Tom and Sambo have passed on, and even the 'Colonel' and 'George' play barnstorm roles from which they escape with relief when the public spotlight is off. The popular melodrama has about played itself out and it is time to scrap the fictions, garret the bogeys and settle down to a realistic facing of facts."[8]

The New Negro is here and in much greater numbers than he was in the 'twenties. The stereotypes are giving way to a Negro with a new sense of his own dignity and worth and a newly awakened pride in himself as a contributor in no mean sense to the progress of our society. He is a Negro determined to fight for his just rights.

And behind this new Negro is the emerging dynamic force of the Negro industrial working class, which is playing an increasingly important role in the councils of Negro leadership.

Of course, this picture of Negro culture is not complete. There are also negative, non-progressive features, expressing the trend of self-isolation, Negro particularism. That the culture of the Negro people is expressed through the medium of the English language is no argument against the apparent fact that theirs is a distinctly Negro culture. English is the language of the Negro American as it is the language of all Americans. All American Negroes speak English. It is their common medium of expression. A common language, not necessarily a separate or distinct language, is the requirement of nationhood. In England, the United States, Canada, Australia, English is the native language. Yet no one will seriously argue that they are not separate nations.

For, with their past behind them, and in the course of their three hundreds years' sojourn on the American continent, the Negroes have adopted the English language as their own in the same manner that they have adopted other institutions of the dominant American nation. They have become transformed from the enslaved descendants of various African tribes and nations, having different levels of economic and social devel-

opment, speaking different dialects and languages, into an eth-
nically homogeneous and tightly welded people. They are today a
people strengthened and hardened by oppression and rapidly
gaining maturity.

Joseph Stalin, who was chiefly responsible for formulating the
successful program for solving the problem of Russia's many
nations, has defined a nation as an "historically evolved,
stable community of language, territory, economic life, and
psychological make-up manifested in a community of culture."[9]
The validity of this definition has been attested by the fact
that it has served as the theoretical cornerstone for the building
of that unique fraternity of free and equal nations known as
the Union of Soviet Socialist Republics.

The Negroes in the United States manifest all these attributes
of nationhood listed in the concise and classic definition of
Stalin. They are "a nation within a nation."

The Status of National Consciousness

True, the actual movement for national liberation among
the Negro people in the U. S. has been comparatively weak.
It has even been argued that the Negro himself rejects the
concept of separate nationality as a classification of his status
in the contemporary American social scene. For, the argument
runs, if the Negroes were a nation, would not the asseveration
of their nationality find definite expression in the demands,
slogans, and programs of their organizations? Since, allegedly,
the capitalistic upper classes are the bearers of the "national
idea," is not the fact that this class among Negroes has never,
in a clear cut and consistent manner, raised the demands of
nationhood, conclusive proof that the Negroes are not a nation?

The fact is that the Negroes are a young nation whose advance
to political consciousness and strength is retarded by imperialistic
oppression. Yet, this very oppression is creating the basis for
the rise of a fully conscious national movement among them.
The weak development of national consciousness, or the lack
of it, is characteristic of young nations. For example, in our
own hemisphere fully a score of new nations have come into
existence within the last one hundred and fifty years. The

acquisition of national consciousness was in most cases a slow and arduous process. It is a fact that some of these nations, particularly in Central America, have yet to develop a vigorous sense of nationhood, and have by no means won full independence.[10]

The anti-imperialistic revolution in India has thrust forward on the political arena of that vast sub-continent a score of distinct and hitherto submerged peoples, energetically demanding a place in the sun—their recognition as nations within the frame of a free India. Outstanding is the case of the Moslems, who, until quite recently, recognized themselves as a religious entity, with only communal and religious differences separating them from the main mass of Hindu peoples. Despite the reactionary distortion of the legitimate Moslem national aspirations contained in the Mountbatten Award, which established two states, Pakistan and Hindustan, on the basis of religious difference only, the movement of the Moslem peoples for the right of national self-determination now occupies a central sector on the front of Indian freedom.[11]

The road to national consciousness of the American Negro is more arduous and tortuous than that of most peoples. It is beset by formidable obstacles both of an ideological and a physical environmental nature.

First, there is the overwhelming and stifling factor of race—the chief weapon in the ideological arsenal of the ruling classes of the oppressor nation. The spurious dogma of Negro racial inferiority is sunk deep in the thinking of white America. It has left its indelible stamp on the nascent Negro nation, befogging the basic concept of the Negroes' status as that of an oppressed nation. The charge leveled against the Negro people, that they are less than human, has forced them into an untenable defensive position, in which much of their energy has been consumed in the assertion of their basic humanity, their right to be considered human beings. To meet this invidious attack they have perforce rallied under the slogans of *racial* equality, *racial* solidarity, slogans which, though militant, do not hit the center of the target—their oppression as a nation in the Black Belt.

Secondly, an additional deterrent to the Negroes' quest for freedom, via nationhood, is that the concept of Negro nationality is a totally new one, and thus outside the bounds of the traditional thinking of American democrats. Thus the idea of Negro nationhood, on American soil, when first projected by the Communist Party, met with attack not only by reactionaries, but also by well-meaning liberals, including many Negro leaders, who felt it to be a retreat before Jim Crow, an acquiescence to segregation.

Finally, perhaps the most formidable retarding factor in the development of the Negro's consciousness of nationhood is the fact that the new Negro nation of the Black Belt finds itself set down in the midst of the strongest capitalist nation in the world, totally engulfed by what the Negro playwright, Theodore Ward, called "The Big White Fog."

Furthermore, as Stalin has pointed out, the national question nowadays is "virtually a peasant question." However, in this struggle against financial exploitation, political enslavement, and cultural effacement of the Negro people by the imperialist bourgeoisie, the mass of the Negro peasantry have lacked the leadership from those classes on which the development of the national movement has historically depended. The Negro bourgeoisie and industrial proletariat are comparatively recent social formations.

For the Negro to claim the rights of nationhood in these conditions would be an act of the highest political consciousness. And yet the fact is that, while eager to combat every manifestation of Jim Crow within American life, the Negro people see the solution of their problems neither in a process of ethnological absorption into the white community, nor in the abandonment of their American homeland for some illusory refuge in Africa or a "49th State," nor in any escapist scheme of mass exodus from the South. On the contrary, they have continued to build their own organizations and agencies affecting every phase of Negro endeavor in the United States, systematically throwing off the feeling and even the terminology of "racial" inferiority,*

---

*For example, the term "Negro race" has more and more fallen into disuse and the term "Negro people" has been gaining general acceptance in the Negro community.

and strengthening the wellsprings of national consciousness. The Negro masses want equality, and increasingly feel that they can and must achieve it as a people in their own right. The emergence of new mass forces and influences, spearheaded by a rapidly maturing Negro industrial working class, has proved decisive in this development.

This growing sense of nationhood has been most dramatically expressed in the appeals of the National Negro Congress and of the National Association for the Advancement of Colored People to the United Nations. DuBois, in his introduction to the N.A.A.C.P. appeal, writes:

> "The United Nations surely will not forget that the population of this group [the Negroes] makes it in size one of the considerable nations of the world. We number as many as the inhabitants of the Argentine or Czechoslovakia, or the whole of Scandinavia including Sweden, Norway, and Denmark. We are very nearly the size of Egypt, Rumania, and Yugoslavia. We are larger than Canada, Saudi Arabia, Ethiopia, Hungary, or the Netherlands. We have twice as many persons as Australia or Switzerland, and more than the whole Union of South Africa. We have more people than Portugal or Peru; twice as many as Greece and nearly as many as Turkey. We have more people by far than Belgium and half as many as Spain. In sheer numbers then we are a group which has a right to be heard; and while we rejoice that other smaller nations can stand and make their wants known in the United Nations, we maintain equally that our voice should not be suppressed or ignored."[12]

Despite the weak growth of national consciousness among Negroes, the road ahead for the Negro people in the United States points to the further, accelerated development of national aspirations. The experiences of World War II, in which the Negro people made great sacrifices in the common struggle against fascist aggression, only provided new evidence that the Negro was suffering from a distinct form of national oppression. The post-war period multiplied the evidence a thousand-fold. Instead of being followed by an unprecedented extension and revitalization of democracy in the United States, the triumph over the fascist powers was followed by a post-war offensive of reaction which, in addition to its assault upon the democratic rights of the labor and progressive movements generally, also set itself the task of "putting the Negro back in his place." Even if the Negro people had chosen to integrate themselves with the nation as a whole, the forces of reaction, spurred on by the program of monopoly capital, put up new barriers to such integration and left no doubt that freedom for the Negro people could only be won by even greater struggles against national oppression, and first of all for land and political power in the Black Belt.

Right of Self-Determination

In fact, it is here that the national character of the struggle is most pronounced. The battle for fundamental agrarian reform is inextricably interwoven with the fight against the most barbarous type of fascist racist oppression of the Negro majority. Here it is not simply a matter of landlordism, but a particular brand of landlordism, that of a *white* ruling clique. In collusion with urban capitalists of the region, and with the clandestine backing of northern reactionaries, this landlordism maintains through the instruments of "white supremacy" (courts, police, militia and extra-legal auxiliaries of the K.K.K. and other such terroristic bodies) a system of special persecution and plunder of the Negro people, rivaled only in the most backward colonial lands. It is a landlordism which glories in the open flouting of the Reconstruction amendments to the Constitution.

This persecution of the Negro in the Southland, as we have indicated, is actually an auxiliary of national oppression of the most voracious kind, equivalent to foreign rule. It is designed for the political suffocation and suppression of a people who comprise the majority of the population of a contiguous land area, a people of common ethnic origin, and with a common history.

Any program envisioning fundamental reorganization of the South's agrarian structure and land relationships must take into full account this "racial" or national factor, which is integrally tied in with the agrarian problem. Such a program must project as its long-range objective the breaking of the class domination of the Wall-Street-backed Bourbon oligarchy and the white supremacy color-caste system by which this rule of arbitrary violence over the Negro people is legally and morally sanctioned.

Democracy in the Black Belt

This means that the corrupt rule of monopoly capitalism and its allies in the Black Belt must be supplanted by the democratic rule of the majority, that is, of the Negro people, with the full participation of their allies among the disfranchised white minority. Without governmental and administrative control in the hands of the most oppressed section of the people, fundamental agrarian reform is impossible, as has been universally proved. Only government institutions that represent and express the special interests of the preponderant Negro population, and enjoy its confidence, can effect a radical change in the structure of southern landownership, so urgently needed by the bulk of the Black Belt's people and southern whites generally.

The question of self-government for the Negroes in the South, however, is inseparable from their character as a nation.

In the last analysis the fight for self-government in the Black Belt is the fight for the right of self-determination by the Negro nation.

What, concretely, is the meaning of the right of self-determination of nations? What should be understood by it? Is it to be identified with separation? As regards the Negroes, is it to be equated to the demand for a separate Negro state in the Black Belt—a Negro republic? Does it run counter to the principle of Negro and white unity, so essential to the struggle for Negro rights and democracy? Is it not a capitulation to Jim Crow or segregation, as many of the critics of this principle contend?

These are some of the questions raised, not only by reactionaries who have donned the false cloak of friendship for the Negro's cause in order better to sabotage it, but by many honest and sincere proponents of Negro freedom.

The right of self-determination means none of these things. Quite the contrary. It implies the application of consistent democracy in the sphere of relations between nations, the elimination of the forcibly imposed distinction between oppressed and oppressing nations; it means the abolition of all and sundry privileges of one nation over the other. Specifically it means simply the right of the people of a nation to determine their own fate, or destiny, free from forcible intervention from without by the people of another nation. A nation has the right to organize its own life in the manner or form it chooses, independent of the dictates of any other nation—to be master in its own house. Finally, self-determination means the recognition of the sovereignty of a people in all matters affecting their internal life as well as in matters involving their relationships with other peoples or nations. This, then, is the content and principle of the right of self-determination.

Quite definitely, this right includes the right of separation, that is, the right to free political secession from the oppressing nation. But self-determination must not be construed as identical with secession and the establishment of an independent state. The right of nations to secede is an inviolable democratic right, but it is not an obligation, or a duty.

> "A nation," says Stalin, "has the right to arrange its life on autonomous lines. It even has the right to secede. But this does not mean that it should do so under all circumstances, that autonomy, or separation, will everywhere and always be advantageous for a nation, for the majority of it population, for the toiling strata."[13]

An illustrative parallel which might serve to bring out the distinction between *right* and *obligation* is afforded in the field of woman's rights. The right of divorce is universally recognized in all advanced nations as basic to the emancipation of womanhood. Every democrat worthy of the name is duty-bound to support this right. But the right of divorce by no means signifies an obligation on the part of women to divorce their husbands. And so it is with nations. Any attempt to reduce the right of self-determination to the demand for secession is in fact to deny this right. It would be equivalent to dictating the form in which the nation should apply its rights.

A study of the national question reveals that the choice of settlement of the problem may be exercised in any one of the following forms, depending on the decision of the nation itself:

A nation may decide upon complete secession, that is, to set itself up as an independent state, or again it may decide on federation with the former oppressing nation, or it may decide upon territorial autonomy within the borders of the former oppressing state, with a varying degree of sovereignty over its own internal affairs, *viz.*, some form of local or regional self-government. There are, of course, varying degrees of autonomy within a state of mixed national composition, depending primarily upon the degree of unification of the respective autonomous people as a modern nation.* Federation implies voluntary association between free and equal nations in the form of a federative state. All these forms of the exercise of the right of self-determination have found a living and truly creative expression in the Union of Soviet Socialist Republics, which assures the economic and cultural development of all of its peoples.†

International experience in the solution of the nationality problem has shown clearly that any program for its solution must include two points. First, it must confirm the unconditional right of the nation to democratic self-determination up to the point of secession and the organization of a separate state. Secondly, it must include a point on territorial autonomy

*"Wherever an ethnic group [in the Soviet Union] exists, its area of settlement is marked off as a political entity. The degree of autonomy which it receives depends upon several factors. One is its size. Another is whether or not it forms a majority even in its own territory. A third is the degree to which its people have progressed toward unification as a modern nation." (William Mandel, *A Guide to the Soviet Union*, p. 472, Dial Press, N. Y., 1946.)

†For an example of how the democratic forces of India, a vast subcontinent of diverse colored nations, envisage this problem, see the program adopted by the Second Congress of the Communist Party of India. (*Political Affairs*, May, 1948, pp. 460-77.)

in the event that the nation should decide on this alternative and consider it to be the most advantageous for its people.

"We demand the freedom of self-determination, . . ." Lenin said, "not because we dream of an economically atomized world, nor because we cherish the ideal of small states, but on the contrary, because we are for large states and for a coming closer, even a fusion of nations, but on a truly democratic, truly internationalist basis, which is *unthinkable* without the freedom of separation."[14]

The recognition of the principle of self-determination implies an uncompromising fight for the conditions for its realization; that means, the fight for equality in all fields, and against all forms of national or racial oppression, in short, complete democracy in the country. The exercise of the right of self-determination is the crowning point of this struggle and symbolizes that the equality of the given nation has been fully achieved.

Self-determination is, therefore, "merely the logical expression of the struggle against national oppression in every form."[15] It is an irrefutable demand of consistent democracy in the sphere of the national problem.

Self-determination as the ultimate solution of the Negro national question is no communist dogma, as the spokesmen of imperialism both open and covert strive so desperately to prove.* Neither is it a mere theory. Quite the opposite. It is a living reality attested by the struggles of the oppressed nations everywhere, and confirmed beyond all dispute in the epic example of the Soviet Union, a country embracing one-sixth of the earth's land surface, in which the national question has

---

* In this respect, an editorial in the *Amsterdam News*, a conservative Negro newspaper of New York, is highly suggestive. The editorial states in part: "A study of the census figures sheds some light on why Bilbo and Co. are anxious for a 'Back to Africa movement.' According to the 1940 Census, there are 180 counties where the Negro is the largest part of the population, which counties represent 4,237,739 persons. . . . When the Negro gets the vote in those counties, we will have a large area in which political self determination will be possible. That explains why the poll tax and anti-lynching bills are fought so bitterly. Bilbo, Rankin, and their neophyte, Eastland, see the handwriting on the wall." (*Amsterdam News*, Aug. 25, 1945.)

been solved. Upon the ruins of the "prison of nations" that had been the Russia of the tsars, where the most rapacious and wildest forms of national and racial oppression prevailed, has now been built that great commonwealth of free and equal nations known as the Union of Soviet Socialist Republics. Here 189 peoples speaking 150 languages, different in tradition, race and color, enjoy the same rights and are forged together in an extraordinary unity of effort and enthusiasm for a common ideal—a multicolored, multi-national fraternity of peoples, a commonwealth of nations based on the free association of races and nations living in peace and friendly collaboration. This democratic solution of the national question, grounded in a socialist economy, is the reason for the unshakable unity displayed by the Soviet peoples in the recent war against fascism. Undeniably the Soviet achievement is a crowning victory for the policy which recognizes the unqualified right of nations to self-determination.

The policy of self-determination as the solution of the national question has found its confirmation most recently in the policies of the new people's democracies which have arisen in post-war Eastern Europe. Czechoslovakia and Yugoslavia, states which prior to World War II had been torn by national strife and dissension, have now been transformed into democratic multi-national states based on equality and the right of self-determination of formerly oppressed nations such as the Slovaks in Czechoslavakia, and the Slovenes, Croatians, Montenegrins, Macedonians, and the peoples of Bosnia-Herzegovina.

The principle of self-determination applies fully to the situation of the Negro nation of the Black Belt. Once the Negro community there is conceded to be a nation, the recognition of its right to self-determination logically and inalterably follows.

It would be scraping the very bottom of the foul pit of distortion and calumny to label this democratic need of the Negro people of the Black Belt a concession to Jim Crow, or to assert that it plays into the hands of the Bilbos and Talmadges. Jim Crow means separation of Negro and white, a separation arbitrarily and violently imposed by the Negro's oppressors.

It is the instrument of imperialist national oppression. But the right of self-determination for the Black Belt Negro, on the contrary, commits its proponents to the most consistent and unremitting fight for every democratic need of the Negro people; it means the obligation to assist in the organization of and to give practical support to their fight against all forms of Jim-Crow oppression and violence to the point of the establishment of their full equality; that is, the realization of the concrete conditions in which the right of self-determination of the Negro nation can be exercised.

In America the imperialist policy of Jim-Crow national oppression of the Negro creates the conditions for the rise of a movement for Negro national liberation. At the same time, imperialist oppression clears the ground for the emergence of the most dynamic force of that movement, the Negro working class, drawing it into the orbit of industry and into direct contact and fraternal relationships with white labor.

This is a glaring paradox in the world of imperialism; but for advanced labor whose perspective is socialism these trends are but part of a single process leading to world unity on a free and voluntary basis.

Self-Government

While the right and exercise of self-determination is the inherent goal of the Negro struggle for national liberation in the Black Belt, self-rule in the partial form of local self-government within the existing federal state is a first and mandatory step in its attainment. It is the *minimum requirement* for the recasting of the South's agricultural set-up along democratic lines, to guarantee to the Negroes the necessary political power for beginning the widesweeping economic and cultural reforms needed in that region.

The precedent for Negro self-government was set historically in the period of Radical Reconstruction, when the newly emancipated Negro, in alliance with southern poor whites and supported by northern democracy, stepped forward to take his place in government, and to establish in the South the only democratic regime it has ever known — the Reconstruction

governments of 1867-77. During this period, Negro self-govern-
ment actually existed in a number of Black Belt counties. Its
rudimentary forms were likewise observed in the Constitutional
Conventions held in ten southern states and by the dominant
Negro representation in the subsequent state legislatures of
South Carolina, Mississippi and Louisiana.

In South Carolina, Negroes composed the great majority in
the Lower House of the three legislatures which sat between
1868 and 1873, and a very large minority of the Lower Houses
which sat between 1874 and 1878. Representation in the state
legislatures of other states was considerably less.

Negroes occupied offices other than in legislatures in the
following states: South Carolina—Lieutenant Governor (twice);
Speaker of the House (twice); Secretary of State, Adjutant and
Inspector-General; Louisiana—Acting Governor (in interim of
43 days—this was Lieutenant Governor P. B. S. Pinchback);
Lieutenant Governor (three times); Secretary of State, State
Treasurer, Superintendent of Public Education; Mississippi—
Secretary of State, Lieutenant Governor, Superintendent of
Education. Other offices were held by Negroes in other states.

From 1868 to 1901, there were a total of 23 Negroes in
Congress, two of whom were Senators. Many of these served
in more than one session of Congress. Some were re-elected
several times.

To the chagrin of its defamers, this "experiment in Negro
government" resulted in the framing of the most democratic state
constitutions in the nation. For example, the South Carolina
convention put through a constitution which included immediate abolition of property qualifications for office holding;
universal suffrage for Negro and white; no discrimination against
Negroes; proportional representation according to population
and not on a property basis; no imprisonment for debt; compulsory universal education; recognition of woman's rights; and
reorganization of state and county governments to provide for
the fullest participation of the people.[16]

The falsification of the true history of Reconstruction, the
concealing of its real lessons from the people has, over the
years, become a built-in part of the whole system of "white

supremacy," by which the Bourbon oligarchs justify their abso-
lutist totalitarian rule. Reconstruction is depicted as a period
of unrestrained violence, bloody terror, carnage, and rapine, in
which the Negro is presented as a naive but semi-savage person
who, freed from a benevolent slavery, roamed the land robbing
and stealing, and venting his lust upon unprotected white womanhood; while in the background, directing this horror, stalked
the most sinister of all figures, the vengeful, swaggering carpet-
bagger exacting his blood-drenched pound of flesh from a ruined
and prostrate South.

A whole literature has been built upon such vicious distortions. Particularly in the South, among poor whites, has this
lying version been accepted as irrefutable fact; the carpet-bag
bogey and its corollary, the threat of "Black Domination," has
been used by generations of Dixie demagogues not only to
frighten little children but a whole white population.

The Negro-white unity achieved during the Reconstruction
"experiment in Negro government," held forth the promise of
a rapid development of the South out of its morass of reaction
and backwardness. It was crushed, however, by the victory of
the counter-revolution of 1877, sealed in the Hayes-Tilden
agreement between northern capitalism and southern reaction.

In the context of the present fight against encroaching
fascism for a truly democratic people's government for the United
States as a whole, the need of the Black Belt Negro for political
self-rule means simply the establishment of the jurisdiction of
the Negro majority over all questions purely of a local and
regional character.

Its realization would of course involve the reorganization of
the present governmental and administrative structure of a
number of southern states whose boundaries now arbitrarily
crisscross the area of contiguous Negro majority breaking up
this area into a maze of governmental administrative, judicial,
and electoral subdivisions, which in no way correspond to the
life needs of its people.*

*The unique powers exercised by county governments in the "deep South"
have been vividly described by W. E. B. DuBois: "County after county has
been erected by the legislature as a corporate center of local government,

Indeed, these divisions are purposely maintained—in many cases are even gerrymandered—by the South's rulers with the aim of continuing the political suppression of the region's predominant colored population. The abolition of these bureaucratic and arbitrarily established boundaries and their replacement by truly democratic ones, conforming not with the needs of the bourbon oppressors but with those of the oppressed, is a key task of American democracy.

Self-government for the Black Belt region implies just such a regrouping of county and administrative districts to guarantee full proportional representation for the Negro people in all areas of government. What honest democrat could deny to the Negro majority in the deep South the self-government that the peoples of other states comprising our federal union now enjoy? For the Black Belt this demand would mean simply majority representation on the governing body or legislature of the region, the right of such a body to make laws in the interests of the majority, to levy taxes, to control the police and militia, jurisdiction over education and public facilities, etc. On whose interests would such rights encroach? Certainly not those of the disfranchised and pauperized white minority. Plain it is that only the Bourbon lynchocrats have cause to fear this legitimate aim of the Negro people—democracy in the Southland. Let there be no mistake. The Talmadges, Rankins, and the rest of their unspeakable tribe clearly understand the real issues involved. And in that understanding lies the explanation for their frenzied beating of the drums of "race war," amidst demogogic cries of "Black Domination." Negro self-government is a simple democratic demand, in full conformity with the principles of majority rule.

until today Georgia is not one state—it is 166 independent counties, counties so independent that if anarchy wishes to stalk in Wilcox County, Fulton County has little more power than a foreign state. The independence and self-rule of these little bits of territory are astounding. They lay taxes, they spend monies, they have partial charge of education and public improvements, and through their dominating power in the legislature they make laws. Only when they touch corporate property, industrial privilege . . . are the reserve forces of capital and politics mobilized to curb them." (W. E. B. DuBois, "Georgia! Torment of a State," 1924, republished in the *New Masses*, Sept. 10, 1946.) This cogent description of Georgia's county setup holds true for most of the Black Belt states.

Negro self-government, in this sense, is conceivable in the frame of our present federal system of government. Clearly, therefore, it can by no means be construed as separation. This demand has nothing in common with the fantastic and reactionary scheme proposed by the 49th State Movement which planned to herd Negroes into a segregated area, set aside especially for them by the federal government. Quite the reverse, Negro self-government for the Black Belt means representative government for the Negro in the area where he now resides and is largely concentrated. Its realization is a prerequisite for genuine democratic unity.

Its realization would lay the basis for the abolition of the odious white supremacy caste system, thus paving the way for a new democratic renaissance of the Negro people surpassing that of their aborted resurgence of post-Civil War times. It would make possible the unleashing of the full potential of creative energy and self-initiative of a people now smothered by Bourbon "race" strictures which are designed to hide the underlying social-class issues of the struggle for democracy in the South.

Self-government is therefore an irreducibly minimal demand of the Negro people of the Black Belt indispensable to their economic and cultural development.

This demand represents the basic interests of the impoverished white minority of the region whose backwardness and distress are anchored in the oppression of the Negro masses, since they can be freed only through uncompromising support for the full rights of the Negro people. Recognition of the right of self-government for the Black Belt Negroes is, therefore, basic to any permanent alliance between them and the southern white working people against the common enemy.

That self-government is a major political goal towards which the Negroes' struggle for democracy in the Black Belt is heading should be apparent to any keen student of southern politics. This need, in its elementary form, is inherent in the widespread demand of Negroes in southern urban communities for the redistricting of political subdivisions in a manner to assure them representation in local politics. And, in its primary stages, the fight for Negro self-government is implicit in the growing demand for representative government in the region; that is, in the fight for electoral reforms, such as the right to vote, to hold office, to sit on juries and for protection against Ku Klux terrorism and lynching. The necessity for such Negro self-government is made patent by the South's bi-color caste system, which dictates permanent inequality for the Negro. The need for it, while not yet clearly expressed, is nevertheless innate in the objective conditions of Negro life in the Black Belt, and will undoubtedly be forced to the surface in the surging wave of unrest now engulfing the colored population of the deep South.

Self-government is a slogan which epitomizes the immediate political demands of the Negroes in the South. It would give the entire movement around these urgent demands of Negro equality —demands being accepted by ever increasing numbers of democracy-loving Americans—their proper focus and import. It would raise the struggle to a higher level, pointing this struggle to its ultimate goal—the achievement of fundamental agrarian reform and the full right of self-determination.

CHAPTER VIII

The Negro Liberation Movement

IN THE PRECEDING CHAPTERS we have described the intolerable plight of the Negro people in the United States. We have sought to establish the full scope of the Negro question and its decisive bearing on the central problems of American democratic development in general. We have examined the basic untenability of the liberal, reformist programs and panaceas arising from their failure to recognize that the system of Negro oppression is an organic part of imperialist-capitalist domination; that the crux of the matter is to be found in the unsolved problems of land and national freedom for the Negroes in the South, and that the solution of these problems is the indispensable condition for the achievement of full economic, social, and political equality for Negroes throughout the country. Finally, we have indicated the objectively necessary line of action required by the historical tasks and aims of the Negro people in their struggle for freedom. The question now is: Where does the Negro liberation movement stand in relation to all this? What social resources can the Negro people muster in this struggle? How do the various social classes measure up to the task?

Stages of the Movement

By the term Negro liberation movement, we mean generally the sum total of the efforts of all organizations, groups, and agencies among Negroes which strive in any manner and to any degree to realize the ideal of Negro equality. Included in this concept is the struggle against all tendencies which conflict with the basic conditions for the achievement of this aim.

In this chapter, we shall limit ourselves chiefly to the organizations and movements which in modern times have sought to effect a unity of these activities on a national scale, around a single program.

In order properly to evaluate the present-day Negro liberation movement it is essential to study it in terms of its historical and social antecedents. Taken as a whole, the modern Negro liberation movement, in which social conservatism has retained a strong, hampering influence, falls roughly into three main stages, the key to which is to be found in the character of the respective class forces shaping each of these stages. Throughout all this, despite the historically conditioned limitations of the class which at the moment was in leadership, there has been a continuous upward line of development within the Negro liberation movement. In the first stage, from the turn of the century to World War I, the organized movement was in the main confined to a small segment of the educated middle class. It was expressed first in the conservative Booker T. Washington school of the late nineties and early nineteen hundreds, then in the dissident and militant Niagara movement of 1906, and later in the liberal reformist activities of the National Association for the Advancement of Colored People founded in 1909. The program of the latter was in the spirit of social conservatism, and, presupposing a peaceful advance of the Negro people to freedom within the structure of imperialism, did not extend beyond moderate reforms. Their strategy, therefore, was the united front from the top with the "enlightened" white bourgeoisie.

World War I, with its accompanying great migration of Negroes from the rural South into urban industrial centers, resulted in the political awakening of large Negro masses and their active involvement in the struggle for Negro rights, reflecting in part the upsurge of the colonial world. The new problems and the new social forces gave rise to the greatest mass movement of Negroes since Reconstruction, which challenged the old conservative programs and the old, narrow, upper-class leadership. The

Negro liberation movement had definitely entered a new stage. The immediate result was the breakaway of sections of the radical Negro petty bourgeoisie and intellectuals from the old-line movement, and their seizure of the leadership of the rebellious Negro masses. In place of the conservative program of peaceful solution on American soil through collaboration with benevolent white rulers, they advanced the slogan of "return to Africa and the establishment of a Negro state in the ancestral land." Opposing collaboration with any section of the white populace, they diverted the mass movement into the utopian, escapist channels of reactionary nationalist separatism. This movement reached its height in Marcus Garvey's Negro Zionism in the critical years immediately following World War I. The social stirrings of more backward sections of mainly non-industrial Negro workers, recent migrants from the farm, found religious expression in Messianic movements, such as those of Father Divine.

However, the main line of development of the Negro liberation movement had to move along other channels. The Negro Zionism of Marcus Garvey could not meet the fundamental problems produced by the general crisis of capitalism which began with World War I and was aggravated by the subsequent economic crisis of 1929. These far-reaching developments within world capitalism were creating the conditions for an entirely new historical stage in the struggle for Negro freedom and the emergence of a new social force, the Negro proletariat, to lead it. The Negro working class was growing in numbers, importance, and political maturity. The time had arrived when this new social force, led by the Communist party, was to begin to place its imprint on the Negro liberation movement. Its philosophy, program, and strategy were diametrically opposed to the conceptions of the bourgeois and petty bourgeois forces that hitherto had dominated the organized struggle for Negro rights. It associated the fight for Negro freedom with the general struggle of the working class as a whole against capitalist-imperialist domination. It based its strategy for victory on alliance with white labor against the common enemy. During the past quarter of a century, the struggle for this path has been the dominant driving force in the Negro liberation movement. An essential part of this struggle has been the battle against the essentially middle-class reformism of social-democracy which has sought to dominate the Negro working-class movement. Keeping in mind this line of development as expressed in the stages broadly outlined here, we can most effectively approach the answer to the questions posed at the beginning of this chapter.

Modern Beginnings

Cut adrift by the Hayes-Tilden betrayal of 1876, which restored the ex-slaveholders to a share of power in the political councils of the nation, the black man had been left to flounder in the treacherous waters of post-Reconstruction reaction and isolation. With the restoration of Bourbon supremacy in the South the Negro had been violently robbed of the hard-won achievements of Reconstruction. The cause of freedom had received a severe setback from which it still has not recovered. It was fully a quarter of a century before the issue was again joined.

Only once in that dark interlude had a beam of hope flickered through. It was the short-lived Populist movement which swept the South in the 'nineties, when Negro and white toilers again sought unity against the increasing encroachments of the northern money kings and their junior partners in the South. But the forces of "white supremacy," enthroned in 1876, were again to prevail.

Out of this morass of hopelessness and despair, Booker T. Washington stepped forward to establish himself as the leader of an opportunistic, gradualist school of thought, destined to dominate the stage of Negro national leadership for several decades.

The Tuskegee Movement, initiated by Washington in the 1880's, as a modest project for Negro vocational training, sought to orient the Negro to the job of improving his economic status; of acquiring skills that would eventually enable him to cope with his new environment of "freedom"; to speed his rise from an illiterate, propertyless peasant folk to an essential place in the new industrial world of post-Reconstruction.

Washington's theory was that Negro progress depended upon

the building of a strong middle class to be founded on the thrift and energy of the Negro people.

> "I believe that the past and the present teach but one lesson—to the Negro's friends and to the Negro himself— that there is but one way out, that there is but one hope of solution; and that is for the Negro in every part of America to resolve from henceforth that he will throw aside every non-essential and cling only to the essential, that his pillar of fire by night and pillar of cloud by day shall be property, economy, education, and Christian character. To us just now these are the wheat, all else the chaff."[1]

Here definitely was the voice of the embryonic Negro middle class, which, though staggered by the shock of the Hayes-Tilden sell-out, was again desperately striving to reform its scattered ranks and break through to a place in the sun. Booker T. Washington's philosophy became its rallying point.

Considering the times, the program of the sage of Tuskegee was by no means wholly negative. On the contrary, it had its positive features. His was an impressive voice of encouragement in the wilderness of isolation, inspiring some courage, some hope, in the routed ranks of Negro freedom. But that this counsel of accommodation and moderation was eventually to clash not only with the needs of the Negro masses but with the interest of the upper strata as well was inevitable. For it was in the realm of political philosophy that the Tuskegee movement was eventually to reveal its negative and reactionary side. The inherent fallacy in the Washington doctrine was its counterposing of the Negro's participation in politics to his economic rehabilitation.

Believing as he did that the success of the Negro must rest upon a sound economic foundation as a craftsman and laborer, Washington felt that the time was not then ripe for the black man to concern himself with such matters as suffrage, social and civil rights. For the Negro to attempt a frontal assault upon the bastion of political inequalities, he felt, would mean to fly in the face of the status quo of white supremacy, which clearly the Negro was in no position to do. He must therefore, at least temporarily, accommodate himself to the situation, seek the good will of the white rulers, curry their favor and thus achieve a measure of tolerance as well as material support for his economic endeavors.

The reactionary features of the Tuskegee plan were to stand out in glaring relief against the backdrop of the sharp deterioration of the position of the Negro people, which accompanied the depression of the 1890's.

The 1890's were a decade of far-reaching structural changes in the economic and political life of the United States. It was in that decade that American capitalism reached its height. Out of the ruins of the panic and economic crisis of 1893 an "America Incorporated" emerged. Giant trusts and monopolies strengthened their hold on the economic and political life of the country; so that "by the end of the nineteenth century, more than two-thirds of all manufactured goods were made by corporations."[2]

The Negro, the weakest segment of the American people, was first to feel the tightening tentacles of the new imperialist octopus. The defeat of the abortive Populist movement in the South in the early nineties ushered in a period of political regression which in the next two decades was to wipe out the last vestige of Reconstruction reforms and to force the Negro completely out of the political picture in the South. The breach made by the agrarian "rebels" in the citadel of the "Solid South" was closed. One-party rule was restored. The Negro ballot became the sacrificial lamb at the feast of reunion.

The champions of "white supremacy," again safely ensconced in the saddle, took measures to assure their rule. New and more effective means for achieving Negro disfranchisement were devised. Constitutional conventions were called. Starting with Mississippi in 1890, new constitutions were adopted in eight states, so that by 1910 the disfranchisement of the Negro in the South was completed. Poll-tax requirements, property and literacy qualifications, and "good character" clauses were the techniques used. The new constitutions included Jim-Crow travel laws, making segregation legal.

This situation brought into sharp focus the innate reactionary content of Washington's doctrine of non-struggle and appeasement on the issue of Negro political rights. For, obviously, the persistence in such a course could only result in the moral and political disarmament of the Negro in the face of the most ruthless and withering attack of his enemies.

The period clearly demanded a basic re-evaluation of old ideas and programs and the mapping out of a new strategy, designed to combat the rising tide of the new reaction. Washington failed to understand the crucial issues of the time. In fact, he sought to by-pass them, continuing his line of conciliation, which meant in actuality to retreat.

Pertinent here is the criticism of DuBois, who in his autobiography wrote:

> "At a time when Negro civil rights called for organized and aggressive defense, he [Mr. Washington] broke down that defense by advising acquiescence or at least no open agitation. . . . His public speeches, while they did not entirely ignore this development, tended continually to excuse it, to emphasize the shortcomings of the Negro, and were interpreted widely as putting the chief onus for his condition upon the Negro himself."[3]

The Atlanta Compromise

In 1895, in the midst of this crisis, Washington made his famous speech at the Atlanta Cotton Exposition, which later was to become known as the "Atlanta Compromise." Bidding for the support of the Bourbon rulers, and purportedly speaking in behalf of the Negro people, he assured his audience that "in all things that are purely social we [the Negro] can be as separate as the fingers, yet one as the hand in all things essential to mutual progress."[4]

Here indeed was a "sane" program, and support for it was not long in forthcoming from the Wall Street mentors of southern Bourbonry. In 1903, Andrew Carnegie contributed $600,000 to Tuskegee Institute, making secure the future of the project. William H. Baldwin, son of the railroad magnate, was to become a prime mover on Tuskegee's Board of Trustees.

What were the considerations behind this lavish philanthropy on the part of northern employer groups?

According to DuBois the idea was approximately as follows:

"It [the Negro problem] must be a matter of business. These Negroes were not to be encouraged as voters in the new democracy; nor were they to be left at the mercy of the reactionary South. They were good laborers and they might be better. They could become a strong labor force and properly guided they would restrain the unbridled demands of white labor, born of the Northern labor unions and now spreading to the South. One danger must be avoided and that was to allow the silly idealism of Negroes, half-trained in Southern missionary 'colleges,' to mislead the mass of laborers and keep them stirred up by ambitions incapable of realization."[5]

The result was that the Tuskegee movement which had once been a modest enterprise to promote vocational training among Negroes had now become, thanks to the support of its big monied patrons, a veritable political machine—a sort of Negro Tammany straddling the path of a rising people.

"Things came to such a pass that when any Negro complained or advocated a course of action, he was silenced with the remark that Mr. Washington did not agree with this. Naturally the bumptious, irritated, young black intelligentsia of the day declared, 'I don't care a damn what Booker Washington thinks! This is what I think, and *I have a right to think.*'"[6]

The scheme was apparent; by building the prestige and power of Washington, northern capitalists proposed to contain the Negro movement, to direct it into channels safe for their interests.

The Revolt of the Young Intellectuals

But a new leadership was aborning. It was to rest in the rapidly growing group of young intellectuals emerging here and there, especially in the North. This group represented the advance echelons of a nascent Negro middle class, which was striving desperately to surmount the obstacles placed by Jim-Crow proscription in its path to social advancement. This young intelligentsia, in the main the product of northern institutions of learning, had long strained at the leash, rebelling against the tyranny of Tuskegee.

The opposition began to crystallize around the *Boston Guardian,* Negro newspaper, established in 1901, under the able editorship of Monroe Trotter and George Forbes. W. E. B. DuBois, then professor at Atlanta University, was more and more attracted to this circle of young Negro dissidents and soon was to become its leader. His trenchant pen was to give their protest literary form in the Negro epic, *The Souls of Black Folk,* published in 1903 and which contained a scathing indictment of the Negro's defamers and a vigorous assertion of his manhood rights.

In 1906, this group coalesced under the leadership of DuBois, Trotter and Forbes to form the Niagara movement. The issue was sharply drawn. Two opposing lines of strategy for Negro liberation had crystallized: militant protest and struggle for full citizenship or continued appeasement and retreat—this was the issue. The banner of revolt was unfurled, and the modern Negro liberation movement was born.

Meeting in the shadow of Harper's Ferry, near the scene of John Brown's famous stand, the Niagrists hurled the gauntlet of defiance at the tormentors of their people.

In a dramatic pilgrimage at dawn, barefooted, to the scene of John Brown's martyrdom, the new spokesmen for Negro rights solemnly vowed:

> "We shall not be satisfied with less than our full manhood rights. We claim for ourselves every right that belongs to a free-born American, civil and social, and until we get these rights we shall never cease to protest and assail the ears of America with the stories of its shameful deeds toward us. We want our manhood suffrage and we want it now. Second, we want discrimination in public accommodations to cease. Third, we claim the right to associate with such people as wish to associate with us. Fourth, we want the laws enforced against rich as well as poor, against capitalists as well as laborers, against white as well as black. We are not more lawless than the white race; we are more often arrested, convicted and mobbed. Fifth, we want our children educated."[7]

With the Niagara movement, the broken thread of organized Negro protest severed by the Reconstruction betrayal was again joined.

But the Niagara movement was shortlived. Its young, sincere, and idealistic leadership was hardly in a position clearly to understand the intrinsic nature of the struggle for Negro rights and the social forces which opposed it.

They were, so to speak, striking in the dark, groping for a way out of the morass of degradation in which their people had become mired. They knew not the main enemy—monopoly capitalism—which lurked behind an ideological smokescreen thrown up by its intellectual hirelings. White labor, the natural ally of Negro liberation, with its trade union organizations saddled by an anti-Negro bureaucracy, was at the time by and large still unconscious of the identity of its interest with the cause of Negro freedom. Hence the challenge of the Niagrists went unheard among the masses of white working people.

But it was not unheeded by the enemy, the big employer interests, which proceeded to rush forces to the danger spot. Its "enlightened" cohorts among the wealthy liberals had already been alerted to the growing danger of an uncontrolled Negro people.

The "overproduction" of Negro intellectuals had already become a menace to "social peace and order." Negro business enterprise, which even today has been able to absorb only a minute fraction of the "educated" stratum of its people, was then in an extremely rudimentary stage. The fear that this new Negro intelligentsia, thwarted by Jim-Crow barriers, debarred from opportunities for which it had been trained, might in bitter frustration fall back upon the restive and sullen black masses, arousing them to struggle, and that such a contingency might well disturb the delicate equilibrium of the regnant social order— that was the problem posed before the dominant white ruling class.

The Negro "talented tenth" was immediately overwhelmed with new pleaders for its cause. It was argued that the educated Negro had a potential use value; instead of a menace, he could, if properly considered, become a shock absorber for Negro discontent, a buffer between the employer class and the rebellious

Negro people. The new liberal friends of the Negro reasoned that the Negro movement under "sane" leadership could serve as a counter-weight to the growing challenge of white labor. The old stratagem of "divide and rule" was refurbished and brought up to date to meet the contingency of the new situation.

This tactic had already been applied to the upper categories of white labor, then represented almost solely by the Jim-Crow-minded top bureaucracy of the American Federation of Labor. And it had paid off with big dividends. These were, roughly, the chief objectives which big business sought to achieve with regard to the Negro question. Operating through its "liberal" wing, it set out to seduce the new Negro leadership.

Having registered its initial protest through the Niagara movement, the young Negro intelligentsia was subjected to the sustained wooing of the "humanitarian" millionaires. This courtship did not long remain on a platonic basis. The bond was sealed by gifts of hard cash.* The golden manna from these new "friends" of Negro freedom began to trickle down. It took the form of increased subsidies for Negro educational, health, and religious projects. Its corrosive influence penetrated every nook and cranny of Negro intellectual and political life. New phil-

* During the first two decades of the twentieth century, northern philanthropy stepped into the picture of southern Negro education in a big way. In 1908, the system of Jeanes teachers was founded, giving impetus to small rural Negro schools in the South. (The Jeanes fund is the popular name for the Southern Education Foundation. Its founder was Anna T. Jeanes.) John D. Rockefeller, through the General Educational Board, donated large funds for the support of state supervisors for Negro education in the South. Money was also given for Negro fellowships, colleges, libraries and other educational facilities. There was also the Carnegie Corporation of New York, which gave significant sums to Negro educational enterprises, libraries, colleges, and various Negro improvement organizations and research plans. Included among these large donors was the du Pont family which donated gifts to Negro educational endeavors in Delaware. There were also the important contributions of the Duke family to Negro colleges in North Carolina. The Guggenheim Memorial Foundation provided Negro as well as white scholars with research fellowships.

But the largest of all philanthropic agencies in the Negro field was the Julius Rosenwald Fund. In 1911, Julius Rosenwald initiated a project in which he proposed to give one-third of the funds for the erection of a Negro school building in each community provided the southern school authorities

anthropy-aided Negro projects were founded and the Negro subsidies of old ones extended. In fact, their weak positions were literally over-run.

Formation of the N.A.A.C.P.

The alliance between the top levels of the aspirant Negro intellectuals and their new-found patrons of the liberal wing of the white ruling class was consummated in the formation of the National Association for the Advancement of Colored People. Doubtless among the white liberal and socialist leaders of the organization were many sincere idealists, devoted to the cause of Negro equality. They were none the less tied by a thousand strings, ideologically and socially, to the interests of the white dominant class. Politically they represented its "enlightened" detachment, committed to the upholding of a system in which objectively the inequality of the Negro had become an integral part. Also, the circle of supporters of the organization included a number of forthright imperialist elements, such as Mrs. Cyrus H. McCormick and Harvey Firestone.

The formation of the new association had been spurred on by an outrageous event in 1908. In the summer of that year, Springfield, Illinois, the home of Abraham Lincoln, was the scene of one of the worst anti-Negro riots in the history of the country. Scores of Negroes were murdered or wounded. The affair shocked the nation.

William English Walling, wealthy Socialist, in an angry challenge to the conscience of white America, wrote at that time:

> "Either the spirit of the abolitionist, of Lincoln and Lovejoy, must be revived and we must come to treat the Negro on a plane of absolute political and social equality, or Vardaman and Tillman will soon have transferred the race war to the North."[8]

and the interested citizens of the community would raise the other two-thirds. The Rosenwald Fund also established libraries for Negroes, assisted Negro colleges and universities and gave generous subsidies to Negro scholars for fellowships and research projects. As regards southern Negro education, the tremendous role of the Rosenwald philanthropic enterprise is described in a comparative study made by Doxey A. Wilkerson, *Special Problems of Negro Education*, 1939, pp. 32-33.

Walling's challenge was taken up by other liberals. In 1909, Walling, Mary White Ovington, and Henry Moskowitz met in New York to plan the organization of a movement that was to become the N.A.A.C.P.[9]

A conference was called for February 12, 1909, the hundredth anniversary of the birth of the "Great Emancipator." The call, drafted by Oswald Garrison Villard, excoriated the mounting injustices inflicted upon Negroes as violating the letter and spirit of the Constitution, and appealed to "all the believers in democracy to join in a national conference for the discussion of the present evils, the voicing of protest, and the renewal of the struggle for civil and political liberty."[10]

A committee of white and Negro liberals was formed, mass meetings were called, literature was distributed and membership solicited.

The following year, 1910, a second conference was called at which was effected the informal merger* of the Niagara movement and the new group. Out of this conference the N.A.A.C.P. was born; Moorfield Storey, the noted Boston white liberal, was elected president.

Significantly, DuBois was the sole Negro among the officers of the newly founded organization, and he was assigned to the post of Director of Publicity and Research; the following year he was appointed editor of its official organ, *The Crisis*.

The "white allies" pre-empted the key positions, thereby assuring themselves the dominant voice in policy. "Thus," observed Ralph Bunche, "the N.A.A.C.P. propelled by dominant white hands embarked upon the civil libertarian course that the Negro-inspired Niagara movement had futilely tried to navigate."[11]

The unadorned fact was that the movement launched by the Niagrists was not only swamped, it was literally "taken over" by these new self-designated friends. The full-throated protest of a rising people, voiced through Niagara, was considerably toned down.

---

* According to DuBois, the new organization was set up "without formal merger" and absorbed practically the whole of the Niagrists, with the exception of Trotter, who "distrusted our white allies and their objects." (See *Dusk of Dawn*, p. 95.)

The N.A.A.C.P., though born under these auspices, could not initially ignore the pattern set by its Niagrist forerunner; albeit this protest thenceforth was to be couched in a more modulated, less belligerent and, on the whole, a more "respectable" tone. The declared objectives of the N.A.A.C.P. at the time of its founding was to "uplift the Negro men and women of this country by securing for them the complete enjoyment of their rights as citizens, justice in courts, and equal opportunities in every economic, social, and political endeavor in the United States. It maintained furthermore, that the U. S. Constitution should be upheld, and atrocious crimes should not be tolerated. This, of course, in a large measure, had reference to lynching."[12]

Between this program and that of the original Niagrists was no discernible difference. It is however a political truism that the criterion of the policy of a social movement lies not primarily in its stated aims but rather in the social class make-up of its leadership and consequently in its practical activities. In this respect, with the launching of the N.A.A.C.P., a new pattern in "race" leadership was set. It was the pattern of white ruling-class paternalism which, as time went on, was to cast an ever deepening shadow over the developing Negro liberation movement, throttling its self-assertiveness and its independent initiative, placing before it limited objectives and dulling the sharp edge of the sword of Negro protest. It was the pattern of interracialism, not from the bottom but from the top, embracing the "cultured elite" of the "races." A brand new technique had been evolved, a technique peculiar to interracial enterprises organized at the top level, in which the direction of policy rested in the hands of the white members of the leading bodies.

DuBois, in his retrospective writings of 1940, indicated the handicap with which the aspirant Negro leadership of the period was faced:

"There was one initial difficulty common to all interracial effort in the United States. Ordinarily the white members of a committee formed of Negroes and whites become dominant. Either by superior training or their influence or their wealth they take charge of the committee, guide it and use the colored membership as their helpers and executive workers in certain directions."[13]

This type of leadership was bound to have its effect upon program and tactics of the organization. The outcome was a line of strategy which concentrated on symptoms of the problem as divorced from fundamental causes and in a tactical program directed toward obviating the cruder and more flagrant forms of the Negro's oppression while compromising with the system which produced this oppression.

Gone was the militant impetuosity and fervor which marked the old Niagara movement. Gone also was its emphasis on Negro rights *now*. The emphasis began to be shifted back to the old doctrine of gradualism. The goal of Negro freedom was to be attained as the result of a slow evolutionary process in which the Negro, through "obvious desert and accomplishment," would gradually reduce the fortress of white prejudice and finally win acceptance by the white rulers and an equal share in American democracy. In a measure, it was a return to the old Booker T. Washington strategy of courting the "best" white folks.

However, there was an important difference in the realm of tactics. Here the new organization pursued an energetic policy of practical defense of the Negro's civil rights. That defense, in the main, was confined to the arena of the courtroom and the fight for legal redress in cases of flagrant violation of the Negro's constitutional rights.

Later the activities of the association broadened to the field of legislative action. Outstanding in this regard has been the struggle for the enactment of federal anti-lynching legislation. Of no less import has been the association's fight for the enfranchisement of the southern Negro. In this sphere its first victory was registered in the decision of the U. S. Supreme Court in 1915, invalidating the notorious grandfather clause.* In later years came the decision of that court on the unconstitutionality of the "white primary." To this record of achievement in the domain of Negro legal rights must be added the significant vic-

---

*Louisiana, in 1898, passed an amendment which was the model for the "grandfather clauses." In effect, it excluded from voting, the descendants of those who had not voted before the Civil War.

tories of the association in the fight against residential segregation. In this field, it has aided in bringing about the abrogation of all local and state laws enforcing the residential ghettoization of the Negro, and finally, in May 1948, scored a partial legal victory when the U. S. Supreme Court outlawed the restrictive covenant, even though the loopholes left show that the fight is far from over. Significant likewise have been the association's campaigns for the improvement and extension of Negro educational facilities in the South, for equal school buildings, equal appropriations, equal salaries for teachers and for the opening of institutions of higher learning to the black man of the South.

That the N.A.A.C.P. as an organization for the defense of Negro civil liberties has played and is still playing an indispensable role cannot be seriously disputed. From the time of its birth, the organization has piled up a record of achievement which has won it recognition as an essential lever of the struggle for Negro liberation. There is a large measure of truth in the statement of the late James Weldon Johnson, one-time national secretary of the association, who stated in defense of the organization:

> "When the N.A.A.C.P. was founded, the great danger facing us was that we should lose the vestiges of our rights by default. The organization checked that danger. It acted as a watchman on the wall, sounding the alarms that called us to defense. Its work would be of value if only for the reason that without it our status would be worse than it is."[14]

But the practice of certain N.A.A.C.P. leaders who speak as the authoritative voice of the whole Negro people on all questions (and it is the fashion in certain circles of white liberals to assume that they do) is certainly open to serious challenge. The facets of Negro liberation are manifold and varied. Any leadership striving to blend these varied endeavors into a composite weapon striking for complete Negro freedom must recognize imperialism as the main irreconcilable enemy. The program and tactics of such a leadership must be governed by the aim of mobilizing the Negro people against that enemy. Only by the pursuance of such a line can the fight of the Negro people for liberation be placed in its proper modern setting in alignment with the progressive forces in the country and in the world. Only in this strategy lies the answer to the important question of allies for the Negro people in their struggle, the acid test for all who claim friendship for the cause of Negro freedom.

It is clear that the policies of the N.A.A.C.P., as at present constituted, fall short of this requirement.

It cannot be denied that the N.A.A.C.P. leadership has shifted in the direction pointed by the times and the awakening Negro people. At the same time, it cannot be gainsaid that this leadership has lagged considerably behind the most advanced sections of the colored population. This leadership had to take cognizance of the deep-going social changes in the country attendant upon the ever sharpening crisis of American capitalism, and the growing social consciousness among Negro people which these changes evoked. Among Negroes, these profound economic changes were symbolized in the rise of a Negro industrial working class, its growing self-assertiveness, its increasing liberation from the enshackling bonds of narrow "race" interests, and its significant strides toward organic unity with its white class brothers. Spelled out in plain terms this meant that an ever widening section of Negroes had begun to see the face of the main enemy and were demanding from those who assayed the responsibility of leadership that they conduct a militant and uncompromising struggle against him. Furthermore, it was a demand by class-conscious Negro labor for a voice in the councils of Negro leadership—which hitherto had been the monopoly of Negro upper class intellectuals—proportionate to its growing influence.

The N.A.A.C.P. leadership has yet fully to meet the challenge of these new forces. Gestures in that direction have of necessity been made, albeit begrudgingly and with considerable reservations.

The strong undercurrent of Negro discontent accompanying the depression of the early 'thirties dramatically forced the issue of policy into the closed council of the organization's governing body, invoking a crisis in its leadership. The crisis was occasioned by the acute divergence between the policies of this leadership and the pressing needs of the Negro masses which it purported to defend.

Stepping forth as the spokesman of the opposition was Dr. DuBois, a founder of the organization. In bitter polemic, DuBois blasted the positions of the Joel Spingarn-Walter White leadership. In contemplative retrospect of this leadership, DuBois writes:

> "The bulk of my colleagues saw no essential change in the world. It was the same world with the problems to be attacked by the same method as before the war. All we needed to do was to continue to attack lynching, to bring more cases before the courts and to insist upon our full citizenship rights. They recoiled from any consideration of the economic plight of the world or any change in the organization of industry.
>
> "My colored colleagues especially were deeply American, with the old theory of individualism, with a desire to be rich or at least well-to-do, with suspicion of organized labor and labor programs. . . . My white colleagues were still liberals and philanthropists. They wanted to help the Negroes, as they wanted to help the weak and disadvantaged of all classes in America. They realized poignantly the dislocation of industry, the present economic problems; but most of them still believed in the basic rightness of industry as at present organized. . . ."[15]

DuBois urged tackling of the basic needs of the Negro people, their pressing demands for economic reform. He demanded a break with the orientation toward upper-class Negroes, upon which the association in later years had come to rely, and who "regarded it as a weapon to attack the sort of social discrimination which especially irked them; rather than as an organization to improve the status and power of the whole Negro group."[16]

In order to effect these changes DuBois called for a radical overhauling of the organizational set-up of the association. Declaring that the leadership was a self-perpetuating clique and that policies for the "welfare of Negroes were being worked out in small committees responsible to no one," he demanded more democracy, more autonomy to local branches, and the drawing of young blood into the leadership. In sum, a radical reorientation in policy, as well as in the domain of organization set-up, was needed "if the organization [was] to fulfill its historic role."[17]

DuBois was among the first of the top stratum of the Negro upper-class intellectuals to see the handwriting on the wall, and to perceive the trend of national sentiment among the Negro masses, although, at the time, his opposition assumed the form of a program of voluntary segregation.

> "The upper class Negro," he observes, "has almost never been nationalistic. He has never planned or thought of a Negro state or a Negro church or a Negro school. This solution has always been a thought upsurging from the mass, because of pressure which they could not withstand and which compelled a racial institution or chaos."[18]

DuBois, having deepened his understanding of social evolution by a study of Marxism, sought a break from the decades-old tutelage of white philanthropy. His was an attempt to strike out on an independent course. That the political program he then espoused bore the earmarks of Negro separatism was mainly due to the still existing isolation of the Negro.

The trends toward Negro-white labor unity at the time were almost solely confined to Communist and left-wing circles. It was to broaden into a mass trend only with the emergence of the C.I.O. in 1936.

That DuBois resigned from the N.A.A.C.P. which he had helped to found (although later he returned to the organization) does not mean that his sharp posing of the issues was without effect in the future activities of that body. On the contrary; his insurgence, backed by the sharp upswing of these trends in the subsequent period, opened a new chapter in the policy of the organization. The status quo of upper-class leadership, though not broken, had been jarred, and the organization, willingly or unwillingly, had to make some concessions to the demands of the new situation or give up altogether the claim of leadership. Pressured by the mounting militancy of the people, dramatically evidenced in the Scottsboro case, the struggles of the unemployed and the battles of the Alabama sharecroppers, the Association embarked on a more energetic defense program. Its internal structure was loosened, permitting more freedom and initiative by the local branches and an increased orientation towards mass recruitment.

With these modifications in policy and organization, the stage was set for the activities of the Association during the period of World War II. Aided by the dominant liberal trend in the country, it chalked up an impressive record on the American Negro sector of the world anti-fascist front, its activities devoted mainly to the fight against Jim-Crow distortions of our war effort in the armed forces and in the campaign for the support of President Roosevelt's policy of Fair Employment Practice.

As a result of its energetic actions, the Association, for the first time in its history, attained the status of a mass movement among Negroes. It emerged from the war with an organization of a half million members, and with more than fifteen hundred local branches scattered throughout the country in the key communities of urban Negro life. Its program, reflecting the pressure of the new mass forces, was widened to include such issues as repeal of the Taft-Hartley anti-labor law, legislation for migratory and displaced farm workers, and the rising cost of living incorporated in resolutions adopted at the thirty-eighth conference of the Association in June 1947.

Nevertheless, it would be incorrect to draw the conclusion that this increased activity was accompanied by any basic alteration in fundamental strategy. The decisive voice in national policy still rests in the hands of a more or less closed top circle of Negro upper-class intellectuals en bloc with white liberals, Social-Democratic reformists, and outright imperialistic elements.

Ralph Bunche, writing in 1940, observed:

> ". . . the evident concern for the opinion of the white supporters of the organization, especially on the part of the National Office, has been a powerful factor in keeping the Association thoroughly 'respectable' and has certainly been an influence in the very evident desire of the Association to keep its skirts free of the grimy bitterness and strife encountered in the economic arena.

> ". . . The South must be subjected to a new agrarian and industrial revolution before any significant changes in the fundamental relationship—political, economic, or

racial—will occur. This is what the N.A.A.C.P. apparently
lacks the understanding and courage to face."[19]

That the orientation of the Association has not basically
changed is evidenced by the co-opting to the National Board
of Eric Johnston, former head of the National Association of
Manufacturers, at present tsar of Hollywood and outstanding
propagandist for American monopoly capitalism.

Broadening the leadership, refreshing it with forces more
representative of the broad masses and of Negro labor, has to
some extent been forced. But the dominant group has sought
to restrict this to such Negro labor leaders as the Social-Democrat
A. Philip Randolph, whose ideas and outlook most closely
approximate those of the entrenched clique. The mandate of
the rank and file of the Negro masses has generally been pursued haltingly and not without considerable resistance by this
controlling group. The National Board has remained in the
hands of the top bureaucracy, which, through co-option and
elections, has retained effective control of the organization's
policies.

Despite these barriers, the floodgates of revolt from below have
been pushed ajar, permitting the increased initiative of the
local branches. These branches, led by a locally elected leadership, in which the voice of Negro labor has been increasingly
represented, especially in many places in the South, have initiated
and led significant struggles and campaigns around local and
national issues, and constitute a continuous militant pressure
upon the national leadership. Of particular significance in
this regard is the movement for the Progressive Party among
large sections of the rank and file and local leaders of the
organization in all parts of the country.

Whither the N.A.A.C.P.? Can it meet the new requirements
and tests which must inevitably emerge in the developing struggle
for Negro liberation? Will it be able to move forward with
the Negro masses whose consciousness of nationhood is bound
to increase under conditions of sharpening imperialist oppression? Will it be able to raise its sights high enough to recognize
the enemy clearly: American imperialism, with its end-aim of
war and fascism? Will it realize its great potential as a demo-

cratic people's force, or will the course of the top policy-makers, characterized by compromise and vacillation on the most vital issues in the struggle for Negro rights, be allowed to convert the organization into a vehicle for reaction? Will the grass-roots upsurge of the Negro masses, expressed in the hostility towards the program of reaction and war promoted by the old, dominant political parties, place an effective stamp on the N.A.A.C.P.? Or will the leadership, persisting in their support of the smokescreen of anti-communism with which the forces of reaction are covering their offensive against the common people at home and abroad, be allowed to impose a course on the organization which can only violate the best interests of the Negro people and isolate it from its true allies, the militant and progressive labor movement? In the last analysis the answer to the question, "Whither the N.A.A.C.P.?" must rest with the mass, progressive forces within the Association. To the degree that these forces are successful in the struggle to translate the program of the organization into deeds, to secure full inner democracy, and to establish unity with the advancing forces of progress, will it play a vital and constructive role among the Negro people.

The National Urban League

Prominent in the list of organizations for Negro improvement is the National Urban League. Founded in 1911 as a social service organization, the League undertook a program of assistance to newly arrived Negro migrants from the South and their problems of adjustment to northern urban life. The organization has a limited field of activities, confined mainly to job placement of Negroes, community improvement projects, schools, playgrounds, public health clinics, and housing projects in Negro neighborhoods. The local organizations have served as employment agencies with their primary task to "find jobs, more jobs and better jobs for Negroes."[20] The League also initiates conferences, investigations, and surveys, and furnishes information and recommendations to government agencies.

Doubtless the League, particularly in many of its local organizations, has made significant contributions in the Negro welfare field, but its dependency upon white philanthropy and the good will of its wealthy white sponsors, together with its non-democratic organizational setup, has operated towards making the League a channel for conservative influence in the Negro movement. To the criticism that the League advocates "a policy of racial expediency and conciliation, which is characterized by extreme opportunism,"[21] its spokesmen have replied that "it is a social service organization attempting to perform a helpful task in a limited field."[22] The fact, however, is that the Negro leaders of the League are at the same time leaders in the Negro community and play a prominent role in its councils and political life. Many of them, to be sure, have participated in progressive causes.

By mutual agreement with the N.A.A.C.P., the League leaves to it such broader issues as the fight for Negro civil liberties. Both these organizations were founded on the initiative of white philanthropists and liberal groups, and follow the pattern of upper-class interracialism, uniting white philanthropists with Negro professional and social workers. But unlike the N.A.A.C.P., the Urban League is not a mass organization, and, even more than in the case of the National Association, the composition of the League's governing boards precludes the possibility of its embarking on a program of fundamental economic and social reform.

The Urban League, founded by representatives of big business, lists among its supporters and its national executive board members such representatives of the Wall Street status quo as William H. Baldwin and Winthrop Rockefeller. The boards of local leagues are heavily weighted with similar elements, although in many places local Negro leaders have played a progressive role. It is significant that along with Wall Street's present drive toward reaction and fascism at home and abroad, the activity of prominent white reactionaries in the League's leading councils has increased. Noteworthy in this respect is the recent prominence in its top committee of Henry R. Luce, multimillionaire publisher and propagandist par excellence for Wall Street's dream of the "American Century." Mr. Luce headed up the organization's fund-raising drive for $450,000 in 1947, and was vice-chairman of the drive in 1948. The connection between the presence of such persons in the top councils of the League and the recent anti-Communist fulminations of certain spokesmen of the League; their stand against the upsurge among the Negro people for progressive independent political action; and their espousal of the Marshall Plan for U. S. imperialist aggrandizement should be obvious to all.

Other Negro Organizations

There are also such business and professional organizations as the National Negro Business League, the National Negro Bankers' Association, the National Negro Insurance Association, the National Teachers' Association and the National Bar Association. There are the Negro fraternities and sororities. All these organizations and movements originated to fill the needs of the Negroes in these respective fields and professions, to a large extent as the result of the Jim-Crow exclusion policies of parallel white organizations. All of them, however, have programs for Negro improvement not confined to their particular groups but for the whole Negro people. Most of them carry on activities toward this end, such as lobbying and petitioning on various Negro issues and participating in concerted action with other groups around issues arising from Negro oppression. This is true also of churches, and the vast network of lodges and social clubs in every Negro community throughout the country.

Prominent among Negro improvement organizations are Negro women's groups, such as the National Association of Colored Women, the National Council of Negro Women, under the leadership of Dr. Mary McLeod Bethune, and the National Association of Colored Graduate Nurses.

Such organizations, though often conservatively led, have played significant roles in the fight for Negro rights. In perspective, they exist as potentially important elements of the united Negro people's anti-imperialist movement that is now emerging.

Interracial Movements

Mention should be made of middle-class interracial movements, which have vastly extended their activities and organization in recent years. In addition to the old-line national organizations, such as the interracial departments of the Y.M.C.A. and Y.W.C.A., the Commission on Race Relations of the Federal Council of the Churches in Christ in America, and the American Council on Race Relations, there has been, in recent years, a mushrooming of interracial organizations on a state and community scale throughout the country. These agencies began to spring up about 1943, immediately following the shocking race riots in Detroit, New York City, Beaumont, Texas, and other smaller communities. Another source of stimulation for this movement was the setting up by President Roosevelt in 1941 of the Fair Employment Practice Committee.[23]

While not part of the Negro movement proper, such groups can be considered as auxiliary to that movement in that they are organized around programs to "lessen friction" and promote "better understanding" and "harmony" between Negro and white. Such organizations, sponsored in the main by white, middle-class liberals and humanitarians, generally follow the pattern of interracialism at the top level, between the "elite" of both groups. In general, they concentrate on flagrant excesses of Negro persecution, while shying away from the fundamental causes of the conditions they deplore, and from the anti-imperialist implications of those causes. In other words, they seek a palliative rather than a cure.

A good example is furnished by the Commission on Interracial Cooperation, commonly known as the Interracial Commission. This organization of southern liberals, with headquarters in Atlanta, was formed in 1919 to combat the social tensions of that period, and is among the oldest of such groups. The Commission at that time set itself the task of working among middle-class white groups to promote better interracial understanding. They tried to bring Negro and white together in a constructive effort to improve racial relations in the region, with the aim "to quench, if possible, the fires of racial antagonism which were flaming at that time with such deadly menace in all sections of the country."[24] A network of local and state commissions were set up around a program of fair opportunity for the Negro on the job, equal pay for equal work, and the elimination of white primary, poll tax and lynching. But at the same time the Commission kept its skirts clear of the crucial questions of segregation and land reform. But the Commission, nevertheless, has had some positive influence in the bitter cauldron of Negro persecution which is the South. Even with its weaknesses, it has served to marshal support for limited reforms among Southern white intellectuals, church circles and women's organizations.

In an entirely different category, however, is the Southern Conference for Human Welfare, organized in 1938 under the influence of New Deal social reform policies, around a program of promotion of interracialism from below, among Negro and white toilers. The Southern Conference became the rallying point for southern white and Negro intellectuals, and now serves as a political center of the most advanced sector of southern liberalism for the new Progressive Party.

The Negro Middle Class

A basic consideration in understanding the course of the leadership of the N.A.A.C.P. and other bourgeois-led Negro organizations is to be found in the character of the Negro middle class. It would be incorrect to say that the Negro bourgeoisie is inherently reactionary. Quite the reverse. For decades the Negro working class was almost completely without expression, not to speak of organization. During this whole period, the middle class was the most progressive force among the Negro people; they were the spokesmen for social reform. To them, the main enemy was not imperialism, which was obscure to them, but the ignorance of the "poor whites" and chauvinistically led American labor which they saw as the main force "keeping the Negro down."

The root causes of the political immaturity of this bourgeoisie, its ideological dependency, its peculiar susceptibility to the blandishments of the dominant white ruling class, are to be found in its stunted economic and social development; it is a non-industrial bourgeoisie relegated to the margins of American economic life.

Clearly, the process of class differentiation among Negroes

could not seriously get underway until the yoke of chattel slavery had been broken by the Civil War. Then, under conditions of most rapacious oppression, the process of class stratification was necessarily a slow and tortuous one.

However, a singular feature of the Negro national question in the United States is that the most advanced and articulate section of the Negro bourgeoisie has developed outside the Black Belt region, and especially in the cities of the North.

This is highly logical, considering the extreme degree of the exploitation and oppression of the Negro in that area, where the total surplus of his labor is hogged by imperialist Bourbon monopoly. The possibility of any real primary accumulation by a Negro capitalist class has thus been obviated; the result has been a trend on the part of the aspirant black capitalists to flee the region in what Charles S. Johnson, president of Fisk University, has described as the "Flight of the Talented Tenth," although some of the wealthiest Negroes are still to be found in the South.

Thus the most enterprising elements of this class have been concentrated in the cities outside of the Black Belt, where they have set up shop administering to the needs of the Negro population in the Jim-Crow ghettos.

The Negro upper class came late to the scene of American economic development, too late to get in on the ground floor of modern industrial enterprise, to share the so-called benefits of "free enterprise"; its misfortune was that it arrived in the epoch of the trusts, when the key points of the country's economic life were already dominated by big business. It, therefore, had to make its way under the handicaps imposed by this circumstance.

With its growth stunted by monopoly capitalism, the efforts of Negro business enterprises had been shunted off to non-industrial pursuits, such as small-scale banking, insurance, real estate, retail merchandising, and the like. The market of the Negro businessman has been limited almost exclusively to the segregated community. Even in this narrow field, big white capital takes the lion's share. The Negro retail merchant is confronted with the overwhelming competition of the big capitalist chain enterprises and their monopolist control of prices, as well as with the economically sounder and more efficient smaller white establishments, which abound in the Negro urban communities. As Bunche has observed: "Negro enterprise exists only on the sufferance of that dominant white business world which completely controls credit, basic industry and the state."[25]

Economically, the Negro upper and middle classes are essentially a marginal bourgeoisie, restricted to the leftovers of the dominant white ruling class; they are a class of small entrepreneurs. Similarly circumscribed is its educated stratum, the Negro professionals—doctors, lawyers, teachers, preachers, social workers, etc.—whose scope of activity is confined almost exclusively to the Negro field.

The result is that the Negro businessman, and to a large degree the Negro professional, finds himself caught in an inescapable contradiction. On the one hand he has what might be called a "vested interest" in Jim Crow, upon which he is economically dependent for his market. At the same time, Jim Crow is the chief obstacle to his social development. The result is a split social personality. The Negro businessman and professional is caught in a vicious circle. He constantly finds himself torn between his immediate economic interest which dictates the maintenance of the ghetto as his main base of operation, and the desire for social equality. These two mutually exclusive and contradictory desires create a dilemma inherent in Negro upper and middle-class thought patterns and programs. Bourgeois leadership has sought to rally the Negro masses to the defense of its segregationalist interests by appeals to "race" loyalty, "race" co-operation and solidarity, for a "buy Negro" policy, thereby fostering a kind of Negro exclusiveness which objectively runs parallel to the Jim-Crow isolationist interests of the imperialist oppressors.*

*This segregationalist tendency was especially evidenced in the widespread movement for jobs which accompanied the unemployment crisis in the early 'thirties. Negro petty-bourgeois leaders sought to limit the scope of this movement to the Negro community. Although the slogan, "Don't buy where you can't work," was a sound one, some of its advocates, such as the notorious Sufi in Harlem and Costonie in Baltimore, combined it

In "hard times," that is, under conditions of economic depression, as a result of the weak and tenuous economic position of this class which makes it the most vulnerable victim among the American middle strata—the least able to withstand the attack of monopoly capitalism—this self-isolationist trend has received sharp emphasis. The result has been the rise of separatist programs which in the past have taken a reactionary escapist and utopian direction, the most extreme expression of which was the Garvey movement.

Such movements have expressed particularly the desperation of the lower Negro middle classes, the small shopkeeper, the unemployed and frustrated Negro intellectual—the petty bourgeois element among Negroes who in such periods are pushed to the wall and faced with economic ruin.

But in more "normal" periods, this separatist, utopian and essentially escapist trend has always existed as a more or less steady undercurrent in Negro upper and middle-class thought. It has been expressed in schemes of Negro business groups for the building of a co-operative economy among Negroes, within the walls of segregation. Thus, there was a plethora of projects for the establishment of some kind of self-sufficient Negro economy through the organization of the power of the Negro consumer, a Negro operated and controlled industrial system within the midst of an imperialist dominated national economy. Plans along these lines were once even sponsored by DuBois.[26]

This ideological dualism of the Negro bourgeoisie has given rise to a peculiar vacillating and compromising trend in their leadership of the Negro movement—a trend which we may designate as Negro reformism. It is expressed in the vacillation between "accommodation to Jim Crow," on the one hand, and the struggle for full equality, on the other—the failure to understand the main enemy, American monopoly capitalism.

In the peculiarly inhibited economic and historical develop-

with slogans such as, "Run the whites out of Harlem," thus seeking to divert the movement along lines of Negro ghetto nationalism. They thereby played into the hands of the real oppressors, by seeking to bring the movement of the Negro workers into a clash with their natural allies, the white workers.

ment of the Negro upper classes is to be found the explanation for the fundamental inadequacy of its policies and programs.

Herein lies the cause for its political backwardness and an answer to the question of why the intellectual representatives of this class, unlike their counterparts in older oppressed nations, *e.g.,* India, have never in modern times projected a program for national liberation of their people, let alone a program setting forth land redivision plus the right of self-determination in the Black Belt as a condition for complete realization of Negro equality.

It is a class which by and large is economically divorced from the Black Belt homeland. Indeed it can be said to have waived all rights to its heritage, written it off as irredeemably lost, and set for itself the realization of modest demands for a greater share in the consumers' market within the Negro urban ghetto.[27]

This ghetto nationalism of the Negro urban bourgeoisie is reflected by certain of its spokesmen in their advocacy of a defeatist Negro mass exodus from the South as a solution of the problem.[28]

Garveyism

The "Back to Africa Movement" was the direct outgrowth of this ghetto nationalist trend, particularly pronounced among lower middle-class Negroes. It was to burst full-flood upon the nation during the crisis years immediately following World War I, to become the program of the greatest mass movement among Negroes since Reconstruction.* This movement was organized in New York in 1916 under the auspices of the Universal Negro Improvement Association, headed by Marcus Garvey.

*"It is impossible to give an accurate estimate of the total membership of Garvey's organization at its peak. Garvey gave the probably exaggerated estimate of 6,000,000 members. William Pickens, on the other hand, one of Garvey's bitter enemies among the Negro intellectuals, charged that the organization never enrolled as many as 1,000,000. Kelly Miller cited the figure of 4,000,000." (Ralph J. Bunche, *The Programs, Ideologies, Tactics, and Achievements of Negro Betterment and Interracial Organizations,* unpublished manuscript, Vol. II, p. 398, prepared for the Myrdal study, quoted by Myrdal, *op. cit.,* p. 748.)

It has become the fashion of certain upper-class Negro intellectuals to brush aside the strident nationalism of the Garvey
movement; to regard it as an artificial incrustation on the
Negro movement, a product alien to the basic thought pattern
of the American Negro. The superficiality of this view is
apparent in that it leaves unexplained the tremendous nationwide sweep of Garveyism and its hold upon the broad masses
of the Negro people of the period. Interestingly enough it is
admitted by these same critics that Garvey "had something."
He was a "clever salesman," a "master promoter," a "dynamic
personality."

The huge movement led by Garvey cannot be explained purely
by the personality of its leader. Yes, Garvey did have "something," and that "something," stripped of all the fantastic and
bombastic trappings which marked the movement, was a deep
feeling for the intrinsic national character of the Negro problem.

Garveyism represented a convergence of two social forces,
distinctly reflected in the 1920 *Declaration of Rights of the
Negro People of the World.*[29] On the one hand it was the
trend of the recent migrants from the peasant South. The
Universal Negro Improvement Association had its main organizations in northern industrial centers, in such cities as Detroit,
Chicago, New York, Cleveland, St. Louis, Cincinnati. The
membership of these organizations by and large was composed
of the new and as yet non-integrated Negro proletarians; recent
migrants from the cotton fields, who had not yet shaken the
dust of the plantation from their heels and still remained largely
peasants in outlook. Embittered and disillusioned by post-war
terror and unemployment, they saw in the Garvey scheme of a
Negro nation in Africa a way out to the realization of their
deep grounded yearnings for land and freedom.

On the other hand, Garveyism reflected the ideology of the
Negro petty bourgeoisie, their abortive attempt at hegemony
in the Negro movement. It was the trend of the small property
holder: the shop keeper, pushed to the wall, ruined or threatened with ruin by the ravages of the crisis; the frustrated and
unemployed Negro professional—doctors and lawyers with impoverished clientele, store front preachers, poverty stricken

students—in sum those elements of the middle-class closest to the Negro laboring people and therefore affected most keenly by the deterioration of their conditions. Garveyism reflected the desperation of these strata before the ruthless encroachments of predatory monopoly upon their already meager markets. It was an attempt by them to seek escape from sharpening national oppression, the terror of "race" riots, mounting lynchings, economic and social frustration. These elements formed the leading echelons of the movement.

Under the generalship of Garvey, the movement was diverted from a potentially anti-imperialist course into channels of "peaceful return to Africa." Here, presumably free from the hardships of oppression which beset the Negro in the hostile "white world," they would have the opportunity to build their own nation under their own leadership and to develop their own culture.

Admonishing the Negro on the futility of obtaining justice in the United States, Garvey maintained:

> "Being satisfied to drink of the dregs from the cup of human progress will not demonstrate our fitness as a people to exist alongside of others, but when of our own initiative we strike out to build industries, governments, and ultimately empires, then and only then will we as a race prove to our Creator and to man in general that we are fit to survive and capable of shaping our own destiny."

> " . . . Wake Up, Africa. Let us work toward the one glorious end of a free, redeemed and mighty nation. Let Africa be a bright star among the constellation of nations."[30]

The Garvey movement likewise expressed the immediate pecuniary interest of its petty-bourgeois leadership. The organization initiated a whole network of co-operative business enterprises, including grocery stores, laundries, restaurants, hotels, and printing plants. Most ambitious of these enterprises was the Black Star Steamship Line. Several ships were purchased and manned by Negro officers. Commercial trade relationships were established with Negro groups in the West Indies and

West Africa. Trade negotiations were also begun with the Republic of Liberia.

Nor was the idea of Negro government confined to agitation alone. Practical preliminary steps were taken on American soil. Garvey proceeded to organize a sort of Negro "Government-in-Exile," pending the reconquest of the African motherland. Thus a Provisional Government of Africa was set up, with Garvey inaugurated as Provisional President.

The West-Indian Garvey proposed for the regenerated Africa a governmental structure which was an amalgam of British feudal forms and the structure of American secret societies. He ruled with the aid of a Potentate and a Supreme Deputy Potentate, a nobility including Knights of the Nile, Knights of Distinguished Service, the Order of Ethiopia, the Dukes of Nigeria and Uganda. A flag of "Black, Red and Green" was adopted as the national colors—"Black for the Race," "Red for their blood," and "Green for their hopes." He set up a skeleton of the army of the future Negro state, founding the Universal African Legion, the Universal Black Cross Nurses, the Universal African Motor Corps, the Black Eagle Flying Corps, equipping these with uniforms and selecting their officers.

The program was accompanied by a feverish cultural revival, the aim of which was to break down all ideas of the black man's inferiority, and to instil in him a sense of pride and self-assertiveness. Garvey excoriated assimilation and amalgamation and preached the glories of African history and the pride of Negro ancestry.

"... Honest students of history," he said, "can recall the day when Egypt, Ethiopia and Timbuctoo towered in their civilizations, towered above Europe, towered above Asia. When Europe was inhabited by a race of cannibals, a race of savages, naked men, heathens and pagans, Africa was peopled with a race of cultured black men, who were masters in art, science and literature. . . ."[31]

The fanfare, parades, bright colors, the ceremony, rituals and pomp, the adaptation of the romantic patterns of Negro secret orders, were designed to appeal to the great mass of downtrodden Negroes. Garvey's program was couched in symbols which the most politically backward Negro could understand. His forte as a leader was due to his clear understanding of the psychology of the Negro of that period. That psychology was mainly a peasant psychology. It was among the Negro peasantry, or, more precisely, people but a step removed from the peasantry, that the Garvey movement found its greatest response.

In all, the Garvey movement represented a mass breakaway of Negroes from the then dominant bourgeois leadership of the N.A.A.C.P. It revealed the deep disillusionment of the Negro man of the street, the returned veteran of World War I, the worker, the sharecropper, the small shopkeeper, with the "close ranks" policy advocated by this leadership during the war years. The Negro veteran felt that he had been cheated, that he fought an illusory battle to "make the world safe for democracy," only to return to a worse slavery than that which he had left.

Apparent, also, was the bankruptcy of the Association's post-war policy of mere protest, which offered the Negro no tangible program for meeting the rampant anti-Negro violence and mass joblessness of the period.

The Garvey movement reflected the widening rift between the policies of the Negro bourgeois reformism and the life needs of a sorely pressed people. It was a mass renunciation of the whole program of interracialism from the top. This mood of the Negro was sharply expressed by Garvey, who denounced the entire incumbent Negro upper-class leadership, claiming that they were motivated solely by the desire for cultural assimilation and banked their hopes for Negro equality on support from the white enemy. Theirs, he maintained, was a policy of compromise between accommodation and protest.

In these circumstances, Garvey, heading the Universal Negro Improvement Association, captured leadership of the rising movement of the Negro people, eventually directing it into the blind alley of reactionary utopian escapism, diverting it from its potentially anti-imperialist course. Instead of the fight for realization of the Negro's national aspirations on American soil through a struggle for land and the right of self-determination in the Black Belt—a fight which demanded the alliance of the Negro people with white labor—Garvey proposed that the Negro waive all rights to his heritage in this country and retreat to Africa. Clearly, this plan meant the desertion of the struggle for Negro rights in the U.S.A. and the widening of the historic rift between black and white labor. It therefore played into the hands of reaction.

But the reign of Garvey was brief. The organization was destined to collapse. Among the factors which brought this about were the subsiding of the economic depression; the ushering in of the "boom" period, with the subsequent easing of the plight of the Negro people; the growing adjustment of Negro migrants to their new environment and their increased integration into industry.

These economic factors brought to a head the basic contradiction, inherent in the movement from its beginning, which was expressed in the conflict between the masses of toilers, their need to defend their rights in America, and the fantastic "Back to Africa" scheme of the Garvey leadership. The decline of the movement found Garvey emphasizing more and more this reactionary phase of the program, to the neglect of the struggle for Negro rights in the United States, a struggle to which the leadership in the initial stages was forced by the pressure of the masses to give at least lip service.

The very logic of the "Back to Africa" program against the backdrop of the movement's decline drove Garvey to a tacit alliance with the southern Bourbons. Thus, in 1924, we find Garvey seeking support for this plan from the most implacable enemies of his people. At that time he made traitorous negotiations with Colonel Simmons, Imperial Grand Wizard of the Ku Klux Klan, in which he sought to enlist the support of that organization for his project. He also tried to secure the co-operation of various southern senators and congressmen. That this "meeting of minds" between Garvey and the southern Bourbons took place on the basis of Garvey's agreement to soft-pedal the agitation for Negro rights in the South in return for their help for the resettlement of the Negroes in Africa, is an open secret.

The final curtain was dropped on the Garvey episode with the failure of the organization's varied business ventures and the subsequent imprisonment of Garvey by Federal authorities on the charge of using the mails to defraud, in connection with the sale of stock for the Black Star Line. This debacle marked the end of Garveyism as an important mass movement.

Offshoots of the movement, however, continued to exist in a number of smaller groups and organizations advocating the Garvey theory or variations of it. Scattered throughout the country are still organizations bearing the name of the Universal Negro Improvement Association. Carrying on in the tradition of Garvey is the National Union for People of African Descent and the National Movement for the Establishment of the 49th State. Another variation of this pattern is the Peace Movement for Ethiopia, formed in Chicago in 1932, which has worked for the support of the notorious Repatriation Bill of Senator Bilbo, seeking mass resettlement of Negroes in Africa. Still another ideological offshoot of Garveyism was the Pacific Movement of the Eastern World, which came to the fore during World War II with the conviction of some of its leaders for collaboration with the Japanese. This movement, which in the early 1930's had exerted considerable influence among the most backward sections of Negro workers in cities like Chicago, St. Louis, and Kansas City, was at the time of the trial proved to have been mainly a paper organization, a cover for the unsuccessful attempt of Japanese agents to influence the Negro people.

That the Garvey movement, the first great nationalist movement among Negroes, was diverted into reactionary, separatist channels was due to the following basic factors:

(1) The immaturity of the Negro working class, which had not yet emerged as an independent force in the Negro movement. (2) The political backwardness of the general labor movement still headed by a white chauvinistic bureaucracy. (3) The fact that the working-class left wing under the leadership of the Communist Party had just begun to strike out on an independent course and had not yet advanced a full and clear program in the field of the struggle for Negro liberation. The "Back to Africa" trend is no longer a significant one in the

Negro movement of today, but in circumstances of sharpening oppression, such trends might again crop up.

The disintegration of the U.N.I.A. did not mark the end of the national aspirations of the Negro people. On the contrary, the movement entered a new stage, this time under the leadership of the new Negro working class signalized in the participation of Negro labor in the historic strike struggles of 1917-19 in the packinghouse and steel industries. The Negro middle class, which had been the dominant force in the formative years of the modern Negro liberation movement, had by now ceased to be such. The petty bourgeois current, left to itself, led only into a hopeless blind alley. In the interval since World War I, new mass forces had come to life, highly conscious of their character as a distinct people and determined to prosecute the struggle for Negro rights on American soil. The rapidly maturing Negro industrial working class was bound to become the spearhead of these forces. The Negro working class is a class with independent political expression and aims directed to active and uncompromising struggle against imperialism. The emergence of this class as an independent political factor marks the appearance of two tendencies within the Negro liberation movement: one which wants to come to terms with the Negroes' oppressors and the other which, under the leadership of the Negro working class, struggles against imperialism.

The advanced echelons of this new Negro working class had appeared as early as 1917 with the publication of the Negro left-wing organs, *The Messenger, The Emancipator,* and *The Challenge.* The organization of the African Blood Brotherhood, with its organ, *The Crusader,* brought together left-wing split-offs of the Garvey movement and the Negro Communists. This movement of the early 'twenties was encouraged by the newly established Trade Union Educational League, representing the left-wing groups in the American trade unions striving for industrial unionism and militant trade union policies. The T.U.E.L., led by William Z. Foster, sponsored the organization of the American Negro Labor Congress in 1925, which sought to unite Negro and white labor on a program for Negro rights and industrial unionism. But the unmistakable inadequacies of these efforts pointed to the need for a fundamental re-examination and revision of policy on the Negro question. The urgency of this was stressed by the approach of the economic collapse of 1929, which the Communists foresaw.

In 1928 an historic turn was achieved in the scientific understanding of the Negro question in the United States. In that year, the Communist Party adopted a program which clearly placed the Negro problem as a question of an *oppressed nation* suffering from an especially oppressive form of subjugation. The program pointed out that in the Black Belt all the objective prerequisites exist for a national revolutionary movement of the Negro people against American imperialism. It established the essentially agrarian-democratic character of the Negro movement, which under conditions of modern imperialist oppression could fulfill itself only by the achievement of democratic land redivision and of the right of self-determination for the Negro people in the Black Belt. Thus the new line of the Communist Party brought the issue of Negro equality out of the realm of bourgeois humanitarianism, where it had been the special property of bourgeois philanthropists and professional uplifters who sought to strip the Negro struggle of its revolutionary implications and to make it a feeble adjunct of safe and sane reforms—all obtainable presumably within the confines of imperialist law and order.

The Communist Party position grounded the issue of Negro liberation firmly in the fight of the American people for fuller democracy and in the struggle of the working class against capitalism. It emphasized the revolutionary essence of the struggle for Negro equality arising from the fact that the special oppression of the Negro people is a main prop of the system of capitalist, imperialist domination over the entire working class and the masses of exploited American people. The Negro people, therefore, are the indispensable allies of white American labor, and the fight of the Negro people for nationhood—quite apart from humanitarian considerations—is a special phase of the struggle for the emancipation of the whole American working class. It is the historic task of American labor, as it advances on the road toward socialism, to solve the problem of land and freedom which the bourgeois-democratic revolution of the Civil War and Reconstruction left unfinished.

This line committed the Communist Party to an indefatigable and uncompromising fight among its own members and in the ranks of labor generally to burn out the rot of white ruling-class theories of white chauvinism which depict the Negro as "innately inferior." The mobilization of the white workers for the struggle for Negro rights is a precondition for freeing the Negro workers from the stifling influences of petty-bourgeois Negro nationalism with its ideology of self-isolation. Only thus, the program pointed out, can the historic rift in the ranks of American labor be breached, and a solid front of white and Negro workers be presented to the common enemy—American monopoly capitalism. Thus the boundary was clearly drawn between the revolutionary and the reformist positions—between the line of effective struggle and the line of futile accommodation.

As the fruit of this program, labor and the progressive movement were able, for the first time since Reconstruction, to tap the profoundly democratic potential of the Negro people's struggle for equal rights. The decks were cleared for the leadership of the Left in the great battles of the 'thirties. It was during this period that the correctness of this program was tested and confirmed. The Communist Party and left-wing trade union forces began to face toward the South, the center of gravity of the Negro problem, and to build organizations there. The League of Struggle for Negro Rights, organized in 1930, became a rallying center for advanced Negro and white militants committed to the struggle for Negro national liberation. The International Labor Defense began to center its activities on Negro civil liberties in the South. These efforts met with overwhelming success, establishing the first breach in the citadel of the "Solid South," in which the imperialist rulers and their Bourbon henchmen had sought to contain the Negro people, to isolate them from their true allies in the ranks of labor.

The Scottsboro defense of 1931, which aroused the entire country and the world, was the result. The epic of Scottsboro, born out of the depths of the great economic crisis, the fight for the lives of nine innocent Negro boys, victims of the usual lynch frame-up, was dramatized by the Communist Party and the International Labor Defense as the expression and symbol of underlying issues of Negro liberation. In this way was developed the first genuine mass movement against lynching, and for the enforcement of the Constitutional rights of Negroes in the Deep South—equal legal protection, jury rights, an end to peonage, etc. The Scottsboro struggle marked the first real bid of Negro labor for leadership in the Negro liberation movement, and its entrance on the field of Negro rights as a politically conscious, independent force. The creative impact of the militant working-class policy of mass struggle which inspired the Scottsboro defense highlighted the pitiable and craven ineffectualness of the reformist liberal policy of exclusive reliance on legal justice and avoidance of the broader issues at stake. The victory of the working-class policy in the Scottsboro case gave an historic impetus to the initiative of the Negro masses in the struggle for liberation, and reinforced it with a new and decisive element, Negro and white labor unity. In the South, the movement awakened the great mass of Negro peasantry resulting in the building of the militant Sharecroppers Union, embracing thousands of debt-ridden and land-starved Negro croppers and poor farmers, impelling them to a renewed struggle for land and freedom against the feudal plantation owners. The heroic battles of Camp Hill and Tallapoosa were milestones in this advance. It was these struggles that paved the way for the subsequent work of the C.I.O. in the organization of labor in the South. The mass upsurge was also expressed in the gigantic struggles of the unemployed during the crisis years in which the Negro working class played a militant and leading role, as well as in the strike struggles of that period.

With the inauguration of the New Deal under President Roosevelt, Negro labor registered important advances, and Negro-white labor unity, dramatized in the Scottsboro struggle, was considerably strengthened. This was expressed in the organization of the C.I.O. in whose founding and subsequent activity Negro workers played a significant role.

The organization of the National Negro Congress in 1936 strengthened this trend. The National Negro Congress, which grew out of a conference under the joint auspices of Howard University's Division of Social Sciences and the Joint Committee on National Recovery, was formed as a national agency at a congress in Chicago. It called for united action of the Negro people in all existing organizations around a program stressing economic and social problems of Negro oppression, as well as equal justice. It became a main agency in the building of the C.I.O., promoting unionization among Negro workers and rallying them behind the program of industrial organization. Its yeoman work in this field was particularly evidenced in its co-operation with the Steel Workers' Organizing Committee in that group's initiation of the conference of Negro and white steel workers in Pittsburgh, January 9, 1937.[32] Local Councils of the National Negro Congress were established in many cities. They played a great part in the fight around local issues of jobs and Negro rights generally. This movement in the pre-war period paced the nation's fight to break down the Jim-Crow barriers which confronted the Negro people on the job.

The achievements of the New Deal period crystallized an historic pattern of Negro-white labor unity which left an indelible stamp upon both the Negro liberation movement and the general trade union movement of the country.

For the past generation, the Communists have fought to raise the level of understanding in the labor movement generally of the Negro question and to win white labor, in its own interests and in the interests of democratic progress, for the alliance with the Negro people in the struggle for equal rights and freedom. Similarly among the Negro people the Negro Communists have striven to establish the understanding of the primary need for such an alliance in active struggle for their rights, and the fundamentally national character of this struggle.*

---

* Earl Browder greeted the New Deal reforms as "the beginning of a deep-going change, a shaking-up of the whole semi-feudal oppression of the Negroes, and the opening up of the vista of *a progressive establishment of Negro equality.*" (My emphasis—*H.H.*) The whole trend was therefore, according to Browder, not toward a sharper oppression of the Negro people but toward their gradual and peaceful winning of democratic rights and finally their "complete integration into the American nation as a whole," eliminating the problem and perspective of self-determination. (*Communists in the*

Under the leadership of Negro labor the Negro people became a vital part of the broad democratic coalition sustaining the New Deal. The alliance of Negro and white in the democratic camp, maintained and extended into a broad anti-fascist coalition during World War II, signalized the attainment of a central position of the Negro liberation struggle on the American political scene.

In this line of development the Negro working class has had to contend not only with the policies of Negro reformism, but also with the efforts of Social-Democracy to take it in tow. In the labor movement generally, Social-Democracy reflects the influence of the frustrated middle class, which at times rebels against finance capital, but shies away from the revolutionary implications of the anti-imperialist struggle, shunning full-hearted acceptance of the working-class position of uncompromising struggle against the exploiting classes. Social-Democrats in the imperialist countries have identified themselves with the imperialist aims of their respective ruling classes, and especially their policy of colonial oppression. The Socialist parties in England, France, Belgium, and Holland are notorious in this respect. American imperialism has found in world Social-Democracy a key instrument for the promotion of its plans for world aggrandizement.

What is the policy of this tendency, represented by the Socialist Party and the Social-Democratic Federation, with regard to the Negro question? Stripped of its humanitarian, pseudo-socialistic phrases, it boils down to a crass rationalization of the status quo of Negro oppression and, in practice, tacit support of the Jim-Crow policies of the imperialistic rulers. This is the reactionary meaning of the Socialist Party formula that the fight for the special demands of the Negro people is divisive in so far as it concerns the interests of the working class as a whole, tending to distract the workers from the struggle for socialism. In practice, this has meant the rejection by Social-Democratic trade union

Struggle for Negro Rights, New Century Publishers, N. Y., Jan., 1945.) Ignoring the nature of monopoly capitalism, Browder visualized a peaceful solution of the Negro question, within the framework of the capitalist-imperialist social setup. This tendency gained some following in the Communist Party, temporarily blurring its program of class struggle, although despite Browder's distortions the Communist Party still remained the staunchest champion of Negro rights.

officials of such vital struggles as that for seniority adjustment for Negro workers and their integration into the leadership of the unions.

This, of course, does not exclude the resort to demagogy, especially by Negro Social-Democrats, in face of the militant upsurge of the Negro people and the heightened political consciousness of the Negro working class. Such demagogy, couched in radical terms and even socialist phrases, has been increasingly used to bolster the largely discredited efforts of conservative Negro reformism. Hence the recent prominence of Social-Democratic Negro "labor" representatives in the leading councils of organizations led by such conservatives.

Prominent among Negro Social-Democratic leaders are A. Philip Randolph of the Brotherhood of Sleeping Car Porters, Frank R. Crosswaith of the International Ladies' Garment Workers, Williard Townsend and George Weaver, both leaders of the Transport Service Workers. There are also a considerable number of local people in the various unions of the A. F. of L. and C.I.O. Others among Negro intelligentsia who are not directly connected with the labor movement are nevertheless influenced by the ideology of Social-Democracy. The common ground for the unholy alliance between these leaders and the white chauvinistic Social-Democrats is their common hatred of the militant "left" and their mutual acceptance of the theory of class collaboration. Here also lies the explanation for their increased prominence in the top council of the N.A.A.C.P. and the National Urban League. Posing as ardent "race men," with long experience in labor leadership, they are in a peculiarly favorable position for playing their designed role.

Obviously, these elements cannot function in the Negro movement without appearing to champion Negro rights, but everything they do shows that they subordinate the interests of the Negro people to the central and all-pervading purpose, which is to throttle the unfolding anti-imperialistic struggle of the masses.

A recent and dangerous illustration of this was the maneuver of A. Philip Randolph on the issue of Jim Crow in the armed forces. Randolph issued a call to the Negro people to engage in "civil disobedience" and refuse to serve in the armed forces unless Negroes were given equal rights as cannon fodder in the execution of Wall Street's imperialist program. It is the sheerest delusion, not to say hypocrisy, to pretend that the world program of the very ruling circles who are seeking to perpetuate Jim Crow and oppression of Negro Americans is a program for liberation and democracy anywhere in the world. In view of this, to propose, as Randolph virtually did, support for the Truman-Marshall plan of world domination in exchange for "equal rights" in the armed forces drafted to enforce this plan is tantamount to a flagrant betrayal of the American Negro. And not only of the American Negro, but also of the millions of colored peoples throughout the world now rising to throw off the yoke of colonial enslavement of which American finance capital, through its outright economic and military aid to decaying empires, has become the chief mainstay. These colored peoples, fighting for national independence, and economic and social reforms similar to those for which the American Negro has been struggling for decades, are finding that the main bastion obstructing the achievement of their aims, is American big business with its Truman-Marshall program. Everyone can read of American plans to use Africa in World War III. They have been stated blatantly in *The United States News* of February 27, 1948. Reporting on the "Growth of Africa's World Role," the journal wrote:

> "Build up of Africa is underway. Things are booming. Money is pouring in to speed production of raw materials. . . . Military plans enter in, too. Uranium, tin, copper deposits, all become important if 'cold war' turns hot."

The magazine further describes military preparations in the Union of South Africa, the Belgian Congo, Rhodesia, British West Africa, East Africa, the French Colonies, etc. The report boasts that "in case of war, or serious threat of war, the U. S. and Britain could move into a series of partially prepared positions in Africa and begin tapping its sources of strategic materials.

> "The U. S. quietly has built up an outpost in Liberia, a country that has had close ties with the U. S. since its founding by freed slaves in 1820. The U. S. already has

spent $25,000,000 in harbor and airport development there. . . . If trouble breaks out in Europe, Monrovia's new harbor automatically becomes a U. S. naval base. Robert's Field, a $6,000,000 air base, built by the U. S. fifty miles inland, then would go into action as a way-station for planes bound for the Middle East.

"Air bases, built by the British and Americans during the war, could be put back into service quickly, too. The U. S. has reopened one war-time base in Libya near Tripoli. From it bombers could reach all the trouble spots of Europe and *strike deep inside Russia.*" (Emphasis mine —H.H.)

"Bases equipped to handle big bombers could be put back into service in Saudi Arabia and Eritrea."

The sinister meaning of these activities in terms of the struggle of the African peoples for freedom is indicated in the political developments in South Africa where, in the elections of July 1948, the white supremacist semi-fascist government of Jan Christian Smuts was replaced by the outright fascist government of Daniel Malen and his Nationalist Party.* The maintenance of such regimes of the colonial exploiters and the strengthening of colonial oppression—this is one of the major objectives of the new army.

Obviously, American Negroes cannot obtain their freedom by helping to enslave other people.

A version of this tactic under different conditions was applied by Randolph in his famous "March on Washington" movement. At a time when our nation's all-out anti-fascist war effort dictated the breaking down of Jim-Crow barriers in defense industries as well as in the federal government, Randolph stepped forward with this "threat of a March on Washington," a tactic cunningly contrived so as to enable him to claim credit for the victory when President Roosevelt proclaimed his Executive Order establishing the F.E.P.C. Clearly, it was not Randolph but

*Jan Christian Smuts, speaking for the British Commonwealth, in the interest of "western democracy," said: "We must stand together, not only among ourselves [the British Commonwealth], but also with the United States, which is now the mainstay of our western group; we must work together with those countries who have the same outlook and the same faith and the same way of life as we have." (*Daily Worker*, April 8, 1948.)

military necessity plus a decade of widening struggle by the Negro people that created the conditions for the President's Executive Order. This fact is admitted grudgingly by Myrdal when he states:

> *"The March on Washington Committee,* led by A. Philip Randolph and created to voice the Negro protest in the war emergency, is in a sense a continuation of the nonpartisan general Negro movement represented by the [National Negro] Congress in its first year."[33]

In the United States, the representatives of Social-Democracy are not confined to the official "Socialists." Quite the contrary, this tendency has a broad social base in the American labor movement. It exists in the stratum of skilled and higher-paid workers, the so-called aristocracy of labor, that section of the working class, which, as Lenin observed, allows itself to be led by men sold to, or at least paid by, the bourgeoisie. This is in accord with the tendency of imperialism to create privileged sections among the workers and to detach them from the main proletarian masses. It is these sections of labor that are most susceptible to the imperialist propaganda of white chauvinism. Hence it is not surprising that the strongest base for this ideology in the labor movement is precisely the reactionary and reformist bureaucracy and the psuedo-Socialist leaders of the C.I.O., the A.F. of L., and the Railroad Brotherhoods, the latter two based upon the craft unions of skilled workers.

Particularly in the South, the officialdom of the A. F. of L. and Railroad Brotherhoods are notorious for their white chauvinistic, anti-Negro attitudes. That the Georgia "Fuehrer-maker" Roy Harris can boast of the "happy working relations" between the A. F. of L. hierarchy in Georgia and the white supremacist manufacturers of the region is indicative of this corruption.

In the South, the corrupt force of ruling-class bribery, direct and indirect, is not confined to the labor aristocracy but extends in a varying degree to the whole of white labor and indeed to the entire white population. The fiction of "white superiority" is here given a modicum of economic substance. Within the general scheme of poverty and human degradation which is the South, the lower-class whites are given a privileged economic and social position in relation to the Negro. Their burden is slightly less onerous.

But the "superiority" granted the white laborer over his enslaved black class brother is proved to be "fool's gold," designed to serve a twofold purpose: (1) to win the mass of southern white labor to active support of the policy of Jim-Crow persecution and slander of the Negro people; (2) to continue the historic rift between black and white in the ranks of the South's laboring classes. "Divide and rule," Dixie style, is employed with deliberate cunning by the Bourbon "riding bosses" of the Yankee absentee rulers to deflect southern white labor and its potential allies, the Negro people, from the fight against the real class enemy; to dissipate its energy in futile and harmful inter-racial strife, thereby frustrating unity and preventing the coalescence of the forces of social progress.

With the increased right-wing orientation of a large part of the C.I.O. leadership, a new beach-head has been established by reaction for the further infiltration of the working class with the dangerous white-supremacist propaganda. A blatant example of this was witnessed in the 1948 convention of the Socialist-run Textile Workers Union of America, which, under the leadership of Emil Rieve, capitulated before the Ku Klux Klan element in the southern wing of the union. At the Atlantic City convention, the high command of the union, according to the New York *Herald Tribune* of May 1, 1948, "quietly withdrew a group of resolutions opposing racial discrimination and segregation, condemning the K.K.K. and calling for anti-lynch legislation and F.E.P.C." In explanation, President Rieve, according to the newspaper of the same day, said that the resolutions were "controversial" and some southern delegates would undoubtedly oppose them. This attitude ties in with the lily-whiteism which, from the day of its launching, has hampered the C.I.O.'s "Operation Dixie" under the leadership of Van A. Bittner. It is entirely in character that the C.I.O.'s anti-discrimination committee is headed by James B. Carey, fervent supporter of the Marshall Plan of enslavement abroad and stout foe of union militancy at home.

Despite the efforts of Social-Democracy, the Negro working class will not be easily swerved from the path which it has blazed in a generation of struggle. Negro labor has reached manhood stature. No longer is it tied to the apron strings of Negro bourgeois-reformist leadership; nor is it likely to tie itself to those of Social-Democracy. Negro labor has stepped forward on the political arena as what Marx called, "A class on its own."

That is the new, decisive factor in the fight for Negro liberation. Some indication of the magnitude of the Negro working class is given in the figures for the spring of 1944, which show that there were over 1,655,000 Negroes employed "in industries in which union recognition and collective bargaining are general practices." This number constituted nearly 31 per cent of all gainfully employed Negroes. They were located mainly in the mining, construction, manufacturing, transportation, communication, and public utilities industries.[34] This class is the factor which has given decided impetus to the whole fight for Negro liberation in modern times. It has sparked the great upsurge of the Negro people of the present post-war period.

Though the Negro industrial worker is not yet the undisputed leader of this movement, he has indelibly marked it with his own militancy and with the independence of his revolutionary spirit.

The ideology of socialism as the final solution of America's Negro problem is developing for the first time among the Negroes. It has become a political factor in their fight for freedom. The influence of this Negro working class has begun to penetrate all areas of the Negro community and all its people, particularly its youth and young intellectuals who have been increasingly attracted to the working-class movement.*

* A significant expression of this fact is the development of the N.A.A.C.P. within the youth branches, many of which have lately been in the forefront of the fight inside that organization for a militant anti-imperialist policy. But a more sound aspect of the growing ferment in the ranks of Negro youth is to be found in the Southern Negro Youth Congress. Organized in Richmond, Va., in 1937, and conceived as a federation of southern Negro youth organizations based mainly on student groups in Negro colleges and universities, the organization took from the start a forthright anti-imperialist stand on the Negro question. During the post-war years, it has stood in the forefront of the Negro movement against white primaries, the poll tax, and lynchings. Now, with its increased orientation toward Negro youth in the factories and in agriculture, it has become a rallying center for the South's Negro youth in the fight for a new people's party.

Negro labor, organically united with the militant and politically conscious section of white labor, is the only force which can rally and unite the scattered segments of the Negro people in its fight for freedom. The Negro industrial working class, in alliance with the masses of the oppressed agricultural population of the Black Belt, and leading them, is the *main driving force* of the Negro national liberation movement.

Clearly, the basic propositions of this book are not at the present time universally accepted as the principles of the Negro liberation movement. While there is common agreement on the necessity to struggle for *equal rights* and for the eradication of all forms of Jim-Crow oppression, there is not agreement as to basic concepts, ultimate goals and concrete implications of the slogan of equality. There certainly is no agreement as to the road to the achievement of equality.

The decisive sections of the Negro liberation movement do not have any *conscious* orientation whatever toward the strategic goal of self-determination in the Black Belt area of Negro majority population. Nearly all non-Marxist Negro leaders sharply reject such an orientation. Among both the Negro minority in the North and the Negro majority in the South, the avowed goal of Negro organizations and leadership is "equal rights," the eradication of all forms of "racial" discrimination, the extension to Negro citizens of the full democratic rights enjoyed by white citizens in all areas of American life, civic, political, economic and social. Moreover, there is the general assumption that this goal of "full democratic rights" can be won through struggles for more and more progressive reforms *within* the framework of existing political institutions and arrangements.

There is manifest, therefore, a wide gap between the predominant reformism of the Negro liberation movement today and the revolutionary political struggles inherent in the principle of self-determination for the Negro nation in the Black Belt. Our analysis has brought out the true revolutionary content of the slogan of *equality*. Under the conditions existing in the Black Belt, this slogan can have no meaning other than national equality, that is, equality between the Negro nation and the white nation, and this can be achieved only through struggle for democratic land redivision and for self-government, including the full right of self-determination.

These fundamental demands of Negro liberation are objectively tied in with the needs of the whole American people as they again enter the fight, on a higher level, to defend their democracy against the threat of a new war and fascist enslavement. The fight for Negro freedom is at the same time an indissoluble part of the fight for socialism, the highest form of democracy, which alone can permanently solve the Negro agrarian and national questions in the deep South. Hence the urgent need for the formation of a fighting alliance between the labor movement and the Negro people, without which neither the victory of labor nor the freedom of the Negro people can be achieved. This need emphasizes the pressing task of the politically conscious vanguard of labor, centering in the Communist Party—*i.e.,* the education of both Negro and white workers in the spirit of unifying solidarity. It means the waging of a relentless, uncompromising fight against the lethal plague of white chauvinism, that is, the idea of "white superiority," the secret weapon of Wall Street and its Bourbon hirelings, which is designed to rally the masses of American white people for active support or at least unquestioning acceptance of the policy of Negro oppression.

The corruptive influence of this Hitler-like big lie of Negro "natural inferiority" has operated to maintain the most harmful division in the ranks of American labor, acting continuously as a brake upon the class struggle. It is a mainstay of capitalist domination over the working class and the masses of American people, a major obstacle of labor unity. The fight against this ideology must be waged in conjunction with the job of mobilizing white labor, that is, the working class of the oppressing nation, for energetic, uncompromising, and all-out support for the fundamental demands of the Negro people. Herein lies the strategy for building the solid, unbreakable front of labor and the Negro people so urgently needed to beat off the growing offensive of monopoly capitalism. It is the only strategy that will enable the class-conscious Negro contingent of American labor to assume the offensive against the "racial," that is, national narrowness, suspicion, and distrust fostered by its own

bourgeoisie, against all whites. Only thus can the Negro proletariat win leadership and hegemony in the national Negro liberation movement, in the interest of that movement and American labor as a whole. It is an essential prerequisite for an effective unity of the Negro people themselves for the achievement of
freedom.

The unsolved Negro question is a focal point of vulnerability
of American imperialism. It is therefore a most vital part of concentration for attack by the working class and the masses of democratic Americans in their fight against the imperialist exploiters
and war-makers. The Negro people themselves are demonstrat-
ing the qualities of a decisive democratic force in American life.
They have broken out of their isolation, and, once again, as at
the close of the Civil War, they are determined to proceed along
the path of great historical decision. And there can be no doubt
that they will give new and vibrant life to their old watchword—
land, equality, and freedom.

REFERENCE NOTES

REFERENCE NOTES

Chapter 1

1. U. S. Census of population, released Jan., 1948. See U. S. Bureau of Census, *Series P-26, No. 9*.
2. See Arthur F. Raper, *Preface to Peasantry*, pp. 4-5, by permission of the University of North Carolina Press, Chapel Hill, Copyright 1936.
3. *Ibid.*, pp. 5-6.
4. Rupert B. Vance, *The South's Place in the Nation*, Public Affairs Pamphlets, No. 6 (revised), p. 7, 1944.
5. See A. G. Mezerik, *The Revolt of the South and West*, p. 91, Duell, Sloan and Pearce, N. Y., 1946.
6. See Karl Brandt, "Fallacious Census Terminology and Its Consequences in Agriculture," *Social Research*, Vol. V, No. 1, Feb. 1938, pp. 21-22.
7. U. S. Bureau of the Census, *Population, Special Report, 1940, Re-*
8. *Ibid.*
9. See James S. Allen, "The Negro Question," *Political Affairs*, N. Y., Nov. 1946, p. 1051.
10. Quoted in *Negro Year Book, 1947*, edited by Jessie Parkhurst Guzman, p. 9, Tuskegee, Ala.
11. *To Stem this Tide: A Survey of Racial Tension Areas in the United States*, p. 2, Pilgrim Press, Boston, 1943.

Chapter 2

1. U. S. Department of Agriculture, *Agricultural Statistics, 1945*, pp. 9, 70.
2. See Katharine DuPre Lumpkin, *The South in Progress*, p. 17, International Publishers, N. Y., 1940. See also The National Emergency Council, *Report to the President on the Economic Conditions of the South*, p. 45, U. S. Government Printing Office, 1938.
3. See Gunnar Myrdal, *An American Dilemma: The Negro Problem and Modern Democracy*, 2 vols., p. 233, Harper & Bros., N. Y., 1940.
4. U. S. Department of Agriculture, *Yearbook of Agriculture, 1940*, pp. 654-55.
5. M. R. Cooper and Associates, "Defects in the Farming System and Tenancy," *Yearbook of Agriculture, 1938*, p. 144.
6. National Emergency Council, *op. cit.*, p. 45.
7. Carter L. Goodrich and Associates, *Migration and Economic Opportunity*, pp. 125-26, University of Pennsylvania Press, Philadelphia, 1936.
lease No. 3, Series P-45, Mar. 29, 1945, p. 45.

8. See National Emergency Council, *op. cit.*, pp. 11-12.

9. Herman Clarence Nixon, *Forty Acres and Steel Mules,* p. 13, University of North Carolina Press, Chapel Hill, 1938.

10. T. J. Woofter, Jr., "The Negro and Agricultural Policy," unpublished manuscript, p. 30, prepared in 1940 for Myrdal, *An American Dilemma.*

11. Gunnar Lange, "Trends in Southern Agriculture," unpublished manuscript, p. 29, prepared in 1940 for Myrdal, *op. cit.*

12. J. Lewis Henderson, "In the Cotton Delta," *Survey Graphic,* Jan. 1947, p. 48.

13. See Rupert B. Vance, *The South's Place in the Nation,* p. 12.

14. Allison Davis, Burleigh B. Gardner, and Mary R. Gardner, *Deep South,* p. 281, University of Chicago Press, Ill., 1941.

15. See James S. Allen, *The Negro Question in the United States,* p. 40. International Publishers, N. Y., 1936.

16. See James S. Allen, "The Negro Question," *Political Affairs,* Nov. 1946, p. 1053.

17. Arthur F. Raper, *Preface to Peasantry,* p. 3.

18. *Ibid.,* pp. 3, 21.

19 Davis, Gardner, and Gardner, *op. cit.,* p. 276.

20. *Ibid.,* pp. 276-77.

21. T. J. Woofter, Jr., *Landlord and Tenant on the Cotton Plantation,* p. xxii Research Monograph 5, WPA Division of Social Research, Washington, D. C., 1936.

22. *Ibid.,* p. 21.

23. Raper, *op. cit.,* p. 103.

24. Rupert B. Vance, *All These People,* p. 215, University of North Carolina Press, Chapel Hill, 1945.

25. U. S. Bureau of the Census, *Census of Agriculture, 1940,* Vol. III, p. 146.

26. See *Fortune,* Mar. 1937.

27. Rupert B. Vance, *Farmers Without Land,* Public Affairs Pamphlet, No. 12 (revised) , p. 15, 1940.

28. T. J. Woofter, Jr., *Landlord and Tenant on the Cotton Plantation,* p. 53.

29. Lumpkin, *op. cit.,* pp. 37-38.

30. Rupert B. Vance, "Cotton and Tenancy," in *Problems of the Cotton Economy,* p. 19, Southern Regional Committee of the Social Science Research Council, Dallas, Texas, 1936 (proceedings of the Southern Social Science Research Conference, New Orleans, La., Mar. 1935) .

31. See Harry Haywood and Milton Howard, *Lynching,* International Publishers, N. Y., 1932.

32. W. E. B. DuBois, *Dusk of Dawn,* p. 264, Harcourt Brace, N. Y., 1940.

33. Davis, Gardner, and Gardner, *op. cit.,* p. 351.

34. Charles S. Johnson, Edwin R. Embree, and W. W. Alexander, *The Collapse of Cotton Tenancy,* p. 9, University of North Carolina Press, Chapel Hill, 1935.

35. Arthur F. Raper, "Race and Class Pressures," unpublished manuscript, p. 180, prepared in 1940 for Myrdal, *op. cit.*

36. Quoted by Walter Wilson, *Forced Labor in the United States,* pp. 85-86, International Publishers, N. Y., 1933.

37. See *Baltimore Sun,* Mar. 29, 1936.

38. Arthur F. Raper, "Race and Class Pressures," *op. cit.,* p. 181.

39. Wilson, *op. cit.,* p. 95.

40. *Ibid.*

41. See *New York Post,* Aug. 29, 1946.

42. See *Chicago Defender,* Sept. 7, 1946.

43. *Ibid.*

44. See Myrdal, *op. cit.,* pp. 228-29.

45. *Ibid.* See also *To Secure These Rights: The Report of the President's Committee on Civil Rights,* pp. 29-30. Simon and Schuster, N. Y., 1947.

46. Wilson, *op. cit.,* p. 90.

47. Harold C. Hoffsommer, *Landlord-Tenant Relations and Relief in Alabama,* No. 9, F.E.R.A., Washington, D. C., 1935, Quoted by Vance, *All These People,* p. 229.

48. Arthur F. Raper, *Preface to Peasantry,* p. 122.

49. U. S. Bureau of the Census, *Sixteenth Census of the U. S., 1940, Agriculture,* Summary, First Series, Table 6.

50. Davis, Gardner, and Gardner, *op. cit.,* p. 293.

51. *Ibid.,* p. 294.

52. Arthur F. Raper, *Preface to Peasantry,* p. 224.

53. *Ibid.,* pp. 91, 111, 184.

54. *Ibid.,* p. 76.

55. *Ibid.,* p. 35.

56. *Ibid.,* pp. 63, 64.

57. *Ibid.,* p. 306.

58. *Ibid.*

59. See *New York Times,* Sept. 16, 1946.

60. V. I. Lenin, *Selected Works,* Vol. XII, pp. 199-200; see also V. I. Lenin, *Capitalism and Agriculture,* Little Lenin Library, No. 30, pp. 17-18, International Publishers, N. Y.

Chapter 3

1. For a detailed treatment of this period, see W. E. B. DuBois, *Black Reconstruction, an essay toward a history of the part which black folk played in the attempt to reconstruct democracy in America,* Harcourt Brace, N. Y., 1935; and James S. Allen, *Reconstruction,*

The Battle for Democracy, International Publishers, N. Y., 1937.

2. The fundamental analysis of this period was made by V. I. Lenin, in *Imperialism, the Highest Stage of Capitalism*, International Publishers, N. Y., 1933.

3. Katharine DuPre Lumpkin, *The South in Progress*, pp. 25-26.

4. *Ibid.*, p. 26.

5. *Ibid.*, p. 27.

6. National Emergency Council, *Report to the President on the Economic Conditions of the South*, p. 54.

7. Lumpkin, *op. cit.*, p. 28.

8. National Emergency Council, *op. cit.*, p. 55.

9. *Ibid.*

10. Lumpkin, *op. cit.*, p. 29.

11. A. G. Mezerik, *The Revolt of the South and West*, p. 57, Duell, Sloan and Pearce, N. Y., 1946.

12. *Ibid.*, pp. 55-56.

13. W. Hustace Hubbard, *Cotton and the Cotton Market*, p. 140, Appleton, N. Y., 1923.

14. *Ibid.*, pp. 140-41.

15. See T. J. Woofter, Jr., *Landlord and Tenant on the Cotton Plantation*, p. XXV.

16. See National Emergency Council, *op. cit.*, p. 46.

17. See Woofter, *op. cit.*, pp. 50-52.

18. See Charles S. Johnson, Edwin R. Embree, and W. W. Alexander, *The Collapse of Cotton Tenancy*, p. 33.

19. W. E. B. DuBois, *Dusk of Dawn*, p. 96.

20. *Ibid.*, p. 55.

21. See Stetson Kennedy, *Southern Exposure*, pp. 37-47, Doubleday, N. Y., 1946; see also Comer Van Woodward, *Tom Watson, Agrarian Rebel*, Macmillan, N. Y., 1930.

22. Johnson and Associates, *op. cit.*, p. 39.

23. I. W. Duggan, "Cotton, Land and People," *Journal of Farm Economics*, Feb. 1940.

24. See Gunnar Lange, "Trends in Southern Agriculture," unpublished manuscript, p. 42, prepared in 1940 for Myrdal, *An American Dilemma*.

25. Johnson and Associates, *op. cit.*, p. 47.

26. U. S. Department of Agriculture, *Agricultural Statistics, 1945*, p. 70; Washington, D. C.

27. See Richard Sterner and Associates, *The Negro's Share*, pp. 11-18, Harper & Brothers, N. Y., 1943.

28. James S. Allen, *The Negro Question in the United States*, p. 103.

29. *Ibid.*, p. 101.

30. Woofter, *op. cit.*, p. 50.

31. See Harold L. Ickes, *New York Post*, May 17, 1946.
32. Quoted by Allen, *op. cit.*, p. 103.
33. See William C. Holley, Ellen Winston, and T. J. Woofter, Jr., *The Plantation South*, 1934-1937, p. 44, W.P.A., Division of Research, Monograph XXII, Government Printing Office, 1940.
34. See Carl T. Schmidt, *American Farmers in the World Crisis*, p. 280, Oxford University Press, N. Y., 1941.
35. See Sterner and Associates, *op. cit.*, pp. 299-300.
36. *Ibid.*, pp. 300-01.
37. *Ibid.*, pp. 307-08, 423.
38. *Ibid.*, p. 306.
39. Arthur F. Raper, *Preface to Peasantry*, pp. 6-7.

Chapter 4

1. See National Emergency Council, *Report to the President on the Economic Conditions of the South*, pp. 6-12.
2. T. J. Woofter, Jr., *Landlord and Tenant on the Cotton Plantation*, p. XXI.
3. *Ibid.*, p. 10.
4. National Emergency Council, *op. cit.*, p. 41.
5. *Ibid.*, p. 43.
6. See Rupert B. Vance, *The South's Place in the Nation*, p. 6.
7. See Stetson Kennedy, *Southern Exposure*, p. 3.
8. U. S. Department of Labor, *Monthly Labor Review*, Oct., 1946, p. 524.
9. See Southern Conference for Human Welfare, *The South is Closer Than You Think* (leaflet).
10. Arthur F. Raper, "Race and Class Pressures," unpublished manuscript, p. 262, prepared in 1940 for Myrdal, *op. cit.*
11. See A. G. Mezerik, *The Revolt of the South and West*, pp. 40-41.
12. *Ibid.*, pp. 36-41.
13. Speech by Dr. Frank Porter Graham, Chairman of National Advisory Committee on Social Security, *Bulletin of America's Town Hall of the Air*, Apr. 1939, Vol. 4, No. 21.
14. George W. Cable, *A Southerner Looks at Negro Discrimination*, p. 32, International Publishers, N. Y., 1946.
15. T. J. Woofter, Jr., *The Basis of Racial Adjustment*, p. 166, Ginn & Co., Boston, 1925.
16. See Resolution of the General Council of the International Workingmen's Association, 1869, quoted in Ralph Fox, *Marx, Engels and Lenin on Ireland*, p. 42, International Publishers, N. Y., 1940.
17. Quoted in *To Secure These Rights: The Report of the President's Committee on Civil Rights*, p. 57.
18. See U. S. Bureau of Census, *Sixteenth Census of the United States: 1940 Population*, pp. 44, 47.

19. National Negro Congress, *A Petition to the United Nations on Behalf of Thirteen Million Oppressed Negro Citizens, etc.*, June 6, 1946.

20. See St. Clair Drake and Horace R. Cayton, *Black Metropolis*, p. 227, Harcourt Brace, N. Y., 1945.

21. Quoted in *To Secure These Rights: Report of the President's Committee on Civil Rights*, p. 56.

22. See U. S. Dept. of Labor, "War and Post-War Trends in Employment of Negroes," *Monthly Labor Review*, Jan., 1945.

23. Quoted in *To Secure These Rights: Report of the President's Committee on Civil Rights*, p. 61.

24. Drake and Cayton, *op. cit.*, p. 204.

25. Lester Velie, "Housing: Detroit's Time Bomb," *Collier's*, Nov. 23, 1946, p. 76.

26. Drake and Cayton, *op. cit.*, p. 202.

27. *Ibid.*

28. *Ibid.*

29. U. S. Bureau of the Census, *Sixteenth Census of the U. S., Vital Statistics of the U. S., 1900-1940*, p. 152.

30. Dorothy J. Liveright, "Tuberculosis Mortality Among Residents of 92 Cities of 100,000 or More Population: United States, 1939-41," *U. S. Public Health Reports*, July 21, 1944, pp. 942-55.

31. See *The Negro Handbook, 1946-1947*, pp. 33-36.

32. See Charles Abrams, *Race Bias in Housing*, pp. 12-13, American Civil Liberties Union, N. Y., 1947.

33. Drake and Cayton, *op. cit.*, p. 184.

34. See *Chicago Defender*, June 23, 1945.

35. National Negro Congress, *op. cit.*, pp. 9-12.

36. *The Public Papers and Addresses of Franklin D. Roosevelt, 1938*, address at Gainesville, Ga., Mar. 23, 1938, pp. 167-68, Random House, N. Y., 1938.

37. *Charleston News and Courier*, editorials, Aug. 26, 1938, and July 20, 1938, Quoted by Rayford Logan, *The Attitude of the Southern White Press toward Negro Suffrage, 1932-1940*, pp. 69, 70, Foundations Publishers, Washington, D. C., 1940.

Chapter 5

1. See Philip S. Foner, ed., *Frederick Douglass: Selections from His Writings*, p. 82, International Publishers, N. Y., 1945.

2. Thaddeus Stevens, Speech at Lancaster, Pa., Sept. 9, 1865. See James A. Woodburn, *The Life of Thaddeus Stevens*, pp. 527-28, Bobbs-Merrill Co., Indianapolis, 1913.

3. W. E. B. DuBois, *Black Reconstruction*, p. 602.

4. Gunnar Myrdal, *An American Dilemma*, p. 224.

5. *Ibid.*

6. *Ibid.*, p. 226.

7. *Ibid.*, p. 225.

8. *Ibid.*

9. *Ibid.*

10. V. I. Lenin, *Selected Works, Vol. II*, p. 235, International Publishers, N. Y., 1943.

11. See constitutions of countries mentioned.

12. Myrdal, *op. cit.*, p. 231 *n.*

13. *Ibid.*, p. 264.

14. Sam H. Jones and James Aswell, "The South Wants the Negro," *Liberty*, Dec. 15, 1945, summarized by *Negro Digest*, Feb., 1946.

15. "Southern Saga," *Wall Street Journal*, Jan. 5, 1948, pp. 1, 6.

16. *Ibid.*

17. Legh R. Powell, Jr., *Journal of Commerce*, N. Y., Jan. 5, 1948, p. 26a.

18. *Ibid.*

19. "Southern Saga," *op. cit.*

20. See *Journal of Commerce*, Jan. 5, 1948, p. 26*a*.

21. "Southern Saga," *op. cit.*

22. C. McD. Davis, *Journal of Commerce*, p. 26*a*.

23. U. S. Department of Labor, *Monthly Labor Review*, Oct., 1946, pp. 482-83.

24. "Southern Saga," *op. cit.*

25. See *PM*, Sept. 1, 1946.

26. "Southern Saga," *op. cit.*

27. *Ibid.*

28. *Ibid.*

29. *Ibid.*

30. Donald V. Fraser, *Journal of Commerce*, p. 26*a*.

31. U. S. Department of Labor, *Monthly Labor Review*, p. 524.

32. A. G. Mezerik, *The Revolt of the South and West*, pp. 130-31.

33. "Southern Saga," *op. cit.*

34. Mezerik, *op. cit.*, p. 40.

35. James S. Allen, *The Negro Question in the United States*, p. 119.

36. See *To Secure These Rights: The Report of the President's Committee on Civil Rights*, p. 59.

37. Labor Research Association, *Labor Fact Book 7*, p. 185, International Publishers, N. Y., 1945.

38. Quoted in Robert Digby, "The Second Chronic Crisis in Agriculture," *Political Affairs*, Feb. 1947 (2nd article), p. 185.

39. *Ibid.*

40. *Ibid.*

41. *Ibid.*, p. 94 (1st article), Jan. 1947.

42. Erik Bert, *The Plantation Economy,* unpublished manuscript.
43. See Gunnar Myrdal, *op. cit.,* p. 260.
44. See William C. Holley, Ellen Winston, and T. J. Woofter, Jr., *The Plantation South,* p. 20.

Chapter 6

1. See Hilary Minc, Polish Minister of Industry, in *Allied Labor News,* Sept. 9, 1946.
2. Quoted by Ernest Kirschten, "Hell, High Water, and the MVA," *The Nation,* Aug. 9, 1947, p. 139.
3. *Ibid.,* p. 140.
4. J. Lewis Henderson, "In the Cotton Delta," *Survey Graphic,* Jan., 1947, p. 50.
5. See V. I. Lenin, "The Agrarian Program of Russian Social-Democracy," *Selected Works,* Vol. II, p. 312.
6. United States Department of Labor, *Labor Unionism in American Agriculture,* Bulletin No. 836, p. 305.
7. *Ibid.,* pp. 292-93.
8. Quoted in *Labor Unionism in American Agriculture,* p. 325. See also Howard Kester, *Revolt among the Sharecroppers,* Covici Friede, N. Y., 1936.
9. Anna Rochester, *Lenin on the Agrarian Question,* p. 26, International Publishers, New York, 1942.

Chapter 7

1. Buell G. Gallagher, *Color and Conscience, The Irrepressible Conflict,* p. 3, Harper & Bros., N. Y., 1946.
2. See George W. Cable, *A Southerner Looks at Negro Discrimination,* pp. 27, 28.
3. See Karl Marx and Frederick Engels, *The Civil War in the United States,* p. 8, International Publishers, N. Y., 1937.
4. N.A.A.C.P., *An Appeal to the World! Statement on the Denial of Human Rights to Minorities in the Case of Citizens of Negro Descent, etc.,* pp. 1-2, N. Y., 1947.
5. St. Clair Drake and Horace Cayton, *Black Metropolis,* p. 396.
6. *Negro Year Book, 1947,* p. 388.
7. See Alain Locke, ed., *The New Negro—an interpretation,* Albert and Charles Boni, N. Y., 1925.
8. *Ibid.,* p. 5.
9. Joseph Stalin, *Marxism and the National Question,* p. 12, International Publishers, N. Y., 1942.
10. See William Z. Foster, "On Self-Determination for the Negro People," *Political Affairs,* N. Y., June 1946, p. 549.
11. See R. Palme Dutt, *India Today,* pp. 384-88, People's Publishing

House, Bombay, 1947; see also "The Second Congress of the Communist Party of India," *Political Affairs,* May 1948, pp. 460-77.

12. N.A.A.C.P., *op. cit.,* pp. 13-14.
13. Stalin, *op. cit.,* p. 24.
14. V. I. Lenin, *Collected Works,* Vol. XVIII, p. 373, International Publishers, N. Y., 1930.
15. V. I. Lenin, *Collected Works,* Vol. XIX, p. 50, International Publishers, N. Y. 1942.
16. See Francis Butler Simkins and Robert Hilliard Woody, *South Carolina during Reconstruction,* pp. 96-102, University of North Carolina Press, Chapel Hill, 1932.

Chapter 8

1. Booker T. Washington, *The Future of the American Negro,* p. 132, Small, Maynard & Co., Boston, 1899.
2. Leo Huberman, *America, Incorporated,* p. 18, Viking, N. Y., 1940.
3. W. E. B. DuBois, *Dusk of Dawn,* p. 72.
4. Booker T. Washington, *Up from Slavery, an autobiography,* pp. 221-22, Doubleday, Page, and Co., N. Y., 1920.
5. Du Bois, *op. cit.,* p. 74.
6. *Ibid.,* p. 75.
7. Herbert J. Seligman, "Twenty Years of Negro Progress," *Current History,* Vol. XXIX, Jan. 1929, p. 616.
8. Quoted by Robert L. Jack, *History of the National Association for the Advancement of Colored People,* p. 4, Meador Publishing Co., Boston, 1943.
9. *Ibid.*
10. Cited by Ralph J. Bunche, "The Programs, Ideologies, Tactics and Achievements of Negro Betterment and Interracial Organizations," unpublished research memorandum, Vol. I, p. 27, prepared in 1940 for Myrdal, *An American Dilemma.*
11. *Ibid.,* Vol. I, p. 29.
12. Jack, *op. cit.,* p. 7.
13. DuBois, *op. cit.,* p. 227.
14. James Weldon Johnson, *Negro Americans, What Now?,* p. 38, Viking, N. Y., 1934.
15. DuBois, *op. cit.,* p. 290.
16. *Ibid.,* p. 297.
17. See Harry Haywood, *The Road to Negro Liberation,* pp. 23-24, N. Y., 1934.
18. DuBois, *op. cit.,* p. 305.
19. Bunche, *op. cit.,* Vol. I, pp. 147-48.
20. Gunnar Myrdal, *An American Dilemma,* p. 839.
21. Bunche, *op. cit.,* Vol. II, p. 265.

22. See letter from Eugene Kinckle Jones (Aug. 8, 1940), cited by Myrdal, *op. cit.*, p. 840.

23. See *The Negro Handbook, 1946-1947*, p. 209.

24. See Commission on Interracial Cooperation, *A Practical Approach to the Race Problem*, Atlanta, Ga., Oct. 1939.

25. Ralph J. Bunche, "Conceptions and Ideologies of the Negro Problem," research memorandum, p. 123, prepared in 1940 for Myrdal, *op. cit.*

26. See DuBois, *op. cit.*, pp. 134-220.

27. See Harry Haywood, *Negro Liberation*, New York, 1934.

28. See Adam Clayton Powell, *Marching Blacks,* Dial Press, N. Y., 1945.

29. Amy Jacques Garvey, ed., *Philosophy and Opinions of Marcus Garvey,* Universal Publishing House, N. Y., 1923.

30. *Ibid.*, pp. 5, 8, 9.

31. *Ibid.*, p. 77.

32. See James W. Ford, *The Negro and the Democratic Front,* pp. 107-09, International Publishers, N. Y., 1938.

33. Myrdal, *op. cit.*, p. 818.

34. See *The Negro Handbook, 1941-1947*, p. 110.

APPENDIX

APPENDIX

SOME DATA ON MONOPOLY CONTROL IN THE SOUTH

The huge steel plants of the Tennessee Coal, Iron and Railroad Company in Birmingham, Ensley, Bessemer, and Fairfield, Ala., its captive iron ore mines in Alabama and its 362,432 acres of captive coal veins in Alabama and Tennessee since 1907 have belonged to the Morgan-launched and Morgan-interest dominated U. S. Steel Corporation. So do the Virginia Bridge Company plants at Roanoke, Birmingham, and Memphis; the Universal Atlas Cement Company plants at Waco, Texas, and Leeds, Ala.; and, since 1943, the American Republics Corporations plants at Port Arthur and Beaumont, Texas. U. S. Steel also has a plant at New Orleans.

Morgan interests likewise control the Commonwealth and Southern Co., leading southern utility company, the American Telephone and Telegraph Co. (Bell System), and the Southern Railway Co.

Republic Steel, a Cleveland-controlled company, has plants and captive mines in the Birmingham area and Gadsden.

The E. I. Du Pont de Nemours & Co. has rayon, nylon, plastic, explosive and chemical plants throughout the South — at Belle, Meadowbrook, Nemours, Weirton, W. Va.; Wurtland, Ky.; Waynesboro, Martinsville, and Richmond, Va.; Old Hickory, Tenn.; Birmingham, Ala.; Bartlesville, Okla.; Houston, Stanton and Orange, Texas. Also under Du Pont control are the General Motors Corp. plants at Memphis and Atlanta, its saw mills in Louisiana and Tennessee, and its timber tracts in Louisiana and Arkansas. So, too, the United States Rubber Co. plants at Hogansville, Ga., Winnsboro, S. C., Shelbyville, Tenn., and Scottsville, Va.

The chemical industry of the South is almost entirely in the hands of large northern corporations — the Du Pont Company, Allied Chemical and Dye, Union Carbide and Carbon, Celanese Corporation of America, the American Viscose Corporation, largest rayon-producing corporation. Dow Chemical Co. has tremendous plants near Houston and has bought four government-owned plants in the area. Monsanto Chemical Co. is also expanding in the South. The American Bemberg Corporation, North American Rayon, and the American Enka Corporation, with plants entirely in the South, are subsidiaries of the Algemeene Kuntzijde Unie N. V., a Dutch concern.

One of the South's greatest natural resources is petroleum. This has fallen almost entirely into the hands of great monopolies.

The Humble Oil and Refining Co., operating mainly in Texas but also in Louisiana and New Mexico, and the Carter Oil Co., producing largely in Oklahoma, are subsidiaries of the Rockefeller-controlled Standard Oil Co. of New Jersey and constitute the entire producing facilities of that company, the largest petroleum company in America, holding in fee and under lease some 20,000,000 acres in the United States mainly in the South. The Interstate Oil Pipe Line Co. and the Plantation Pipe Line Co. are also subsidiaries of Standard Oil (N. J.).

Standard Oil Co. of California, also a Rockefeller company, has under lease 613,903 acres in Texas, 246,346 acres in Mississippi, 217,656 acres in Louisiana, 733,899 acres in Georgia, and 207,062 acres in Alabama, and additional acreage in other southern states, although this company operates at the present time almost entirely in California and has actual southern oil wells in operation only in Texas, Louisiana, and Mississippi. The rest of its acreage is for future use.

Rockefeller interests also control the Socony-Vacuum Oil Co., Inc., which holds about eleven million acres of land in the United States, about seven million acres in the South. Of its 10,621 oil and gas wells operating in the United States, 5,708 at the end of 1945 were in Texas, 1,758 in Oklahoma, 278 in Louisiana and 20 in Mississippi.

The Coronado Corporation, owning and operating oil properties in Texas, Louisiana, and Alabama, is owned by the Stanolind Oil and Gas Company which is owned by another Rockefeller company, the Standard Oil Co. of Indiana. Standard Oil (Ind.) has producing or prospective acreage in Arkansas, Georgia, Florida, Kentucky, Mississippi, and Alabama though its chief producing properties at present are in Kansas, Oklahoma, Texas, New Mexico, Wyoming, and Louisiana. The Mexican Petroleum Corporation of Georgia with a refinery at Savannah, and the Pan-American Refining Corporation with refineries at Texas City, Texas, and Destrehan, La., are other subsidiaries of Standard Oil (Indiana).

Another Rockefeller company, Atlantic Refining Company, owns oil rights on 3,665,000 acres in the U. S., much of it in Alabama, Arkansas, Florida, Louisiana, Oklahoma, Texas, and Mississippi. A smaller Rockefeller-controlled company, the Ohio Oil Company, has oil and gas lands or leases on production in Kentucky, Arkansas, Louisiana, Oklahoma, and Texas.

Joining hands with Rockefeller interests in joint exploitation of oil resources in the Near East is the Texas Company, fifth largest American oil corporation, which operates mainly at present in Texas, but also has extensive operations in Oklahoma and Louisiana. It has more than 10 million acres of oil producing or potential producing land owned in fee or under lease in the United States, mainly in the South.

Gulf Oil Corporation with millions of acres under lease in the South is a Mellon concern. Mellon also controls the Koppers Co., with many southern plants and the Virginian Railway Company.

Shell Union Oil Corporation, which is controlled by the great Royal Dutch petroleum company, holds in fee or under lease 365,743 acres in Louisiana, 122,292 acres in Oklahoma, and 907,593 acres in Texas.

These companies and a few others not quite so large are rapidly acquiring control of all the potential oilfields in the South. Thus the Socony Vacuum Oil Company holds under lease 1,678,976 acres of land in Florida where in 1946 it had not tried to drill a single well; and in Mississippi nearly 800,000 acres only 800 of which were "proven."

Another great industry of the South is the manufacture of pulp and paper from wood supplied by the South's forests. This industry is one of the less concentrated of America's industries so far as ownership is concerned. But the world's largest paper company, the International Paper Company, with assets amounting to over 250 million dollars, has huge plants in Mobile, Ala.; Camden, Arkansas; Panama City, Florida; Moss Point, Mississippi; Georgetown, South Carolina; and three plants in Louisiana. It owns one and a half million acres of timberland in the South.

The Union Bag and Paper Company, world's largest producer of paper bags, also controlled by northern capital, has its principal plant at Savannah, where, prior to its current expansion, it produced each eight-hour day nine hundred and sixty tons of Kraft pulp, 500 tons of Kraft paper, 400 tons of Kraft boards and 14,500,000 paper bags. This company owns in fee or holds under long term lease 468,269 acres of woodlands in Georgia, South Carolina, and Florida.

Also Wall Street-controlled is the West Virginia Pulp and Paper Company, which between 1923 and 1943 bought 345,800 acres of timberlands in North and South Carolina and has huge plants at Covington, Va., and Charleston, S. C. This company pays $1.00 a year for the lease on its Charleston, S. C. plant which started operations in 1937. The lease runs for fifty years with an option to renew for another fifty years.

The Container Corp. of America, third largest paper producer in this country, has plants at Fort Worth, Texas, and Fernandina, Florida. It also controls the Sefton Fibre Can Company with a plant at New Orleans.

The Brunswick Pulp and Paper Company which began operation at Brunswick, Georgia, in 1938 is jointly owned by two northern corporations, the Scott Paper Co. of toilet-tissue fame and the Mead Corp. The Mead Corporation has plants of its own at Lynchburg and Radford,

Virginia; Nashville, Knoxville, Harriman, Kingsport and Newport, Tenn.; and Sylva, N. C.

The Champion Paper and Fibre Company, a fifty million dollar northern corporation, has mills at Houston, Texas; Canton, N. C.; and Sandersville, Ga. It owns about 75,000 acres of timberland and holds a contract for preferential right to purchase another million and a half acres in Texas.

Rubber is a relative newcomer to the South; Goodyear Tire & Rubber Co. which accounts for about one-third of all rubber sales and is controlled by the Cleveland financiers, has a tire and rubber plant with nearly 3,000 employees at Gadsden, Ala., and tire cord plants at Cedartown, Cartersville, and Rockmart, Ga., and Decatur, Ala. At the end of 1947 it was still operating a government-owned war plant at Houston, Texas.

Firestone, which is a family-controlled northern corporation depending on a Ford connection for its market, prior to the war got 30 percent of its production from its Memphis plant. It also has plants at Gastonia, N. C., and Bennettsville, S. C., and at the end of 1947 was still operating government-owned synthetic rubber plants at Lake Charles, La., and Port Neches, Texas. The B. F. Goodrich Company has large plants in Alabama, Georgia, Tennessee, Kentucky, and Oklahoma. The U. S. Rubber Company has three mills in Georgia and other plants in South Carolina, North Carolina, Virginia and Tennessee.

The South's industries most closely allied to agriculture, such as the fertilizer plants and the tobacco plants, the cotton oil mills and the cotton compresses, are dominated by giant corporations.

Prices paid to southern farmers for the tobacco crop are pretty much determined by the big tobacco companies whose giant southern plants supply the nation with cigarettes. In 1934, according to the Agricultural Income Inquiry of the Federal Trade Commission published in 1938 (Part 1, *Principal Farm Products*), Liggett & Myers, the American Tobacco Company, and R. J. Reynolds, makers of Chesterfield, Lucky Strike, and Camel cigarettes respectively, bought nearly half the United States tobacco crop, and nearly 70 per cent of the crop sold for use in this country. The six leading companies bought 58 per cent of the total crop and more than 87 per cent of the crop sold domestically.

The compressing and warehousing of cotton is dominated by another giant $160,000,000 corporation, Anderson, Clayton & Company, largest merchandiser of cotton in the world with buying organizations in the United States, Brazil, Mexico, Argentina, Peru, Paraguay and Egypt. In 1933, this company bought 10 per cent of the American cotton crop. It employs about 6,000 men and women in this country and 6,500 abroad. Its subsidiaries include chains of cotton compress plants and warehouses located in Georgia, Texas, Louisiana, Alabama, North Carolina, Tennessee, Arizona and California. It also operates cotton oil mills and cotton gins in Texas, Oklahoma, New Mexico, Arizona, and California. The stock of this company is handled through J. P. Morgan and Co. and the Morgan-interest controlled bank, the Guaranty Trust Co. of New York.

Swift & Company, the great meat packer, with sales that led the nation in 1946, has some 40 cotton seed oil plants and refineries in the South, 12 fertilizer plants, 11 packing plants, nine dairy and poultry plants and eight ice-cream processing plants. These are only its principal southern properties.

Armour & Co., which in 1946 led the nation's meat-packing industry for profits, has large packing plants at Atlanta, Ga.; Birmingham, Ala.; Fort Worth, Texas; Lexington, Ky.; Memphis, Tenn.; Oklahoma City, Tifton, Ga.; and a rendering plant at Fort Worth, Texas. It has fertilizer works at Albany, Atlanta, and Columbus, Ga.; Greensboro, N. C.; Houston, Texas; Jacksonville, Fla.; Nashville, Tenn.; Navassa, N. C.; New Orleans, La.; Augusta, Ga.; Birmingham, Ala.; Columbia, S. C.; Montgomery, Ala.; Norfolk, Va. It operates cotton seed oil plants at Forrest City, and Pine Bluff, Ark.; Jackson and Memphis, Tenn.; and shortening plants at Chattanooga, Tenn.; Helena, Ark.; Jacksonville, Fla.; and Norfolk, Va. It has a leather unit at Charlotte, N. C. and 20 southern dairy and poultry units. These are just its principal plants.

Wilson & Company, third largest meat packer, has plants at Oklahoma City and Columbus, Ga., and a cottonseed oil and compound lard refinery at Chattanooga.

The Cudahy Packing Company, last of the Big Four, has plants at Albany, Ga., Leedwood, near Memphis, Tenn., and Victoria, Texas.

The Buckeye Cotton Oil Co. with plants in Alabama, Arkansas, Georgia, Mississippi, North Carolina, and Tennessee is owned by the soap monarchs, the Procter and Gamble Co. So is the Traders Oil Mill Co. of Fort Worth. Procter and Gamble also has soap and glycerine plants at Macon, Ga., Dallas, Texas, and Portsmouth, Va. During the war it operated three government munitions plants in the South.

These companies together with the Wesson Oil and Snowdrift Co., owners of 69 cottonseed crushing mills and 100 cotton ginneries, seven peanut shelling plants, seven shortening plants, 28 fertilizer plants, and miscellaneous other plants labelled under various names, operate together to control the price of cottonseed paid to the farmer and play an important part in credit extended to the cotton grower.*

* Note, Wesson Oil and Snowdrift Company owns the Southern Cotton Oil Company, the Refuge Cotton Oil Company, the International Vegetable Oil Co., and many others.

While southern textiles remains one of the least concentrated of American industries, the ten largest corporations owning in 1948 probably not more than about a fifth of the spindles and possibly a fourth of the looms, it should be noted that much of the southern textile industry is owned by northern corporations or under northern control.

The southern textile industry was orginally native but northern companies moved in increasingly after 1910. By 1931 at least 6 per cent of the spindles and 3.7 per cent of the looms were northern owned; in South Carolina 13 per cent of the spindles and 10 per cent of the looms; in Georgia 20 per cent of the spindles and 14.4 per cent of the looms; in Alabama 36 per cent of the spindles and 37 per cent of the looms. Nearly half the silk looms and a quarter of the silk spindles in the South were northern-owned. (See Ben F. Lemert, *The Cotton Textile Industry of the Southern Appalachian Piedmont*, p. 155, University of North Carolina Press, Chapel Hill, 1933.)

There are indications that the depression years served to increase the degree of northern ownership considerably. The later war years and first two post-war years, however, saw a veritable revolution in southern textiles, with whole chains of mills passing into northern ownership and merging with northern capital, as well as a general integration of the industry. Between a fourth and a fifth of the productive capacity of the textile industry were involved in such changes of hands during these years. One leading newcomer to the south was the war-born Textron, Inc., a Rhode Island Company, which owns the Manville-Jenckes Company and Textron Southern, Incorporated, organized in 1946 to take over the Gossett mills in North and South Carolina. Another was J. P. Stevens & Co. J. P. Stevens & Co. of New York were the leading cotton commission merchants during the recent war. In August 1946 they merged nine textile companies in the Carolinas and a producing subsidiary in Massachusetts.

Sources for this material are as follows: For interest group control and some other information: *Economic Concentration and World War II*. (Report of the Smaller War Plants Corporation to the Special Committee to Study Problems of American Small Business, U. S. Senate, 79th Congress, 2nd Session, Report No. 6; U. S. Government Printing Office, Washington, 1946.)

For individual company data: Moody's Manual of Investments, American and Foreign, *Industrial Securities*, Moody's Investors Service, New York, 1945, 1946, 1947 and 1948, and *The Wall Street Journal*.

For textile industry, some material was secured from the *Journal of Commerce*, the *Textile World*, the *Manufacturers Record*, Standard and Poor's *Industry Surveys*, and Davison's *Textile Blue Book*, 1940.

INDEX

INDEX